# GENDER, POWER AND ORGANIZATION

Work organizations are a major site of gender politics for professional women and men, and although there are more women in senior positions than ever before, these increased opportunities have not been gained without psychological consequences. Evidence-based and theoretically driven, the new edition of *Gender, Power and Organization* raises important questions about gender and power in the workplace, and the psychology of women's advancement. Twenty years on from the first edition, it re-examines gender relations at work and asks why, despite many years of feminist critique and action, we are able to understand the dynamics of the workplace but fail to make them more representative. The struggles women face in professional and public life remain intense, not least because many men experience an increasing sense of threat to their long-term aspirations and professional positions.

Using examples from recent research and the author's own consultancy experience, this important volume offers a fresh exploration of the psychology of gender and power at work, from the development of gender identities and roles, to explanations of bullying and sexual harassment in the organization. It provides an accessible survey of the subject for professional managers and students of leadership, psychology, management, sociology, gender and women's studies.

**Paula Nicolson**, a Chartered Psychologist, Fellow of the British Psychological Society, organizational consultant and leadership coach, is Emeritus Professor of Health and Social Care in the Department of Social Work, Royal Holloway, University of London, UK.

# GENDER, POWER AND ORGANIZATION

A psychological perspective on life at work

**Second edition**

*Paula Nicolson*

Routledge
Taylor & Francis Group

LONDON AND NEW YORK

Second Edition published 2015
by Routledge
27 Church Road, Hove, East Sussex BN3 2FA

and by Routledge
711 Third Avenue, New York, NY 10017

First Edition published 1996

*Routledge is an imprint of the Taylor & Francis Group, an informa business*

First edition published in 1996 by Routledge

*British Library Cataloguing in Publication Data*
A catalogue record for this book is available from the British Library

*Library of Congress Cataloging-in-Publication Data*
Nicolson, Paula.
  [Gender, power, and organisation]
Gender, power and organization : a psychological perspective on life at work / Paula Nicolson. — Second edition.
    pages cm
  Includes bibliographical references and index.
  1. Sex role in the work environment.  2. Women in the professions.
3. Professional socialization.  I. Title.
  HD6054.N53 2015
  155.3'3—dc23
  2014046021

ISBN: 978-1-84872-322-1 (hbk)
ISBN: 978-1-84872-323-8 (pbk)
ISBN: 978-1-31572-656-4 (ebk)


Typeset in Bembo
by Apex CoVantage, LLC

# CONTENTS

*Acknowledgements*                                              *vii*

Introduction: gender and career in organizations                  1

1   Biography, biology and career                                17

2   Femininity, masculinity and organization                    35

3   Gender at work                                               56

4   Still in the shadow of the glass ceiling?                    87

5   Sexuality, power and organization                           108

6   Gender, power and leadership                                127

Conclusions                                                     145

*References*                                                    *151*
*Index*                                                         *173*

# ACKNOWLEDGEMENTS

Caroline Dryden originally persuaded me to submit the proposal for the first edition of this book nearly 20 years ago during a conversation in a crowded pub. The book has now achieved a second edition so I would like to thank her once again.

Sue Walsh originally convinced me of the importance of psychoanalytic insights into the relationship of gender to power, and we had some interesting arguments to that end.

Since that time I have been further persuaded and consequently trained as an organizational consultant in psychoanalytic and systemic approaches at the Tavistock and Portman NHS Foundation Trust. I would like to acknowledge everyone I worked with there – staff and students.

They and numerous others provided stimulation and support during the intervening years. I want to include my grateful thanks to all my colleagues and friends in the Psychology of Women Section, the universities of East London and Sheffield, Royal Holloway, University of London, the legal profession and the National Health Service.

I also want to acknowledge the late Barrie Newman who gave me invaluable insights into relevant aspects of sociology, although I am not so sure he would have really liked what I made of it all.

Derry Nicolson, Kate, Malachi and Azriel have all helped to cheer and inspire me and along with Michael Strang from Taylor & Francis they all helped to bring the project to fruition.

## Note

This book contains quotations from Nicolson, P., Rowland, E., Lokman, P. F. R., Gabriel, Y., Heffernan, K., Howorth, C., et al. (2011). *Leadership and better patient care: Managing in the NHS*. London: HMSO. Reproduced with permission. http://www.nationalarchives.gov.uk/doc/open-government-licence/version/3/

# INTRODUCTION

## Gender and career in organizations

During the early 1990s I wrote about gender, power and organization with passion having found myself working in an organization, a university medical school, with few female colleagues and a male head of department who transparently demonstrated that he valued the opinions and contributions of young men far more than he did those from women of any age. This raised ideological and personal challenges for me, at least in part because our medical students comprised 50 per cent women and I myself had academic ambitions. What messages were women students and colleagues receiving from senior staff such as this professor? What was going on in an organization that claimed to *pride* itself in its encouragement of young women entering the medical profession? How did any of this behaviour fit with late-twentieth-century rhetoric about equal opportunities for all?

Consequently the first edition of this book was both cathartic and a fascinating learning experience as I worked my way through these tangled paradoxes in theory and practice. I began to realize that I was far from alone in finding myself and other women marginalized and excluded from the *real* organizational issues such as decision-making and future leadership roles. As you will observe, many writers in the late 1980s and early 1990s from whose work I drew inspiration highlighted that gender, power and organization are intrinsically linked in a dynamic way. This position may perhaps only be apparent when attuned to the issues that really matter in any workplace – power and influence, and probably financial reward. Thus:

> At any given moment, gender will reflect the material interests of those who have power and those who do not.
>
> *(Brittan, 1989: 3)*

> Organisational processes are central to the understanding of gender relations, and . . . organisations are gendered.
>
> *(Witz and Savage, 1992: 3)*

> The power dynamics inherent in traditional conceptualisations of gender was theorized in the writings of those who noted that 'difference' was often equated with women's subordination or inadequacy.
>
> *(Radtke and Stam, 1994: 5)*

Both *gender relations* and *organizational dynamics* are typically about the achievement and maintenance of power on behalf of men, accomplished because the ability to influence and control human and material resources exists where power and subordination are inseparable. Power, though, once considered to reside in particular individuals or groups of individuals for very specific reasons, such as their particular knowledge or expertise, or their ability to coerce (French Jr and Raven, 1959), is more frequently understood now as socially constructed and dynamic. That is, power shifts from person to person and from group to group depending on the context and specific events (Burrell, 1988; Foucault, 1982). Thus, in a twenty-first-century bank, when there is a focus on rebuilding trust, power might reside in a well-considered CEO (chief executive officer). However, when there is a crisis or loss of confidence in that person it is the company board members who are likely to hold power. Even more so in a group or a team, such as that company board, power shifts between people and groups of people, according to the team's immediate needs and outside threats. On the whole, though, power transfers from one group of men to another similar one.

But despite a reconsideration of what constitutes power, an understanding of its dynamic nature and the role of feminist-inspired activities in the popular imagination, have things changed for *women* at work in the twenty-first century? Have gender and power relations become less oppressive because we understand them better? Women and men's experience of organizational power have of course changed over the past 20 years, but as what follows in the second edition of this book demonstrates, patriarchal power (literally the power of the father) has managed to evolve to resist such challenges despite illusions of equality. Thus we are still some distance from gender equality at work and at home. Some more recent examples show this in universities, public life and the British National Health Service (NHS):

> University walls bedecked with portraits of elderly male grandees may seem like echoes of the dusty past, but the persistent under-representation of women in leadership roles in the UK academy suggests otherwise.
>
> *(Grove, 2013: 30[1])*

> Twenty years ago The Hansard Society's independent Women at the Top Commission, chaired by Baroness Howe of Idlicote, concluded that the parlous state of women's political representation in Britain was 'wholly unacceptable in a modern democracy'. In the years since little has changed at Westminster: women MPs still comprise less than a quarter of the House of Commons.[2]

In a study of leadership in the NHS, this man's view of himself and his abilities underlie some of the differences that are still evident between women and men. They came as a shocking reminder to us as the research team.

Q: (Young female research assistant) And do you see yourself as a leader?
A: (Man in his late 30s) Oh yes certainly. I can remember the time when I realised that I should be in management. I was working in a \*\*\*\* clinic in [the name of an Acute Health Care Hospital Trust] and it was so inefficiently run and I said as much to the manager. She said "if you think you can do it better then why don't you manage?" So I said "OK I will!" And I think I'm pretty damn good at it. I don't play by the rules, I don't have any formal qualifications, but I can get things done. I'm not perfect – I shout, I swear and mostly I'm just very, very cheeky, but I'm good with people and that's what you need in this job.

*(Nicolson et al., 2011)*

Everything that is wrong with that particular man's analysis of himself and career trajectory will be discussed in Chapter 6 where I explore some contemporary thinking about leadership and gender relations. For now I want to use this extract to highlight the way that women and men present themselves both to themselves and the outside world because from it we can see that self-confidence, arrogance and what appears to represent a complete lack of awareness about the outcome of his behaviour upon others is the opposite of emotionally and socially intelligent leadership and management.

In contrast to this man lies a high-profile and interesting case, which may serve to highlight some of the contemporary discourse around gender and power. The case in point is that of the former British Labour government Education Secretary, Estelle Morris, who resigned from her post in 2002 saying the job was too important for the role to be occupied by second best (i.e. herself).[3] She was by repute an intelligent, popular and committed member of Prime Minister Tony Blair's cabinet who had resolved to improve standards in state education. In her resignation letter she said:

> In many ways I feel I achieved more in the first job than in the second (an expanded role). I've learned what I'm good at, and also what I am less good at. I'm good at dealing with the issues and in communicating to the teaching profession. I am less good at strategic management of a huge department and I am not good at dealing with the modern media. All this has meant that with some of the recent situations I have been involved in, I have not felt I have been as effective as I should have been, or as effective as you need me to be.

She is reported to have had sleepless nights worrying that her mission to improve education was being hampered, not least because the media seemed to be against her, although it was probably the complexity and enormity of the task she had set herself that led to so many potential pitfalls. It is also reported that civil servants broke down in tears when she left. But she was as hard on herself as the media was on her.

Even if men as a sex were intrinsically more gifted in the way they managed power, as a report on gender balance in FTSE companies makes clear:

> Our top companies need to continue to demonstrate that within this competitive, global economy, boards that have a better gender balance are able to make better decisions which can only lead to better performance. This can only be beneficial for individuals, for companies and for the economy as a whole.
>
> *(Sealy, 2013)*

While on the surface much about gender relations at home and at work has changed since the 1990s, equivocality and inconsistency continues to surround women's advancement in public life and business, while some men's more traditional patriarchal view of how to achieve career success frequently triumphs. But if the individual man succeeds, does that also mean the organization is also best placed to be effective?

The intervening decades since the first publication of *Gender, Power and Organization* in 1996 have seen many more women entering the workplace, taking up increasingly senior positions across public, private and third sector organizations. However, problems remain about the nature of women's everyday *experiences* of leadership and management on all levels in a range of organizations. The NHS now has a far higher proportion of female chief executives than formerly, a higher number of women sit on commissioning boards and more women occupying senior clinical posts in medicine and nursing. The head of the International Monetary Fund, Christine Lagarde, and Deputy Governor of the Bank of England, Nemat Shafik, are female with the latter reported to be mother of twins suggesting that motherhood should be no barrier to successfully negotiating a career in the senior management of male-dominated industries. Women entrepreneurs across the globe have gained prominence it seems so that many are now household names both for their main work, such as Nicola Horlick, who set up and runs financial and arts enterprises, *and* for writing about their achievements, such as Sheryl Sandberg, Chief Operating Officer of Facebook, who is also a mother.

We can also see from the report on the FTSE companies quoted from above (Sealy, 2013) that women's achievements and increased organizational status are taken seriously in the twenty-first century and are not 'just' a feminist issue, as frequently portrayed in the 1990s. Nemat Shafik is reported to have remarked that women and girls should not look up to a glass ceiling but switch their gaze straight ahead to a 'sticky door' which is blocking women from breaking through that glass ceiling. This follows Hillary Clinton's view that, although it is still present, the glass ceiling has been shattered into millions of pieces.[4]

Women, however, *do* experience explicit discrimination, subtle and not-so-subtle bullying and isolation, and many middle-ranking professional women still lack the ability to 'play the promotion game' as Jack Grove (2013) reported about university academics. Evidence more widely also supports the view that the 'battle' for everyday gender equality in organizations is far from won (Sambrook, 2007). Gender equality has become buried in the rhetoric that points to the greater numbers of women CEOs, professors and senior professionals such as doctors and lawyers, business leaders and politicians, but neglects the important details of women's and men's *experiences*, particularly in relation to each other, at work (Harter et al., 2006; Smithson and Stokoe, 2005). While Shafik's view that the sticky door was being pulled open at the other side (presumably at least in part by women like herself and men concerned with greater equality and diversity of talent at the top) it is by no means clear that strength in this direction is applied unequivocally.

These dominant discourses, indicating the equality struggle has been won, generally fail to examine the high levels of stress women in particular have to endure to achieve and maintain their achievements in organizations (Hansen et al., 2006; Sharp et al., 2012). They also fail to focus on men's experiences of working with more women while women senior to them are increasing in numbers and influence, which impacts considerably on the dynamics of gender relations in such cases (Leon et al., 2006).

Gender politics, and changes in gender politics, have psychological consequences for all involved. They also impact upon the organizational *systems* women and men work within. By changing the gender balance and more importantly the *gender–power balance*, psychological factors come into play upon day-to-day experiences of those who work in organizations of all kinds, and have an impact upon decision-making (Ackoff, 1998; Barge and Fairhurst, 2008; Byers and Fitzgerald, 2002; Collier and Esteban, 2000; Gillis, 2006; Sharp et al., 2012).

The second edition of this book therefore provides an examination of the psychological impact of the work setting on (mostly) professional women and men currently engaged in organizations where women are apparently both entering and succeeding in increasing numbers. I remain particularly concerned with women who have achieved or aspire to power, and expressly about the *psychological* dimension of the impact of redistributed power for women, as well as the men and the organizations in which they work.

I also pay attention to organizations and members of the workforce who may not be described as professional but where equal pay for equal work, equal opportunities and non-sexist behaviour are still far from current reality. Behaviour across organizations represents dominant cultural value systems with implications for all who work there.

## Demographic changes and power dynamics

While women and men have always co-existed in various capacities in extended families and friendship groups, their relationships in the workplace are relatively new. Women in Western society have entered the (official) workplace in increasing numbers only since the late 1950s, although this entry has been rapid. By 1975 46.2 per cent of women in OECD[5] countries were working outside the home for a wage and this rose to over 65 per cent in 2013 with 65.7 per cent of women working outside the home in the UK. This pattern is set to continue.[6]

However, this has not been on equal or gender-free terms. Typical of female work is that it is part-time and in stereotyped occupations, such as clerical, secretarial, nursing, health-care, teaching, child-care and social work, sales and manufacturing (OECD, 1979) and there appears to be very little change since then with no evidence that women are moving into previously male-dominated work.[7] These typically female occupations have provided some opportunity for professional career progression, but men who enter these professions consistently rise to the top relatively quickly while women remain in the junior posts (Arulampalam et al., 2007). There is also a close relationship between relatively low-paid and 'typically female' occupations such as teaching and nursing which has persisted (Arulampalam et al., 2007; Pillinger, 1993; Smith et al., 2011). The global recession after 2008 has led to shifts in employment patterns with men working fewer hours and women often being employed, but for less pay than a man might receive for similar work (Bell and Blanchflower, 2013.)

Although men have traditionally succeeded over women in terms of their pay, seniority and status of their profession, women are now entering the preserves of male power such as politics and management, and professions such as medicine, law, academia and accountancy, but the picture is far from one of equality.

In the medical profession, for example, while women have trained as doctors in increasing numbers since the 1970s, there has been relatively little change over the decades in the gender proportions at the top of the profession in either the UK or USA (Department of Health, 1991; Rees and Monrouxe, 2010; Silver, 1990; Tsouroufli et al., 2011). In 2011 43 per cent of all doctors in England were female with the prospect that women will outnumber men in the profession by 2017.[8] However the increase in the proportion of female doctors entering the profession has slowed down from 61 per cent of medical students being women in 2003 to 55 per cent in 2012.[9]

But what does this mean for the control of the profession? Female doctors were most visible in the group under 30 years of age with only 28 per cent of the profession in the over-50 age group. This suggests that women fall behind, perhaps because of child-care concerns.

Within the branches of medicine where status and remuneration are high (e.g. surgery) only 3 per cent of consultants were women in the late 1980s, while in psychiatry where the patient group and opportunities for lucrative private practice in the UK are low, around 25 per cent were female (Health Trends, 1991/2). Even so, most of those with high status and reputation are still men.

Women academics in the 1990s were about seven times more likely to be temporary contract researchers than they are to be professors; and even then women only comprised around 35 per cent of contract researchers, 15 per cent of lecturers, 6 per cent of senior lecturers and 4 per cent of professors (AUT, 1990). In 2013 a report by *Times Higher Education*[10] suggested that only one in ten professors across UK universities was female with some universities gaining near parity although others had almost no women academic staff at that grade.

In the USA 35–50 per cent of all new employees in public accounting were women (Lehman, 1990) but only around 2 per cent achieved the status of senior partner in prestigious companies (Maupin, 1993). The legal profession in the USA and UK demonstrated a similar pattern with only 3.6 per cent of women in the UK being High Court judges (Holland and Spencer, 1992).

In the USA only 0.5 per cent of top people in the highest category of management are women (Fierman, 1990) and there are similar figures for female chief executives in the UK (Davidson and Cooper, 1992).

The Hansard Society's report on who runs Britain[11] showed that 22.5 per cent of MPs, 15.6 per cent of High Court Judges, 10 per cent of bank CEOs, 5 per cent of national daily newspapers and 0 per cent of the Bank of England Monetary Committee members were women in 2013. 51 per cent of the British population are women and the authors of the *Hansard* report reiterate that such lack of diversity weakens democracy and public confidence.

This book is not, however, primarily about the identification, political and social challenge of inequality of numbers because this contest continues to be taken up effectively elsewhere (e.g. Davidson and Cooper, 1992; *Hansard*, 1990.[12] It is about the *psychological consequences* of this gender–power imbalance for senior and ambitious middle ranking women and men in management and the professions (Marshall, 1984; Nicolson, 1996, 2003; White et al., 1992).

## Successful women: are they different?

What happens to women who distinguish themselves in their organizations or in the public political arena? What is it about some women that they smash through into power at work and in politics? Successful and aspiring women appear to differ from others in several ways: they differ from their peers who enter the professions but who are side-tracked or drop out. They are separated from women who choose not to enter professional life in the first place but opt for the more traditional family/ non-career employment route. They differ from those women who choose semi-professional work like administration or secretarial/personal assistant. Most significant is that they are unlike their main work peers who are men. Being so different has major psychological consequences. There are still too few role models, not only at work, to provide inspiration about all other aspects of life as well.

In this book I re-examine the ways that the continuation of patriarchal structures, which support male-dominated hierarchies, *still* resist women's progress, regardless of advice from Sheryl Sandberg. I also examine how male success (and high-profile but minority female success) has psychological implications for women's experiences in terms of the sense of self-esteem, perceptions of their own and other women's femininity and gender identity, the impact of these issues on their physical and emotional health, and how achieving against such odds has an impact on women's everyday life. The general theme is not new (see Marshall, 1984; McKenzie Davey, 1993) but nevertheless neglected, and the more opportunities there are for women to achieve, the more scrutiny women's *experience* of career accomplishment is required so that success may be sustained.

DeLamater and Fidell wrote about the problems of professional women as having a 'cumulative impact . . . as she moves from childhood to occupational employment' (1971: 7). They suggested how girls are socialized into being people-oriented and dependent, while work, and particularly success at work, was perceived to be masculine, and as such undesirable for women. They suggested too, that 'Socialisation to traditional feminine values results in lower occupational aspirations for women' (ibid.). Their edited collection demonstrated that the end of the 1960s brought with it an awareness of gender and power as issues for social science.

What has changed since that time? We know that many women's aspirations have been raised and there are role models of successful career women who are also mothers and look feminine including successful political leaders such as Hillary Clinton, Condoleeza Rice, Angela Merkel and Benazir Bhutto (Genovese and Steckenrider, 2013). However, the conflicts and contradictions inherent in women's lives, subjectivities/identities and experiences as professionals in patriarchal organizations have taken on a similar pattern to those reported years ago.

In 1996, in the first edition of this book, I identified that, despite changes in the law and the aspirations of women, there were still barriers – psychological, social and structural – to women's career success. Back then I quoted the *Hansard* report of 1990 to support this. That *Hansard* report had argued that women 'face general barriers which transcend differences of occupation and sector – out-dated attitudes towards women's roles in society, sex discrimination, inadequate provision of child care facilities or support for the care of elderly dependents, and inflexibility in the organisation of work and careers' (1990: 20).

The Hansard report in 2012[13] indicated that the number of women MPs has only been growing at a rate of 4 per cent every 13 years so that it will be another century before parity of representation will be secured.

What I want to know now is how far things have changed for the better since 1996 for women, men and gender–power relations at work and whether there are any positive or negative psychological consequences.

## Post-feminist times

The barriers to gender equality in the workplace identified in the 1990s had a psychological impact, and women paid the heavier price either through loss of career potential, or in more personal ways. This is different from the experience of men. While by no means all men succeed in their ambitions, the majority of people who *do* succeed in their careers are still men. The personal and professional costs of career failure for men are recognized as attacking masculine identity. There is sparse theorization of the influence of career success or failure on feminine identity. Masculinity is equivalent to success, achievement and power, while femininity remains perceived by men and women as dependent passivity. This has implications for self-esteem, gender relations at home and at work, and is critical for women who challenge traditional gender expectations. Thus, although the potential cost of thwarted ambition is painful for men, and may skew their own self-evaluation, the lack of a similar career-expectation model for women denies them a framework through which to explain their experiences and emotions to themselves and others. A woman who fails to achieve promotion or appointment to a senior management post or to become a High Court judge, for example, is seen, and probably sees herself to some extent, as lucky to get that far. This way of thinking is particularly problematic because of how women have to struggle for their success (Sharp et al., 2012) and develop intricate coping and image management strategies that appear to be essential to women's organizational achievement (Cassell and Walsh, 1991; Fairhurst and Grant, 2010; Marshall, 1984).

My interest in this particular aspect of organizational psychology arose from personal experience. As an academic, a feminist and a psychologist taking up a post at a medical school in a psychiatry department in 1990 I experienced extreme culture shock. Following life in a psychology department with its share of strong female and male colleagues, I was suddenly an outsider: not a man but a woman, not a psychiatrist but a psychologist and to cap it all was not particularly interested in experimental research but with research interests in non-traditional areas, represented in the way I studied women's accounts of motherhood and postnatal depression.

There seemed to have been no precedent in the department I joined for someone like me. Women were expected to be seen, work hard and definitely not heard. If they were not prepared, or were unable, to fit this template there seemed to be no end to the hostility and envy. I was appointed to a reasonably junior position, and thus could afford to avoid a high-profile presence. I wondered how much worse the feelings of hostility might have been if I had arrived as head of the department?

The experience of entering the medical school had made me contemplate the practical, day-to-day aspects of the relationship between psychology, power and subordination in organizations. It was not too difficult to realize what was considered to be my place, although I did make very positive alliances with mostly senior medically qualified men who were concerned to raise the profile of female clinicians through supporting women while they were medical students and in their early postgraduate years.

I eventually became a professor in this Russell Group (i.e. research-intensive and elite) university in 2001 when I was 50. That is rather later in life than such a promotion would be for a man. Men who are going to achieve professorial status generally do so at least 10 years before I did and I have been witness to ways in which this happens.

Reggie, my head of the department at the time of my appointment to a personal chair, had been supportive over my promotion to senior lecturer and subsequent readership and indeed had seemed very pleased for me and applauded my achievements. He gave his support to my professorial application too, and the papers were processed accordingly. However, the day before the deadline for them to be submitted to the senior central promotion committee he came into my office with a downcast look. He sat down, accepted the coffee I offered and said he had something difficult to discuss with me.

Erik, a colleague in his mid-30s, seen as a potential high flyer, had also applied to be promoted at the last minute. At this university each department could only give vigorous support to one candidate so this meant Reggie wanted me to step aside until the following year. Reggie suggested I would understand his choice to sponsor Erik because (of course) otherwise Erik would be moving on (and up) and we would lose him if he were not made a professor now. I was thunderstruck initially and then absolutely furious. I had worked hard – been successful at gaining research grants, writing and editing books and journal papers and was a well-appreciated teacher and PhD supervisor. I also knew that if I allowed myself to be leapfrogged by a younger man this year it would probably happen again the following one. What was I to do? Were middle-aged women who were producing the goods, but likely to remain at their university rather than hold it to ransom, so much less valuable than younger (as yet less successful) men who were likely to move on?

I consulted the university rules and found they did allow an individual unsponsored application for promotion to a personal chair to be submitted directly to the Human Resources Department and Vice-Chancellor, although this procedure was almost never successful.

I refused to let the matter drop, and looking back it still surprises me how much Reggie's assumption about the value of the young man in contrast to me filled me with rage. Serendipitously, a new Vice-Chancellor had recently come into the post who had wanted to 'do things his own way' in contrast to his predecessor. After much effort (phone calls, meetings and emails) eventually my promotion came through and was also backdated.

Even though Erik had achieved his personal chair, Reggie stopped speaking to me after that – which made everyday work quite uncomfortable. It seemed though that my case had become something of a *cause célèbre*. Even after I had moved to another university, several women who had been trying to get promoted contacted me to ask advice on how I did it. The 'case' had apparently achieved notoriety and I was pleased to see that some of these women subsequently made a successful case for themselves.

The material for this book though is not based on a single research project or anecdotes from my own and others' personal experience, but has emerged from a range of sources. Initially my experience of culture shock gave rise to discussion with friends, each of whom in different ways recognized similar experiences to my own. Although few of us worked in the same cities, we had (and continue to have) an unwritten agreement to be available on the end of the phone (and nowadays email) as soon as possible to discuss organizational issues that are precipitating problems. These appear to be almost exclusively related to gender issues on some level, and have provided essential food for thought.

As a consequence of my 'self' interest, I have given serious attention to women and professional power over recent years. I became involved in providing supervision/consultancy to individuals and groups of women in senior posts in male dominated professions. This frequently involves detailed discussion of the stresses and strains of everyday working life, and although not all of these are directly attributable to gender discrimination as such, they *are* attributable to the fact that women are in the minority, that they do not have a long tradition of networking and mentoring other women, that they feel isolated but are not always prepared to admit it, and that women's *lives* (rather than their biological and psychological make-up) on the whole do not prepare them for senior professional and managerial roles. I am also involved in providing support to some senior men who manage women and men in their organizations who are aware of dilemmas that gender management might throw up.

Also, a key component of my previous academic research, with my colleague Christopher Welsh, had been to examine gender discrimination and sexual harassment in medical school and in clinical settings, for medical students and doctors. We observed the strategies for survival that women had to adopt as they rose up the medical hierarchy, which involved distancing themselves from junior women, from problems of sexism and moving towards an individualized sense of responsibility for achievement and combating sexism (Nicolson and Welsh, 1993). These findings persuaded me to concentrate on the psychological consequences for women of the need to achieve success, rather than the experience of the forces of discrimination at the start of a career. Since then I have been the lead researcher for a large project on leadership in the NHS which demonstrated in further detail how discrimination in hospital contexts operates and how women and men experience their relationships (Nicolson et al., 2011).

Over the years I have had the benefit of being able to draw upon the work of those who have conducted research and written about gender and career before me. Their work is wide ranging and covers a broad spectrum from home–work conflict, to coping with sexism, the development of coping strategies, organizational culture and unconscious aspects of organizational and interpersonal life. Extracts from the interviews they conducted as well as the authors' own analysis of the importance of these extracts have been invaluable in mapping out the arena within which women's experiences may be understood. See, for instance, the work of Beverly Alimo-Metcalfe, Cary Cooper, Marilyn Davidson, Ginny Dougary, Jenny Firth-Cozens, Wendy Hollway, Judi Marshall, Jane McLoughlin, Celia Morris, Barbara White and others mentioned below in what follows (Fairhurst and Grant, 2010; Fletcher, 2004; Ford, 2010; Schnurr, 2008).

I have divided this edition of the book into seven chapters, which are not mutually exclusive.

Chapter 1, 'Biography, biology and career', sets out the core theoretical framework developing a critical position towards traditional, positivist academic psychology's contribution to career and organization. It reviews theoretical perspectives for understanding power in organizations and how this is demonstrated and practised, and embedded in the culture of systems and the individuals working in them.

I propose a material–discursive–intrapsychic (MDI) approach to understanding the experience of both individual and organizational development, which I have used elsewhere in the context of human growth and development (Nicolson, 2014) (following the work of Ussher, Yardley, Giddens and others).

This chapter thus explores the interaction between the bio- and socio-material contexts of a person's life with the meanings they give to positioning themselves within these contexts and explaining consequent experiences. In so doing it draws upon behavioural, social and biological psychology and the ways in which the evidence from these approaches has been used to exploit gender differences and maintain inequalities discursively across the private and public spheres.

The chapter goes on to situate the material and discursive contexts within psychoanalytic ideas, particularly those of Freud, Melanie Klein and post-Kleinians such as Wilfred Bion, John Bowlby and Donald Winnicott.

Finally, the influence of systemic culture will be explored – making the link from the family to the organization.

All subsequent chapters draw on these theoretical positions as their starting point.

Chapter 2, 'Femininity, masculinity and organization', draws upon this framework to explore how women and men differ in terms of the meaning given to their bodies and gender identity and how this subsequently impacts upon their career and organizational relationships. It examines what is meant by masculinity and femininity and the relation between the two in the workplace.

Chapter 3, 'Gender at work', explores further how femininity and masculinity are acted out at work on both a conscious and unconscious level. This includes the means by which stereotypes are employed to disadvantage women, particularly in terms of home/work spill-over, leadership characteristics, and the development and failure of support networks for women and men. It focuses upon the importance of envy and competition in work organizations and shows how this often sets men against women to the disadvantage of women. Finally, the enduring theme of sexuality and professional life is explored.

Chapter 4, 'Still in the shadow of the glass ceiling?', focuses upon the contradictions in the lives of many women, some of whom shatter this particular barrier while others retreat to different ways of being.

I return also to earlier themes although shifting from the critique of the status quo to the examination of solutions. The role of a feminist stance for understanding organizational life is discussed, particularly the meaning and consequences of success and power for women and men.

Chapter 5, 'Sexuality, power and organization', highlights research and examples of sexual harassment, abuse and bullying using contemporary examples from research, high-profile legal cases and anonymized evidence from my consultancy work.

All are discussed within the theoretical framework described in Chapter 1.

Chapter 6, 'Gender, power and leadership', explores how female and male sexuality are positioned and the ways in which some systems undermine women's leadership through exploiting discourses of sexuality. This chapter also explores the ways in which emotion is managed by individuals (consciously and unconsciously) and its role in the organizational system. It re-examines how the formative influence of early experiences of family life (whatever its form) contribute to our experiences of 'belonging' to an organization and the ways in which we practise those experiences.

The final chapter, 'Conclusions', draws together the evidence from demographic changes, abuse of gender–power relationships and the continued influence of patriarchy in organizational systems reiterating the relevance of an MDI take on this evidence for dynamic and systemic change.

All the chapters will be evidence-based and theoretically driven. They will also be illustrated by examples from research (my own and others'), consultancy and issues raised by media events and legal cases to make the evidence and theory behind it come alive.

## Notes

1 UK figures but indications are that the situation is not much different here.
2 http://hansardsociety.org.uk/wp-content/uploads/2013/03/Women-at-the-Top-briefing-paper-2012.pdf.
3 http://news.bbc.co.uk/1/hi/education/2359695.stm.
4 http://independent.co.uk/voices/comment/forget-about-that-glass-ceiling-women-should-be-pushing-through-the-sticky-door-9203314.html.

5 The Organisation for Economic Co-operation and Development was set up in 1960. Participating countries included USA, UK, Canada and many Western European countries.

6 www.oecd-ilibrary.org/;jsessionid=22boph8fieb2q.x-oecd-live-01content/table/emp-fe-table-2013–1-en.

7 http://economist.com/node/21530159.

8 http://kingsfund.org.uk/time-to-think-differently/trends/professional-attitudes-and-workforce/medical-workforce#consultants.

9 http://gmc-uk.org/SOMEP_2013_web.pdf_53703867.pdf.

10 http://timeshighereducation.co.uk/news/gender-survey-of-uk-professoriate-2013/2004766.article.

11 http://hansardsociety.org.uk/research/women-at-the-top/sex-and-power-2013-who-runs-britain/.

12 http://hansardsociety.org.uk/research/women-at-the-top/sex-and-power-2013-who-runs-britain/.

13 http://hansardsociety.org.uk/research/women-at-the-top/women-at-the-top-2011/.

# 1

# BIOGRAPHY, BIOLOGY AND CAREER

## Introduction

Below I set out the core theoretical framework, the material-discursive-intra-psychic (MDI) approach that I use to develop a psychological analysis of gender, power and organization in the fast-changing world of the twenty-first century.

- I review ways in which patriarchal organizations can be understood through an MDI lens.
- I also explore how biography, biology and career can be examined and explained through this framework.

In this chapter, biography, biology and career, the interrelationships between the gendered social context (from that of the family, the organization and the socio-political culture) and the developing individual woman and man are explored. Biography refers to an individual's life up to the point of discussion and includes a sense of the meaning that person gives it. Biology refers to sex and gender as well as health. Career is primarily about work career but also about other aspects including informal organizational relationships and dynamics, family life and leisure.

Clues to gendered behaviours, power and social and organizational changes lie variously in understanding biographies, biology and career through a series of lenses that take account of how 'family' and 'organization' exist chronologically (Archer and Lloyd, 2002; Carter and Levy, 1988; Martin and Ruble, 2010); that is, how early socialization and family interactions and relationships impact on adult experiences, emotions and behaviour in work organizations (Carless, 1998; Eagly and Carli, 2003; Ely, 1995; Evans, 2002; Gerber, 1991). Thus, in a simplistic case, a girl might see the adult man/father as head of the household. A boy might see his mother or sister in need of protection (Dryden et al., 2009). As children develop and become independent of their family they shed (at least consciously) some of these ideas.

However, there is also a powerful level at which impressions and family power relations experienced and witnessed in infancy and childhood remain with us, outside chronological development and beyond what we might see as 'rational' thinking and behaviour. In other words, without a conscious awareness we frequently 'bring our family to work' (Ackerman, 1972; Bettman, 2009; Eriksen and Jensen, 2009; Goldner et al., 1990). A female manager, without thinking, might treat or experience her male boss as she would her older brother or father and so on. These relationships exist on an unconscious or at least semi-conscious level and are shot through with power and gender dimensions (Klein, 1946; Nicolson, 2012; Segal and Klein, 1973).

However, it is not just the individual who carries forward those early experiences. Families themselves have life cycles that in many ways mirror the processes that occur in organizations thus underscoring and emphasizing the early patterns in all of us that influence expectations of others and our relationships with them (Dallos and Draper, 2010). Dallos and Draper propose that families evolve and develop, and negotiate their way in their internal and external worlds. These interconnected areas are the social, cultural and spiritual; the familial (how relationships are managed within the family); and the personal (personal beliefs and experiences).

To take these ideas further, then, in what follows I develop this representation to set out the core theoretical framework, of a material-discursive-intrapsychic (MDI) approach as the means to analyse those interrelationships via a critical lens also involving psychosocial development and systems theory (Nicolson, 2014). Making sense of the story of each of our lives and decision-making, from our early days through various stages of our career, comes through an analysis and understanding of biology, psychology, culture, politics and history. These are the components described in the MDI approach.

We develop our biography, the story of our life, as we both live it and make our own sense of it, in the social, biological and psychological contexts we experience and inhabit. Further, we engage with our physical and social worlds through thinking, imagining and feeling and all of the others who interact with us in our worlds, families, school, social groups and in work organizations, are reflected upon and consequently influence us similarly. The MDI framework takes account of all these dimensions. So what do I mean by MDI?

## The material

The 'material' is two-fold. It refers first to the *physical social context* in which we develop and live, involving ingredients such as the community, the quality of the built environment and our economic status; and second to the *biological materiality* of our bodies and health, which includes our sex, age, physical abilities, intellectual capacities and appearance (Luyt, 2003; Ussher, 2006; Yardley, 1996). These lists are not mutually exclusive.

The material context, represented by our own biological make-up including individual characteristics such as our sex, our body shape, size, colour, ethnicity and health, also includes the physical, economic and political culture that gives meaning to the biological. All of these elements, as you will see, are located within historical contexts, and different meanings are attributed to social and biological contexts over time.

The material context

| Physical environment | Housing, family type and size, economic status, community, physical environment and location of the organization. |
|---|---|
| Biological environment | Genetic status, sex, ethnicity, appearance and the meaning we, and others, attribute to it. |
| Interpersonal environment | Number and quality of friendships, work culture, personal status, community culture and family. Power dynamics, communication strategies and patterns and relationships. |

The material context is made up of overlapping elements and, as I suggested above, the material is not mutually exclusive but has common characteristics with the discursive and intra-psychic elements.

Gender (Ely, 1995) is an important part of the material context that also links with our *discursive* and *intra-psychic* status in that it forms a bridge between our understanding of our sex and what being a man or a woman means in the social context in which we live. Gender and its practices (that is, how we behave and think in gendered ways) have involved different experiences embracing different values across time.

To illustrate this there are many examples but I have chosen one from the nineteenth-century Spanish novel *Fortunata and Jacinta* by Benito Pérez Galdós. The former is born into poverty although possessed by physical beauty. This brings her to the attention of a rich, spoilt, society man, Juan who, despite having an affair with Fortunata resulting in her pregnancy, goes on to marry his cousin, Jacinta, a social equal. Despite their physical passion Juan does not continue the affair with Fortunata until she herself has married, which gives him (he thinks) protection against any demand she might make to have a legitimate relationship with him. Their relationship ends mostly in tragedy for all involved but Fortunata and several of the other women in this complex story identify female rivals for the love and attention of men as their enemy. Women in the nineteenth century practised gender in different ways from the late twentieth- and early twenty-first-century feminists, and did so according to the biological material conditions of their time such as their appearance and the socio-material conditions of their social and economic status.

A more contemporary example of how the material context impacts upon power is perhaps well illustrated by the British political elite in the early twenty-first century, most of whom are public school educated men from economically and socially privileged backgrounds. The more populist among them also appear to have appealing physical characteristics that suggest the 'jovial man next door' who might chat to you informally, or the humorous 'rake' – both types of whom seem able to charm women and men in a non-threatening way. These men are portrayed as somehow 'harmless' as they are affable and apparently accessible. But this is not a reflection of reality in that such men, still representing a sexist patriarchal culture, are just as inaccessible and unrepresentative in the twenty-first century as they were in the nineteenth.

## The discursive

The 'discursive' refers to the way our worlds and behaviours, or social practices, are talked about, portrayed and constrained by the dominant discourses in society (Foucault, 1982) so that some ideas, such as those about gender roles for instance, constrain our imagination and actions precluding alternative discourses (Bettman, 2009; Girard, 2009).

Gender, if you are thinking discursively, is a social construction in that it is subject to popular and influential belief systems, as with Fortunata above for instance, or the men who are 'entitled' to power. It is frequently suggested by the mass media, casually, that gender is 'hard wired' into our brains (Hyde, 2007; Schore, 2001). This discourse evolved from the relatively recent burgeoning of theories connected with the mapping of the human genome and the increased ability to use brain scanning to observe the effects of specific stimulation and patterns in brain activities (Baron-Cohen, 2004). But discourse, as a constraint on behaviour and psychological functioning, is not only related to contemporary technology as with the discourses surrounding the genome. Each historical period characterized by predominant value systems and political ideologies involves discursive practices that impact on how we act and think about our lives (Fine, 2011). As Cordelia Fine argues, 'that there must be hardwired psychological differences between the sexes also appears to enjoy impressive scientific support' (p. xxi) as the explanations fit neatly into a story that we can see represented in our lives at home and at work.

But discursive practices supported through popular rhetoric change over time. It is likely, for example, that a girl at school in the 1960s would have been encouraged to excel in needlework or cookery rather than technical subjects which might have made her think that an interest in engineering was undesirable. Similarly a boy might have been subtly discouraged from taking part in 'softer' school subjects such as art or modern languages, in favour of science through watching images on television or hearing discussion in which men were scientists and girls linguists. What we don't know is how many female engineers might have reached the top of their professions today if a different set of messages had been around.

Contemporary rhetoric, to some extent, eschews the idea of feminism in favour of a belief that success in this apparent post-feminist era is up to each individual regardless of gender. This discourse is more pervasive in the twenty-first century than it was in the mid-1990s when this book was first published (Dias and Blecha, 2007; McRobbie, 2004).

Feminism, which for many, like myself, represented a means of asserting equality between women and men in a range of social and psychological spheres, has been subject to discursive change. It was in the 1950s a means of liberating women from domestic drudgery and demonstrating that women were as able as men to work successfully outside the home (Sayers, 1986); in the 1980s and 1990s it became a rallying cry for the ambitious woman to have faith in herself and her 'sisters' in arms (see Nicolson, 1996). By the twenty-first century feminism was, to some, discredited in that younger women were, paradoxically, influenced by the vision of themselves as equal and just as likely to succeed as their male counterparts. Sadly, and frequently, it isn't until young women become mothers that they realise the extent to which they might have been duped by contemporary post- and anti-feminist discourse (Nicolson, 1998, 2003).

It is easy to see how a discursive perspective is also valuable to feminists. Post-modern critiques, which take apart, or *deconstruct*, ideas and meanings of taken-for-granted concepts such as 'power' or 'marriage' or 'success', enable the identification of linguistic repertoires leading to exposure of structural power relations (Edley, 2001; Wetherell and Edley, 1999). By this I mean that we can begin to understand the power of mere 'talk' as a means of influenc-ing what we all take to be immutable social or psychological truths. This involves statements such as leaders are made not born, success is making more money than your colleagues, power means getting people to do what you want and so on. At various times in recent history all of these ideas have been influential and have had an impact on how we see ourselves and evalu-ate our behaviours in relation to others.

Thus, such an emphasis on language and power in discourse accounts for the continuity and contradictions in human interactions and emotion (Weedon, 1987). So, in the process of deconstructing the 'subject-as-agent and the unitary individual . . . [discourse] provides a critique which gets under-neath what is taken for granted by those terms' (Hollway, 1989: 31). That is, we always need to look under the surface of what is being said and believed, particularly when it appears that an idea or a particular practice is indisputable.

It is also significant though to see how some feminists have found this approach to deconstructing gender–power relations to be unacceptable. Questions have been raised about the complex tension between a discur-sive approach to gender–power relations and the personal experience of subjectivity, or being a person with a sense of identity and continuity. My belief is that to exclude a *sense of the individual* from critical and feminist psychology is unproductive in the long term, and increases the widening gap between feminist psychologists and the women who might benefit from their analysis of gender–power relations (Dryden et al., 2009; Tunaley, 1994). However, I do not want to throw the baby out with the bathwater and have therefore tried to emphasize the discursive context as important within a framework that also takes the bio- and socio-material and intrapsychic contexts just as seriously. Even so it needs to be stressed that the theory and practice of discourse analysis has been exceptional in denting the positivist barriers of academic psychology, while being mindful of the danger of los-ing its grounding in everyday life (see Lewis, 1995). For these reasons using discursive practices within the MDI framework takes the best processes of deconstruction of rhetoric and discourse but takes identity seriously as well (Nicolson, 2010).

## The intrapsychic

The 'intrapsychic' refers to the world of conscious and unconscious experiences that comprise our internal worlds. These involve our sense of who we are, reflected in our biographies (Gough, 2004; Hyde, 2006; Theodosius, 2006), our emotional responses to relationships that seem understandable and those that are apparently irrational, and feelings that we cannot always explain to ourselves or to others (Segal, 1993). While this perspective owes much to classical psychoanalysis it goes beyond looking at defence mechanisms and the unconscious drives. To understand the impact of each of our internal worlds upon the ways we live our lives we need to revisit the very early minutes, days and months of life. Birth itself is a traumatic experience – passing through a narrow passageway into (frequently) a brightly lit, noisy environment where you are weighed, measured, cleaned up and eventually fed. The latter is something you need to learn fast if you are to survive. Equally you are dependent on the will and abilities of those adults who will keep you safe, warm and nourished. The uncertainty surrounding such early and highly dramatic experiences frame the ways in which we make sense of a whole variety of social interactions that eventually become part of our internal intellectual world. But the origins of these lie in a primitive, preverbal sense of trust and safety and from that a primitive feeling of our worth and who we are to become (Klein, 1953, 1959/1975).

It is clear also that a central task of infancy is making the most of opportunities to make attachments, if possible, to adults who are caring and interested in your welfare. If these attachments are positive then it is likely that throughout life such a person will have the desire and ability to work co-operatively with others whom they trust but do not entirely depend upon (Bowlby, 1988). Those of us who make positive attachments in this way are also likely to be empathic and understand others' feelings, behaviours and motivations (Fonagy, 2000). For those who have negative experiences and experience neglect and/or abuse from those who are supposed to care for them may develop a disorganized attachment pattern which will not be particularly conducive to their development or careers (Bifulco et al., 2003; Shemmings et al., 2012).

## Beyond MDI

In a variety of ways all individuals exist in some relation to their social context so that being comfortable with one's own gender is a prerequisite for emotional health and there is evidence of distress for those who are not so. However, being an ambitious and successful woman has been seen as inimical to femininity, or at least it was in the late twentieth century.

How far have things changed? Can an MDI approach provide a means of making sense of the complexities of gender and power in contemporary organizational life? In my textbook about human growth and development (Nicolson, 2014) I explored how this approach enables all of us to make sense of who we are and our biographical development in our individual ways while taking account of the constraints our socio-political-historical context places upon us. In the context of who we are psychologically and biologically, alongside our location in history and culture, we begin to *negotiate* our biographies as we move through life and through our careers. By this I mean that although there are patterns that might be observed that predict career outcomes, which include gender, class and ethnicity, within our culture (or material worlds) we negotiate (or make decisions) all the time about how to manage the places in which we find ourselves (Hunter, 2005).

A further element to include in the MDI analysis of biography, biology and career is that of the *lifespan*. While much has been written about the lifespan, and similar models such as the life course and the life-cycle, two key theoretical contributions underpin a theory of biography. The first is the model of 'psychosocial development' developed by Erik Erikson (1950/1963, 1959/1980; see also Gough, 2004) and the second the processes involved in human attachment behaviours and desires developed by John Bowlby (1977, 1982) and many others (e.g. Ainsworth et al., 1978; Bifulco 2004).

By considering the process of development through the lifespan we also take account of human needs and abilities to form attachment relationships and it is these that interact with the material and discursive context that provide the ingredients that comprise our biography and career (Fonagy, 2001).

Finally, *systems theory*, which takes account of the relationship of the individual in their role (as child, parent, community member, manager and so on) in the context of the family (Dallos and Draper, 2010) or organization (Campbell et al., 1994). This approach is particularly useful for considering the social interactions that support or curtail an individual's sense of biography and career (von Bertalanffy, 1950). Thus, each of us exists within a system so that changes in the system impact upon the role, communications, behaviours, authority and boundaries within elements of the system as well as the boundaries between the system and the outside world. So, in a relatively open system with porous boundaries, changes in legislation to improve equality of opportunity would have an impact on how the system is arranged. For instance, a human resources department might instigate new training for managers and checks and balances at various levels of the hierarchy. In a closed system the outside influences would find it difficult to penetrate the culture and consequently the internal practices are likely to be opaque. The latter is the type of organization where corruption among the leaders could take a hold. However, that type of system is also likely to be in decline because it lacks the stimulation and nurturance that the outside world might provide.

## Gender and sex in biography and career

Discourses of sex, gender and gender relations have major implications for women's personal and professional lives. Less often studied in the twenty-first century, dilemmas surrounding the practice of sex roles and the continued existence of sex-role stereotyping have been eclipsed by the potentially more exciting studies of the (so-called) hard-wiring of gender in the brain (Gallagher and Frith, 2003). Studies of sex roles over recent years have focused on specific attributions made to gender in cases of domestic violence, abuse and rape, for example (Anderson, 2005; Brown and Testa, 2008; Capezza and Arriaga, 2008). There are also studies of men doing 'typically' female work such as male nurses (Evans, 2002; Loughrey, 2008) and characteristics of women as leaders, traditionally a 'masculine' activity (Eagly and Carli, 2003).

Social, biological and psychological influences on our lives come together in a complex way in relation to *sex* (Archer and Lloyd, 2002). Differences between the way women and men experience these competing and complementary forces are emphasized in both scientific literature and in everyday life, where they are taken for granted and frequently characterized as the 'battle between the sexes' (Gill et al., 2008; Kirsten and Tamar, 2009; Martin and Ruble, 2010; Paechter, 2006).

Dame Glynis Breakwell (now one of the few contemporary university vice-chancellors) vividly described the female sex role as performed in the 1980s thus:

> Make no mistake about it, the role is meant to be performed. Sex roles are no theoretical fiction concocted by psychologists or sociologists

or even by militant feminists. They have just baptised a creature that women have always been able to delineate. When asked, women can describe the dimensions of their own sex role. What is more, they can describe the punishments incurred for any infringements: the emotional blackmail and social shame.

*(Breakwell, 1985: 2)*

But why does designated sex appear to make so much difference to the life course of individuals? Why are women punished for stepping outside the boundaries of recognized sex roles? How does sex and sexuality influence professional relationships?

Most of us are born female or male and that designation is called our 'sex' which is initially dependent upon genetic endowment, and subsequent characteristics upon hormone distribution prior to birth and at various stages of the life cycle. Biological and anatomical differences between women and men are strikingly visible. Female and male bodies have much in common that makes them both human, but they are also different in incisive ways; specifically in connection with their reproductive organs. The physical characteristics of females and males represent clear anatomical distinctions: body fat and hair distribution, reproductive functions and genitals (Archer and Lloyd, 2002). However, the anatomical distinctions are not simplistic. They represent social and ideological constraints as well as biological ones.

## Gender

*Gender* is different from sex in that it refers to the *social* characteristics whereby women and men exist in a dynamic structural relation to each other. While biologically designated sex has a significant part to play in the way human experience is defined, that explication is subject to layers of psychological experience mediated by personality, socialization, sexuality and gender divisions which are themselves socially constructed.

Gender, then, is a *process* through which social life is organized at the level of the individual, family and society (Morris and Thomas, 2005; Shapiro and Applegate, 2000; Zaretsky, 2000). This means it is also crucial in the structure of organizations. It prescribes and defines the parameters of individual human experience in that women's lives are different from men's (Nicolson, 1992a, 2012; Rohrbaugh, 1981) and through the recognition that individuals are in possession of a gendered self or subjectivity through which they themselves interpret their own experiences and operate constraints (Bolton, 2000, 2001; Dangor et al., 1998; Hollway, 1989).

Anatomy, as well as embodiment, is characterized by the ways women and men *use* their bodies to express everyday femininity and masculinity and experience sexual sensation. For example, we emphasize our physical shape and attributes which have been socially defined as attracting sexual partners, through dress, hairstyle, posture, make-up and physical movement. This results in women's passive/responsive qualities being emphasized as are men's potentially aggressive/active ones (Choi and Nicolson, 1994).

Anatomy/biology has a clearly social *meaning* encapsulated in the discourses on gendered behaviour (Sayers, 1986) so that when we look at a woman, the female body symbolizes an entire 'social history' through which others can understand her and through which she makes sense of her own life (Fine, 2011; Ussher, 1989).

Anatomy provides a set of physical symbols through which sex and gender, meanings and representations are communicated. The social meanings given to anatomical symbols operate in a deterministic way so that whether the argument is based upon biological, social or psychological factors, anatomy *is* destiny (Nicolson, 1994; Orbach, 2010).

It is this idea of 'destiny' that is intriguing and especially important here. While the notion that social meanings are attributed to biology is far from reductionist in perspective, it may still be seen as determinist in that social ideas about sex, gender and sexuality are neatly bound up in the concept of female reproductive life. When we see a woman we assume certain personality traits, certain behaviours, certain limits to her experience and most important we see her in some relation to motherhood rather than professional success (Nicolson 1992b, 1993a). Women's biological capacities to bear and feed children are presented in patriarchal societies as the determining features of what is 'natural', and conversely what is 'unnatural'. Childlessness and traits contrary to the nurturing role, such as aspiring to and achieving social power, are presented as unfeminine and somehow 'damaging' to potential femininity (Ehrenreich and English, 1979).

## Gender relations

Gender relations are *power* relations, through which men and male values have superordinate status over women and female values, and socialization into gender roles is an integral part of the maintenance of the patriarchal power structure (Fine, 2011; Hollway, 1989; Leonard, 1984). Women and men experience their worlds through these contextualized relationships, and therefore it is arguably the role of academic psychology to explore their psychologies *within the gendered context*. However, scientific knowledge reflects a value system that not only fails to tackle effectively the disadvantages in women's lives, but, through its knowledge claims, privileges male experience over female. Thus, most of what counts as legitimate psychological knowledge mirrors this privilege (for instance in relation to cognition and the menstrual cycle where, despite critique and contrary research evidence, researchers continue to investigate women's cognitive problems during the pre-menstrual period (Ussher, 1992a)).

All women are positioned and position themselves within the discourse on female reproduction and associated 'qualities', although femininity itself is arguably less prescribed than masculinity which is defined through 'what it is not' (Archer, 1989) (see Chapter 3). Femininity, however, is constantly under surveillance and consequently regulated through patriarchal exploitation of the intrinsic relationship between reproductive function and acceptable womanhood. Feminine women have to behave in what are deemed socially appropriate ways and what is seen as suitable for one generation may not be the case for the next one.

## Sex roles

Sex roles represent an intricate pattern of involvement between sex, gender and everyday experience. Women and men have expectations placed upon them from a range of constituents, identified collectively as 'society'. These include parents, the family, peers and institutions such as school, university, religious bodies and work organizations. However, these expectations are neither easy nor comfortable to fulfil, nor are they value free (Auster and Ohm, 2000; Breakwell, 1985). To 'become' a girl/woman and to 'become' a boy/man cannot be left to biology alone (Archer, 1989; Krane et al., 2004). Women and men have to learn what is expected of their sex; they also have to negotiate with themselves and their immediate social context what it is possible and desirable to do as members of each sex.

Further, sex differences are not neutral categories. As Leonard (1984) argued over 30 years ago, entry into the social order for females means that they are from the start expected to defer to males, to accept the leadership of males, to be, in a word, subordinate. Women, as a consequence of gender–power relations, then, are more likely to accept the patriarchal/male version of their lives as their 'reality', although they experience and manifest contradictory responses. Thus, many women have come to believe that child-care and home-making are their destiny, or that despite intellect and competence they are not suited for senior management. This does not mean they are content with these beliefs, but probably that they accept their distress as a personal failure rather than a power issue. How far is this notion of deference still the case – at home and at work?

While it might not appear to be so blatant for many Western heterosexual couples in the twenty-first century there is clearly a discourse of gender-deference with many non-Western cultures (Hill and Ly, 2004) including families living in Western countries from minority communities some of which is enacted through violence, particularly domestic violence by men towards their female partners and daughters (McFarlane et al., 2005; Nasrullah et al., 2009; Nicolson, 2010).

The interface between gender identity, sex-roles and discrimination is additionally complicated. Gender is a crucial means of categorization and social stratification in all societies (see Bleier, 1984; Fine, 2011); it is central to individual identity, life expectations and opportunities (Martin and Ruble, 2010; Rohrbaugh, 1981). Sex-role stereotypes in Western societies reflect what women and men do, while at the same time they serve as the basis for inequalities and social sanction (Braidotti, 2008; Brown and Testa, 2008; Kirsten and Tamar, 2009b). As Breakwell asserts, it is difficult for women and men to step too far beyond stereotypical behaviours without dire consequences. Women who achieve professional success have made an important step beyond the bounds of conventional femininity and women's role requirements.

How do women senior managers cope with junior male colleagues who subvert their operations just because they object to a female boss? How do business-women negotiate sufficient reward for themselves when work-related lunches and exclusive club membership feels alienating and stressful rather than a 'bonding' experience?

## Becoming gendered

Lifespan development and career are related concepts. Career progress and the context of a person's life are clearly and unequivocally linked to their family and the broader social context as well as a sense of identity and personal integrity. Studies of lifespan development which tend to focus upon male development, position women primarily in the context of their nurturing role in the family (Erikson, 1968; Levinson, 1986) and thus have little to offer to the theorization of women's professional achievement.

The overwhelming fact about adult psychological development is that it involves *accumulation of experience*, and that experience is crucial to the way individuals act. Studies of child cognitive (e.g. Kohlberg, 1966; Martin et al., 2002) and social and behavioural development have shown that gender is salient to the way children and adolescents adapt their cognitive and behavioural strategies. Psychological development and socialization in the family, school and wider social context guarantee that these strategies are incorporated into an individual's repertoire of knowledge, which is a major source of gender differences in behaviour and temperament (e.g. Bem, 1974; Gilligan, 1982; Nicolson, 2014).

The consequence of socialization and development in a specific context for professional women is likely to mean that some aspects of their beliefs about and experience of gender become increasingly difficult to sustain. They are no longer fitting the expected gender lifespan path, and their chosen route is less clear for them than it is for their male colleagues. Even so it is important to remember that, despite socialization and development through common life stages, each person has their specific means of being themselves.

Studies of gender issues in school, higher education and training provide data on differences in intellectual, social and personality aspects of performance and behaviour at various points of the life course. Research on behavioural differences at school between boys and girls shows girls working more consistently at academic work, although very few distinctions in personality or intellectual ability between the genders have been demonstrated irrefutably (Maccoby and Jacklin, 1974).

There is, however, evidence that teachers' expectations and behaviour towards boys and girls differs, and working-class girls in particular are expected, and consequently expect, to be primarily mothers who may work, but simply to subsidize the family income (Beckett, 1986). There is also some data to suggest that girls and young women feel they are less intellectually able than boys and young men (Beloff, 1992); and believe that menstruation disadvantages them in terms of exam and other cognitive performance (Richardson, 1992; Walker, 1995) although there is little conclusive evidence that this is so.

## Sex-role stereotyping

Girls in our society are socialized to be more oriented towards people, to be other-directed and dependent, whereas boys are raised to be more independent, aggressive and achievement-oriented. Girls develop a negative self-image when they accept society's more positive evaluation of males, particularly that to succeed at 'work' is to demonstrate masculine traits, something most women are reluctant to do (DeLamater and Fidell, 1971: 7).

Sex-role stereotyping is pervasive. Scientists, social opinion leaders and everyday beliefs reinforce traditional views of women's and men's characteristics, and these beliefs make a crucial contribution to organizational structures. Broverman et al.'s (1970) small-scale but influential study demonstrated the view that health professionals have about the 'mentally healthy adult' and social desirability for women's behaviour. Women, if they are to be acknowledged and acknowledge themselves as *suitably* feminine, are unassertive, interested in their appearance, dependent, illogical and focused on home and the family. While this equated with images of femininity, it is not representative of the successful career person. Subsequent studies of sex roles have shown that while these characteristics cluster together as a gross stereotype, they cannot be dismissed as such because they represent much of what women actually do and expect in their lives (Archer and Coyne, 2005; Schnurr, 2008). Girls are socialized actively into being feminine (Beckett, 1986) and the experience of psychological development involves girls in recognizing what girls do, and thus beginning to identify their own thoughts and behaviours with this (Bem, 1981; Hargreaves, 1986; Kohlberg, 1966).

Classical psychoanalytic theory, which has had a greater influence on popular culture than on academic psychology itself, also suggests that normal and healthy femininity equates with passivity. 'Normal' women are passive and responsive to men in their actions, personality, sexuality and other relationships. Freud himself was clear that women who achieve in careers may suffer from 'penis envy' (1931) which will have long-term negative psychic consequences. This theory went as follows:

> The little girl, frightened by the comparison with boys, grows dissatisfied with her clitoris, and gives up her phallic activity and with it her sexuality in general as well as a good part of her masculinity in other fields. The second line leads her to cling with defiant self-assertiveness to her threatened masculinity. To an incredibly late age she clings to the hope of getting a penis some time. That hope becomes her life's aim; and the phantasy of being a man in spite of everything often persists as a formative factor over long periods.
>
> *(Freud, 1931, quoted in Bocock, 1983: 53)*

Freud, and followers of his theory and practice claim power, influence and assertiveness in the public sphere to be 'naturally' the province of men. They argue that women 'naturally' gain their greatest satisfaction from giving birth and motherhood, particularly if they should have a boy. These issues are explored more fully in later chapters when considering the interface between gender identity, beliefs and experience from an intrapsychic perspective.

## Subjectivity

How does the gendered person negotiate their psychological development and social interaction? How do women and men make sense of their gender in the world of work? Psychologists traditionally have talked about personality, intelligence and situational variables as influencing behaviour and experience in organizations, and make claims to select suitable candidates for management positions through the use of psychometric tests and standardized interviews (Alimo-Metcalfe, 1994). This process relies on the assumption that the person/individual is somehow an objective, measurable and observable entity and mainstream psychology has adhered stubbornly to the validity of the unitary individual whose personality, behaviour and cognitive abilities might be objectively measured (Dewsbury, 2000; Frosh, 2003; Henriques et al., 1984/1998). However, critical psychologists from discursive and intrapsychic positions have provided strong challenges to the fixed notion of the unitary individual. 'This concept describes a fictitious character, the bourgeois individual, whose integrated wholeness, unique individuality and status as a subject with actual power to shape events has become null and void' (Sampson, 1989: 3). Instead of concepts such as 'personality' or 'self', critical writers have focused upon the dynamic interaction and fluid boundaries between the social and the individual, and identified *language* as the means by which interactions take place (Potter and Wetherell, 1987). Language and social discourses produce the means by which the social and the individual interconnect and disconnect, and these processes occur over time and during the course of specific actions.

In the context of this project, I am concerned to demonstrate the complex and contradictory ways in which a sense of being a gendered individual in a male-dominated culture and organization influence the ways in which integrity and survival are negotiated. Women's and men's traditional roles and responsibilities in relation to the male boss or patriarch (at home and at work) are integral to the experience of being a female or male *subject*. Gender discrimination, subordination at work and the experience of being socially and professionally marginalized or privileged further influence everyday experience and become integrated into a sense of subjectivity/ identity in an intra-psychic way. Resistance to patriarchal processes occurs as women refuse to accept the pre-existing categories and roles, while at the same time women's lives are circumscribed by gender-role expectations.

Femininity is a contradictory experience and, as such, individual identity or subjectivity is experienced as a connection/dislocation between the social and the subjective. Masculinity too is problematic for discursive practice and intrapsychic experience for those men who find themselves eclipsed by other men and more importantly by women.

As Harré and colleagues, in their critique of mainstream psychology, suggested:

> a human mind does not emerge out of processes internal to the human individual. It is a shaping of the activities of the whole person, including their brain and nervous system, by sociolinguistic influences. In the course of this shaping a person acquires a fragment of the rules and conventions of their society, in accordance with which they form projects for action and choose the means for realising those projects.
>
> *(Harré et al., 1985: viii)*

Deconstruction and discourse analysis as a method in social science and psychology, in particular, has demanded detailed scrutiny of the concepts of 'self', 'identity' and 'subjectivity' which can no longer be taken for granted. The terms 'self' and 'identity' were traditionally associated with mainstream notions of the unitary individual, and while some post-modern, deconstructionist social scientists would stress that there is nothing *but* text (see Sampson, 1989 for discussion) an MDI approach provides evidence of and access to a reflexive self/identity/subjectivity (see Nicolson, 2014) which in turn engages a person in biographical accounting of the relationship between their development over the lifespan and their present-day experiences in organizations.

What is important is to stress the fluidity of the boundary between subjective experience and the social world, and particularly the relationship between gender as a social process and gendered experience (see Georgakopoulou, 2005; Gill et al., 2008; Henriques et al., 1984/1998; Tunaley, 1995). Thus, there is no essential biologically determined female or male experience, but being a woman or a man, including for women the capacity and reality of child bearing, and for men the capacity for aggression, is a socially constructed and dynamic process.

## An MDI analysis of gender in biography

A major task of this book examining the lives and careers of professional women in what is still a male-dominated context is to analyse experience as one of dynamic and ongoing interaction between discourses of gender and power, and the experience and meaning of being an individual in a social context (see Craib, 2001; Nicolson, 1994). This is particularly salient when there is conflict and contradiction between the experience of being a woman and the social construction of femininity that explicitly prioritizes the non-assertive and non-rational part of human action and emotion (see Bem, 1974; Broverman et al., 1970; DiLillo and Peterson, 2001; Nicolson, 1992a).

The dilemma for many professional women is how to negotiate and give meaning to their sense of femininity and gender identity in the world of power and intellect, when that world has defined them out.

It may be summarized thus:

> Bearers of the heritage of the 'Age of Reason' as we are, it can be argued that it is fundamentally contradictory for us in the West to think about women as rational or to perceive them as askers of questions or thinkers. Nor do these images fit the views and stereotypes about traditional femininity. The basic question is: how do feminine identity and intellectual thinking go together?
>
> *(Wager, 1985: 2)*

In what follows I argue the case for women to continue to claim their *right* to the world of intellect, authority and power, which is still denied them under current social practices that position the normal woman as emotional, nurturing and passive and the difficult, unfeminine harridan as disturbing the boundaries around the rightful territory of men. It is stressful to be seen as marginal to patriarchy, and the successful woman is marginalized because she is unfeminine and as a consequence of having to 'toughen herself up' to get anywhere against the existing male strongholds.

# 2

# FEMININITY, MASCULINITY AND ORGANIZATION

## Introduction

Below I examine how, within an MDI framework, meanings and practices of masculinity/masculinities and femininity/femininities have an impact on women and men in their professional lives.

Such meanings and practices involve:

- First, a *bio-material* context, where femininities (Barnes, 2002) and masculinities (Zaretsky, 2000) operate on the level of the *biological/anatomical body*. That is, hormones, genitals and secondary sexual characteristics such as facial hair or breasts demonstrate the body and give it a biological meaning (Archer and Lloyd, 2002).
- Second, a *discursive* framework, at the level of the *gendered body*. That is, the way that the biologically sexed body is given a social meaning. Thus, the shape, size and appearance of the body, particularly in terms of sexuality (including desire and attraction/attractiveness), reproductive role related behaviours, the meaning attributed to hormonal/menstrual cycles through the life span, and the way women and men use their bodies to express themselves in a variety of interpersonal interactions are discursively constructed (Choi and Nicolson, 1994; Ussher, 2003).

- Third, a *discursive through to intra-psychic* context that implies femininity and masculinity are associated individually and socially, with certain *traits/characteristics*. Femininity according to pervasive stereotyping equates with being 'passive' while masculinity means 'active'. Sex-role theories in psychology contribute to this by listing feminine, masculine and androgynous characteristics, and although female sex and femininity do not necessarily coincide, a woman whose main characteristics did not include feminine ones would probably be concerned, as there is an underlying popular belief system that women are like other women and men are like other men (Bem, 1987; Broverman et al., 1970; Freud, 1973; Thomas, 1986).
- Fourth, there is the level at which *gender–power relations* operate within all three material, discursive and intra-psychic contexts. Femininity/women and masculinity/men co-exist in a constant power dynamic, which shifts its focus depending upon action and circumstances, but is nonetheless ever present (Bell and Newby, 1976; Davies, 2003; Fox and Suzy, 2012; Hollway, 1989; Leonard, 1984; Wood, 2001).
- Fifth, intra-psychically, femininity (Brownmiller, 2013; Freud, 2010) and masculinity are contained at an *unconscious* level as a product of all these aspects of human experience and consciousness (Davies, 2003; Frosh, 1994; Gough, 2006; Hearn, 2004; Sayers, 1986, 1990, 1992; Seidler, 2004).

There are multiple ways of examining and accounting for masculinity and femininity, from exploring hormones and physical sex characteristics (Fine, 2011) and testing the validity of sex-role stereotypes (Auster and Ohm, 2000) to a focus on evolutionary psychology and the role of sexual reproduction (Auster and Ohm, 2000; Gallagher and Frith, 2003; Potts, 2005). However, those who continue to research and develop theory find the concepts remain problematic. This is in part because materially and discursively history, politics, biological, psychological and medical sciences develop and change. This is particularly clear to me because, even since the first edition of this book was published in 1996, thinking and practices, including my own, have changed considerably. Thus, this second edition is focused upon gender relations in organization more so than it is on a feminist perspective per se. The reason is not because the feminist project is over by any means, but the focus has shifted and women's relationship and subordination to men's power is less clear-cut than in the 1990s, as we shall see. However, this is not to say that fundamental patriarchal power relations have been overthrown. Maguire made the point that gender, in the form of definitions of masculinity and femininity, is omnipresent even though the details comprising the definitions might have changed.

> What are 'masculinity' and 'femininity'? Every society has ways of distinguishing the sexes – socially, culturally, psychologically. Historically, however, the way this division has been drawn has varied enormously. What counts as maleness or femaleness in one period or cultural setting can look radically unlike its equivalents in other times or places. And similarly, how an individual comes to identify him or herself as belonging to a gender also varies greatly.
>
> *(1995: 1)*

Sigmund Freud seemed to find thinking about masculinity and femininity a lot easier: 'You cannot give the concepts of "masculine" and "feminine" any new connotation. The distinction is not a psychological one; when you say "masculine", you usually mean "active", and when you say "feminine" you usually mean "passive"' (Freud, 1973: 147–148). It is tempting to reject Freud's assertion as an out of date concept representing the work of an advocate of patriarchy. But would that be a mistake? He is not talking about a biological inevitability here, as some have taken it to mean, but that masculinity and femininity are discursive constructions, in his words *connotations*. This discourse of femininity/masculinity has contemporary significance. The oft-reported Sheryl Sandberg (Luscombe, 2013) has been criticized for expecting less well remunerated women to manage their lives as effectively as she does. She is referred to frequently as 'ballsy', a direct reference to her behaviour and success in aping masculinity rather than being a typical woman who has smashed that proverbial ceiling of glass with a feminine style. Christine Lagarde (Walt, 2013), again often described in the press as an exceptional woman, is spoken of as possessing 'formidable people skills' (p. 18). To be exceptional is not to be normal, while 'formidable' has connotations with the stereotypical view of masculinity (active, powerful, dominant and so on) rather than femininity (passive, soft, emotional). Formidable people skills sound, to me at least, as if she is terrifying rather than skilled!

Lagarde herself is reported in the same article as speaking in simple terms and applauding the fact that women, when they meet, talk about things they do on a daily basis rather than talking in opaque terms about the politics and technology of the work they do. These examples are perhaps more connected to images of femininity, not quite akin to passivity, but they do indicate discursive constructions of gendered expectations of behaviours and role (Afifi, 2007; Genovese and Steckenrider, 2013; Martin and Ruble, 2010; Paechter, 2006; Sharp et al., 2012).

From birth, it seems, we are compelled to seek confirmation of our gendered identity (Fine, 2011; Nicolson, 2014). From the time we recognize whether we are female or male, before we are sure we know how those in each category are meant to behave, all human individuals actively pursue the project of 'becoming gendered' (see Chapter 3) (Butler, 1990; Lempers and Clark-Lempers, 1997; McDowell, 1993; van Roosmalen, 2000). At the same time, we are aware of the contradictions that separate experience and desire from social constraints (Coward, 1993; Edley, 2001; Orbach, 2010; Walkerdine, 2003).

## Anatomical and biological aspects of gender

> That women bear children and men do not is probably the most important biological difference between them.
>
> *(Sayers, 1982: 7)*

> The definition of women as weak, inferior and inherently unstable because of their dangerous sexuality and 'bleeding wombs' has long been the basis of society's and psychology's understanding of female adolescence, concealing reality behind the myth. It is during adolescence that the young woman first experiences a split between her body and her self: between her own experience and the archetype she is expected to emulate.
>
> *(Ussher, 1989: 18)*

It is difficult to separate anatomy and biology from their meaning – either their meaning to individuals or to society (Nicolson, 2014; Orbach, 2010). The crucial aspects of anatomy/biology in relation to gender are the way that men and women are physically different, and that those differences are endowed with value that consistently disadvantages women (Nicolson, 1998; Ussher, 2003).

Women's bodies, with the capacity for child bearing and breast-feeding, are clearly different anatomically and biologically from men's. These anatomical and biological differences are the source of different behaviours associated with reproductive function. This is not in dispute. What is challenging, however, are the various ways in which the female *body* has been positioned as subordinate to that of the male (Ussher, 1989, 2002, 2006). This is often achieved in relation to women's reproductive *capacities* by patriarchal science operationalizing female possibilities as if they were deficiencies. Thus, for instance, the menstrual cycle has been socially constructed by scientists, health professionals and the media as a disability (Nicolson, 1995a).

This myth, or discourse, has permeated popular knowledge. It has been particularly important in constraining some women's beliefs about their own professional life, because the idea that women are intellectually weak at certain 'times of the month' has been used implicitly and explicitly to count against women aspiring to senior roles. Who would want a barrister suffering from pre-menstrual tension to be their advocate? The idea of the surgeon or test pilot bursting into tears during the difficult part of the operation or flight is horrific. However, consistent evidence that only around 5–10 per cent (Warner and Walker, 1992) of the female population have menstrual disorders continues to be ignored in favour of these misogynist images. The same is true of the idea of cognitive impairment around the time of menstruation, even though it has been shown to be scientifically insupportable (Sommer, 1992; Walker, 1997).

However, not having menstrual periods is no safeguard for the image of the competent woman. Older post-menopausal women, who have brought up their children or who have simply taken longer to decide upon a career path, are also discriminated against for their lack of youth and femininity – the counterpart of their lack of fertility (Gannon, 1994; Hvas, 2006; Rostosky and Travis, 1996; Ussher, 1989; Walter, 2000).

As Jane Ussher argued:

> The discourse which defines women through their reproductive function conceptualises the biological event of menopause as the end of a woman's useful life. As fertility and femininity are immutably linked here, women who lose their fertility often experience the simultaneous loss of their femininity a major part of their identity as a woman.
>
> *(1989: 104)*

Masculinity, on the other hand, is positioned as positive and competent in youth, middle and old age. This is not to say that all men are destined to be successful in their professional lives; far from it. Masculinity is about competition, often to the 'death' of the rival. It is not uncommon for newly appointed senior managers to openly express hostility to rivals, particularly towards those in slightly junior positions who might be 'in waiting'. The male body is built to fight, and whereas the older woman is seen mainly in terms of her faded femininity, the older man, if he is no longer in the running for power, is seen as wise and experienced. However, masculinity is a highly pressured discourse, and men and boys need to be good enough to meet the criteria (Cross and Bagilhole, 2002; Davies, 2003a; Yarnal et al., 2004). Failed masculinity is a disgrace while failed femininity might actually mean a woman is 'ballsy' and overtly powerful.

## The meaning of the body

Feminist social science, psychoanalysis and post-structuralist critiques have all made significant contributions to understanding the meaning of the gendered body, and feminists in particular to the power connotations of these meanings (e.g. Orbach, 2010).

I want to introduce the importance of the unconscious (or intrapsychic) in the process of giving meaning to the gendered body and particularly to the way women and men interrelate in organizations.

The meaning of the gendered body is discursive, a process rather than a set of facts, and this process takes place throughout an individual's psychological development, and responds to social development and change. The gendered body has a social meaning and personal/interpersonal meaning. It is difficult for an individual to experience one without the other. Thus, we give our own body meaning that develops through our reflexive work in relation to different levels of consciousness, which becomes embedded albeit in a dynamic way as part of our biography. However, the meaning we give our own body is bound up inextricably with the social construction of the female and male body. We evaluate ourselves accordingly.

The late Precilla Choi, who wrote extensively about female athletes and body builders, demonstrated the contradictions women face through the paradox of being fit and physically active which frequently results in visible muscular strength (Choi and Salmon, 1995; Krane et al., 2004).

## The body at work

As women demanded access to power, the power structure used the beauty myth materially to undermine women's advancement.

*(Wolf, 1990: 20)*

Women, valued by men and women alike according to cultural standards of 'beauty', are traditionally seen as valuable in relation to their reproductive capacity.

*(Buss, 1994)*

Popular writers like Naomi Wolf and scientists like David Buss agree, although they express it differently: women are subject to age-related prejudice not because of lack of ability but because of appearance and all it means to the masculine mind. In the popular media, including television news presentation, there has been an ongoing debate about whether older women are cast aside in favour of younger women or men.[1]

In the UK one presenter of a programme called *Countryfile*, Miriam O'Reilly, successfully sued the BBC in 2013 for dropping her because she was approaching 50 years of age. Harriet Harman, a British Member of Parliament, publicly backed the view that women in general were removed from television at that age. More commonly, though, women over 40 frequently find themselves unable to find work in frontline secretarial jobs[2] it is said because the 'boss' (man) wants an attractive woman to display. There is increasing evidence, probably as a consequence of such practices, of a rush to plastic surgery or botox injections to hold back the observable ageing process.[3] This is not of course a new phenomenon, but in the twenty-first century women are beginning to fight back by publicly recognizing and challenging this age/sexism.

Naomi Wolf still believes there is still no other way used to judge women's worth than beauty, which is the beauty of the young, proven by the dominant discourse that for an older man to have a young female partner to replace a wife of his own age equates to 'trading up'.[4]

This, therefore, continues to present a major dilemma for women who wish to be successful at work; being valued and valuing themselves at all stages of their career and life cycles. The 'beauty myth' proposed by Wolf represented an important cultural focus in relation to the female body. Women are valued by men for their beauty in popular culture, which is also associated with youth and reproductive capacity in the currently popular evolutionary science (Buss, 2000).

Men still have the economic power, which means that many ordinary women need to compete with other women on beauty terms in order to achieve scarce male attention and ultimately to survive. As women get older their value is less. This results in highly lucrative global industries aimed at sustaining and enhancing female beauty, where the industry itself has a vested interest in maintaining this beauty-requirement. The discursive construction of beauty for women is ever present (Acker, 1990; Orbach, 2010; Sharma and Black, 2001).

All of this influences women's and men's everyday experience in the workplace. Women have to be attractive, but if they are too sexually attractive they are dangerous and/or dismissed as mere objects of male desire (Ussher, 1989).

If they rebel, and refuse to compete in the beauty game, they are seen as ugly harridans, and if they are in positions of high visibility they are disposed of.

The 1980s in Europe and the USA was the decade of power dressing. Power dressing, or wearing business suits, might then have been the 'answer' for aspiring professional women wishing to be attractive rather than sexy. Faludi, discussing these repercussions associated with John Molloy's (1977) *The Woman's Dress for Success Book*, said:

> for the next three years, women's magazines re-cycled scores of fashion stories that endorsed not only the suits but the ambitions they represented – with headlines like YOUR GET-AHEAD WARDROBE, POWER! and WHAT TO WEAR WHEN YOU'RE DOING THE TALKING.
>
> *(1992: 210)*

As both Faludi and Wolf pointed out, there was a fashion industry and media backlash against power dressing, although many women who did wear suits (a uniform similar to that of professional men) felt both comfortable, and that it suited their behaviour and aspirations. Women were accused subsequently of looking masculine, although the kinds of suits women wore were 'masculine only in so far as it established for women something recognizable as professional dress' (Wolf, 1990: 45).

Wearing more traditionally feminine clothes, particularly those that accentuate female characteristics (tight jumpers, short skirts), leaves the woman in danger of provoking sexual harassment (Wolf, 1990) and not being taken seriously as a professional.

As Wolf says:

> If, at work, women were under no more pressure to be decorative than are their well-groomed male peers in lawyer's pinstripe or banker's gabardine, the pleasure of the workplace might narrow; but so would a well-tilled field of discrimination. . . . Since women's working clothes – high heels, stockings, makeup, jewellery, not to mention hair, breasts, legs, and hips – have already been appropriated as pornographic accessories, a judge can look at any younger woman and believe he is seeing a harassable trollop, just as he can look at any older woman and believe he is seeing a dismissible hag.
>
> *(1990: 45)*

All women and men create and re-create their images throughout their careers. Undergraduates wearing jeans, with pink spiky hair, do not become academics, business-women or lawyers without changing their image to a more conservative one. The emphasis, as women and men enter the professional world, is upon specifying their *difference*, although this in turn reproduces inequalities. It is clear what the professional man is expected to be, but the woman is left floundering with the strong possibility of falling into the trap that she does not look the part.

But what is the significance of the difference between the ways in which the female and male bodies need to be represented? Despite understanding the politics and economics of gender and the implicit sexualized relations, there are important unconscious aspects of gender similarities and difference that provide symbolic meaning to the bodies of women and men.

## Different bodies, different minds

> When you meet a human being, the first distinction you make is 'male or female?' and you are accustomed to make the distinction with unhesitating certainty.
>
> *(Freud, 1973: 146)*

The differences between the male and female body are usually obvious, and this is accentuated through the way the individual is dressed and how they hold, move and generally control their physical presence. However, that the need for certainty in differentiating between the sexes is so important reveals the political significance of the gendered meanings given to the subjectivity of the person occupying the body.

Psychoanalysis more than any other perspective in psychology links the body, mind/emotion and the social realms of sex/gender. Feminists, concerned with the way that femininity has been intrinsically linked to masculinity in a subordinate relationship, have turned to psychoanalysis and an intrapsychic perspective to contest this intellectually and politically. Evidence achieved in this intrapsychic enterprise has served both to expose and implicate its proponents, particularly Freud; and to employ psychoanalysis to untangle the problem of subordination in the unconscious.

### Freud and femininity

Freud's work focused on the connections between human sexuality and its psychic development, and to explain this he describes the processes linking the body to the *social* and the achievement of masculinity and femininity and heterosexuality (see Freud, 1922). His method for attaining evidence consisted of his clinical case studies, and he extrapolated from these to develop his theoretical ideas.

Basically Freud's explication of sex/gender was as follows. The human psyche has a tripartite structure – the ego, the superego and the id (see Freud, 1922). The infant is born with the id in place, which is the source of unconscious instincts and drives. During the first year of life the ego (or the self, the link with others and reality) begins to develop, and around the ages of five/six the superego or conscience begins to form. Although girls and boys are born with different genitals, they have no knowledge of this at first,[5] and thus there is little to distinguish their early psychic development. Their psychic development occurs through the journey of the libido through the bodies erogenous zones: the mouth, the anus and the genitals. After the 'genital stage', during which the differences between girls and boys are ultimately recognized (around the ages of five or six), there is a period of sexual latency which ends with the emphasis in adolescence on heterosexual genital sexuality. It is during the genital stage that Freud's ideas on femininity and masculinity are incisive.

Underlying psycho-sexual development is the infant's belief that everyone has a penis, and it is this belief and the discovery that not everyone does, that brings about differential crises in girls and boys which makes them identify with the same-sex parent and separate themselves from each other. But because of these bodily differences, and the *value* of the penis, identification has different implications for both the psychic nature of each sex, and the relations between the sexes. The one sex (male) *has* the desired penis while the other (female) *lacks* a penis.

Freud is clear that there is a pathway to normal womanhood and a path to normal manhood. These are achieved at the point where genital differences are noticed in the self and the same- and other-sex parents.[6] For the boy, who has unconscious sexual desires towards his mother, the recognition of the girl's lack makes him fear similar consequences – castration. To avoid the rivalry and the wrath of his father the boy identifies with his father's masculinity, positioning himself with all men as different from women. This is the Oedipus complex (Britton, 1994; Edmunds and Ingber, 1977; Loewald, 2000; Nicolson, 2012).

Teresa Brennan summarized the Oedipus complex and its consequences as follows:

> The boy resolves his Oedipus complex by anticipating the future: he will have a woman like his mother one day; and this prospect enables him to defer the present unrealisable attachment in favour of a possible

future goal. He defers at the same time as he 'smashes' his Oedipus complex by diverting the hostility originally directed towards his mother towards his father. Some of this hostility also finds its way into his sexual drive, which he splits off from his affectionate feelings towards his mother and represses. . . . The lynch-pin in the repression of the masculine Oedipus complex is the threat of castration. This threat, which can be a matter of reality but is usually phantasy, is what prompts the boy to repress his desire for his mother, identify with his father, establish a superego, and ideally redirect his drive into sublimation.

*(1992: 12)*

Freud was less decisive in his account of girls' resolution of their sense of lack, and it is the contradiction in his accounts of the development of femininity which is both intriguing and abhorrent to feminists (see Mitchell, 1974).

As Brennan summarizes again:

Because this threat has less power in the feminine case, as the girl is already castrated, she has less motive for establishing a superego, and none for giving up her attachment to her mother. Indeed, the problem becomes why she should repress her phallic sexuality, as Freud of course maintains she does, and why she turns from her mother 'in hate', and forms an Oedipal attachment to her father. . . . Freud's main explanation for the girl's repression of her phallic sexuality and for her turning from mother to father is penis-envy. . . . She blames her mother for refusing to supply her with a penis, and turns instead to her father.

*(1992: 12–13)*

The girl's phantasy is that the father will supply her with a baby to substitute for the missing penis. Hence for Freud 'normal' femininity is enacted through childbirth and motherhood and other desires are *neurotic* affirming the unresolved *envy* of the penis.

Freud's clinical work and hence his case studies, which provided the evidence for his theoretical stance, was almost exclusively with women. Thus despite his persistent claim that he had theorized 'normal' masculinity and femininity, he was constantly faced with women who were not in accord with this norm. His response was to deem that they were 'neurotic'. In addition, he consistently reiterated the idea that femininity was a 'riddle':

> Throughout history people have knocked their heads against the riddle of the nature of femininity . . . Nor will you have escaped worrying over this problem – those of you who are men; to those of you who are women this will not apply – you yourselves are the problem.
>
> *(Freud, 1973: 146)*

His view is that the male is naturally 'active' and the female 'passive' by virtue of their genitals and their function during sexual intercourse. This is only contradicted in women's 'active' behaviour in relation to caring for infants/children (p. 148). Women have made no other contribution to society it might appear. 'It seems that women have made few contributions to the discoveries and inventions in the history of civilization; there is, however, one technique which they may have invented – that of plaiting and weaving' (Freud, 1973: 167).

His evidence for the psychological importance of anatomical distinction in different characteristics in women and men is what he calls women's *castration complex*. When girls see the genitals of the other sex they consider themselves to be seriously wronged and 'fall victim to "envy for the penis", which will leave ineradicable traces on their development and the formation of their character' (Freud, 1973: 159). For Freud, these ineradicable traces may be seen in subsequent desire 'to carry on an intellectual profession' (ibid.). The seriousness of this lack is the turning point in a girl's development, and Freud argued that there were three potential pathways of development from that point: sexual inhibition or neurosis, change of character in the sense of a masculinity complex and normal femininity (p. 160).

Neurotic sexuality is to take on the 'active' role in relationships that Freud argues comes from failure to abandon clitoral sexuality in favour of vaginal. This is only resolved 'if the wish for a penis is replaced by one for a baby' (p. 162). The masculinity complex occurs when the girl continues to behave in an active way into adulthood, the extreme of which he sees as female homosexuality. Normal femininity is passivity and motherhood.

Of course the issue is why Freud has these 'problems'. They are only problems for *women* as they represent the strains of patriarchal culture on freedom of choice and ability to achieve according to merit.

### Feminism and Freud

Mitchell, in *Psychoanalysis and Feminism*, argues that despite Freud's clear plea for the patriarchal status quo, through the judgement that women have to achieve femininity and may only do so through being wives and mothers, 'a rejection of psychoanalysis and of Freud's work is fatal for feminism' (1974: xv). This is because Freud is not offering 'a recommendation for a patriarchal society, but an analysis of one. If we are interested in understanding and challenging the oppression of women, we cannot afford to neglect it' (ibid.).

She argues that Freud himself neither 'invented' the myths underlying the bourgeois family and patriarchal social structures, nor did he unequivocally recommend their continuation. His thinking changed over the years, and he identified contradictions in his own work, as well as inspiring others such as Deutsch, Horney and Reich to take issue with traditional notions of female sexuality, passivity and 'women's place'.

Janet Sayers has reiterated Mitchell's point in relation to psychotherapy:

> It is no surprise to learn that feminists often reject this phallocentric account of women's psychology – at least for the first dawning of their heterosexual and maternal desire. So too do many psychoanalysts. Yet in doing so they have opted for psychological theories and therapies that assume and in the process overlook sexual difference and inequality.
>
> *(1992: 196)*

Nancy Chodorow (1994) has further stressed feminist abhorrence to the essentialism of Freud's psychoanalysis, but asks why the same critics remain intrigued by psychoanalysis, particularly its contribution to understanding gender divisions (Chodorow, 2000).

Certainly psychoanalysis and feminism are increasingly paired in the research/theoretical literature (Brennan, 1993), and there appears to be a consistent interest in Freud's work. However, recently, post-Freudian psychoanalysis has taken centre stage, particularly in relation to understanding sexual difference and accounting for female subordination.

## Discourse and psychoanalysis

> Femininity and masculinity are ways of experiencing the world. They are constructions which are built around anatomical difference, signifying only because they are given significance in the context of the power relations that constitute the social environment. Masculinity and femininity are subjective positions, central to our concepts of self because we are constructed in a world divided along gendered lines, but in principle they are just positions, ways of seeing and speaking about what we see.
>
> *(Frosh, 1992: 154)*

It is this sense of gendered experience that has been made possible to discuss in relation to the physical body through the work of post-structuralist psychoanalysts following the work of Jacques Lacan. Lacan, a psychoanalyst, was among the first to question the assumptions traditionally made about Freud's work. He was interested in exploring notions of the ego, which he understood in terms of the more dynamic subjectivity, and was influential in using this in relation to sexual difference.

Grosz (1990) argued that Mitchell's (1974) account of Freudian theory owes an unacknowledged debt to Lacan. Lacan focused upon the relations between women and men, through which he developed a strong theoretical analysis of femininity. His contribution was distinguished by his attention to the importance of *language* as symbolic of structural relations.

Central to his ideas in this context is the notion of the *phallus*. For Lacan, the phallus was distinct from the biological penis, and represented ideas about masculinity in the *symbolic order* under patriarchy. During the post-Oedipus phase, according to Lacan, when the boy identifies with men in general, the penis becomes seen as somehow 'detachable' or a generalisable phenomenon which represents the masculine. It becomes a 'signifier',[7] not owned by anyone, although available to men rather than women. Girls/women therefore 'identify as the "second sex", as the "other" of men's agency, desire and sexual exchange' (Sayers, 1986: 86). In Lacan's version of the castration complex, as the child separates from the mother s/he positions her/himself in relation to the mother's or father's possession of the imaginary phallus. In other words, the possibility of having a phallus or not (which depends on sex) positions a child in relation to their gender in accord with patriarchal symbolic order. 'Through the phallus, each sex is positioned as a speaking being, "giving reality to the subject"; through the phallus, the reality of anatomical sex becomes bound up with the meanings and values that a culture gives to anatomy' (Grosz, 1990: 131, quoting from Lacan, 1977). Through possession of the phallus, the subject (male) comes to occupy the position of 'I' in relation to the object 'Other' (female). Masculinity, then, is a powerful, active and potent force. The person possessing the phallus is affirmed as the subject who is able to *desire*. Femininity is about acceptance of the lack of phallus and resolution to being the object of that desire. This may only be achieved through the illusion brought about by feminine trappings such as clothing and make-up. These, according to Lacan, conceal the 'deficiency' and enable the woman to secure 'access to the phallic. Ironically, in this aim of becoming the object of the other's desire, she becomes the site of a rupture, phallic and castrated, idealized and debased, devoted to the masquerade (an excess) and a deficiency' (Grosz, 1990: 132). Thus the woman can be the phallus but only in appearance, because in reality she is not. She can only maintain the masquerade if she is the object of desire.

As Jane Ussher (1995) says:

> This leads to Lacan's apocryphal statement – 'The woman does not exist'. It is a depressing picture – woman is all appearance and sham, or she does not exist at all. Within Lacanian theorising she is all surface and no substance; the misleading object of desire, that promises everything but ultimately offers nothing.
>
> *(Ussher, 1995: 2)*

However, Ussher went on to argue that the phallus itself is also a representation because it is an unattainable phantasy, and although there is little doubt that the symbolic significance of the penis is important, it may be that men fare far worse than women. Having a penis (i.e. being a man) is no indication of warding off the sense of 'lack'. Indeed the lack of phallus will be felt even more acutely in those who have a penis. Following Frosh (1994) mastery and potency are problematic for men, as individually they have, literally, to measure up to the fantasy of the full phallus (see also Ussher, 1995).

This is crucial to gender relations in the workplace, particularly in relation to success and failure. Men have prepared themselves for age/stage career pathways carved out by preceding generations. Men have the potential for power, but more frequently the potential for failure and bitterness. Women have nothing so potent that they need to measure up to, although as the objects, or potential objects of desire, their energies are exploited and plundered in competing with other women for the right to be the object of a powerful man.

## Discourse and the unconscious

The phallus, the symbol of male power, is the inheritance of the male. The phallus enables the man to position himself as the powerful subject, the active, the desirer of the female object. Women may aspire to this by making themselves desirable, but any belief that they possess a phallus is masquerade. Thus, there are both male and female ways of looking at the world. The male from the position of authority and power, the female from the position of the 'other', whose only access to power is through being desired but being desired as a woman with all the implications that femininity brings. Thus, in professional life and work organizations, where the climate is competitive, the power resides with possessors of the phallus. However, while all women are excluded, so are some men. It is often the case that these women and men continue to attempt to achieve what they are unaware is the impossible. This results in misuse of energy and finally bitterness. However, as the object of male desire, some women are likely to be perceived as achieving phallic power by unfair means, and these powerless men may turn their bitter energies onto women, which makes the women doubly disadvantaged in terms of their energy expenditure.

## Sex-typed behaviours

> women have adapted themselves to the wishes of men and felt as if their adaptation were their true nature. That is, they see or saw themselves in the way that their men's wishes demanded of them; unconsciously they yielded to the suggestion of masculine thought.
>
> If we are clear about the extent to which all our being, thinking, and doing conform to these masculine standards, we can see how difficult it is for the individual man and also for the individual woman really to shake off this mode of thought.
>
> *(Horney, 1967/1993: 56–57)*

Gendered bodies have a meaning and are positioned within the social order. Femininity equates with lack/deficiency and masculinity with power. It is men who set the agenda, they are the 'I', they possess and desire. Women and femininity are defined through this construction of masculinity.

Here I want to reiterate and develop some of the aspects of sex-typed behaviours associated with gender relations in professional life and to place them in the context of biography and the discursive consciousness. Often there is a close link between stereotypical beliefs and what women and men actually do, and believe they should do. As Rhoda Unger suggested, it is likely that 'stereotypes are a component of a larger conceptual process involving how we view the causes of our own and others' behaviour' (1979: 51).

Men behave as if they were powerful, or at least heirs to power, almost from the start of life. Women behave as if they were not autonomous and potentially influential beings, but are the objects of the powerful. This is the result of socialization in the context of patriarchal power relations (Leonard, 1984; Lester, 2008; Martin and Ruble, 2010).

Psychological development, and socialization into becoming gendered and making sense of gendered behaviour continue throughout adulthood. Work organizations such as business corporations, town halls, universities, hospitals, legal practices and schools are influential in adult socialization and provide a powerful context for psychological change (Nicolson, 2014).

Women and men entering professions or large companies experience shifts in their subjective experience and their sense of subjectivity/identity through being part of the culture. They see what happens to the people around them. Who is promoted and who is overlooked. As time passes they evaluate their own progress in relation to others, but also reflexively and discursively monitor their own emotional and behavioural strategies and experience. They cannot, however, do this independent of gender. As Frosh (1992) summarized: there are gendered ways of experiencing the world.

What is important though is whose view counts, and clearly it is that of *powerful* men. Men are successful if they are able to take hold of the available power. Successful men may be criticized on an interpersonal basis for being selfish, too ambitious, ruthless or underhand. Less successful men also reflect on their experience and some may indeed feel that their masculine status is under threat. However, it is likely that they will have their own means of asserting power – at home, in their departments over junior staff, nurses, secretaries and female peers. Women are in the paradoxical position of being at risk of losing their femininity if they succeed or are striving to succeed, and also if they fail in their quest for promotion and influence. In both cases they will be seen exhibiting non-feminine behaviour because a successful woman cannot by (patriarchal) definition be nurturant; while someone thwarted in the attempt to achieve success is positioned as bitter, competitive and envious because they do not have essential ingredients to fulfil themselves. This is not feminine because 'little girls are not like that'. Femininity is about *accepting the lack*. Anything short of that is perversion/neurosis.

However, it is not only psychoanalytic theorists who have addressed the issues surrounding the beliefs and behaviours surrounding masculinity and femininity. As Bem (1974) began to suggest in the mid-1970s, the notion that femininity and masculinity are static qualities that only apply to attributes demonstrated by biological females or males is absurd. Her concern with research on stereotypical gendered behaviours focused on women and men's abilities to employ different characteristics according to circumstances. This meant that men could be masculine/aggressive/active on the rugby field, but exhibit tenderness and gentle behaviour towards, for example, babies and kittens. Women were able to be assertive or nurturant when the situation demanded. Bem further stressed the centrality of androgynous qualities such as intellect, honesty and interpersonal competence qualities in all people. She made the assumption that it was possible for men and women to operate primarily in an androgynous way.

However, separating femininity and masculinity from biology, and using them, along with androgyny, as concepts that relate to personality and behaviour, meant that she side-stepped the problems of gendered power and inequality and thus the meaning of *femininity* and *masculinity*.

Alison Thomas (1985, 1986) argued that Bem's contribution is limited.

> Bem offers no satisfactory way of independently ascertaining the meaning of the person's gender-schema . . . Bem has in fact overlooked an important cognitive issue – namely, whether or not her subjects actually share her own definitions of femininity and masculinity as represented in the Bem Sex Role Inventory.
>
> *(Thomas, 1985: 2)*

Thomas herself suggested that gender has a meaning for each of us – individually and collectively. She extends the notion of gender characteristics by raising questions about the interpretation of traditional feminine qualities. Thus, in a critique of Bem she states:

> What, critically, is not taken into account is whether or not the person concerned, describing herself, perhaps as 'nurturant', actually shares Bem's view that this is a feminine trait and sees it as relevant to herself. If she does not . . . then any inference about her self-perceived femininity is rendered invalid. She may indeed appear feminine, as judged by normative standards, but whether she construes herself as feminine or not cannot be established without first finding out her own constructions of what is or is not 'feminine'. This is where it becomes necessary to acknowledge the importance of personal representations of gender, and specifically, ideologies of gender, in any serious attempt to understand what gender means in self-perception. In other words, to consider the political along with the personal.
>
> *(Thomas, 1986: 4)*

Thomas's own work demonstrated that beliefs about gender and self-concept are complex. Individual women and men *do* operate reflexively and gender is a crucial aspect of their personal biographies. However, she has arguably focused too heavily on the cognitive aspects of gender schemas and masculinity and femininity, at the expense of social experience/intersubjectivity.

As Mead (1935), social constructionists from phenomenological sociologists such as Berger and Kellner (1964) through to Harré (1993) and Shotter (1995), to psychological discourse analysts such as Potter and Wetherell (1987), and psychoanalytic theorists (Freud, 1973; Lacan, 1977) have all stressed, society/social discourses 'pre-exist' the individual in some way, and the process of living as a gendered person is not one of choice. The body, language and power relationships all conspire against volition.

## Gender–power relationships

In a game where you cannot win, the sensible thing to do is to refuse to play.

*(Breakwell, 1985: 118)*

Power relations are both intentional and nonsubjective. If in fact they are intelligible, this is not because they are the effect of another instance that 'explains' them, but rather because they are imbued, through and through, with calculation: there is no power that is exercised without a series of aims and objectives. But this does not mean it results from the choice of an individual subject.

*(Foucault, 1978: 94–95)*

Participants in social interactions are aware of the fact that power is a crucial part of the dynamic, that it resides with individuals within the social organization, and that those with the power will maintain their influence (Bell and Newby, 1976). Most formal and informal meetings – at home, socially and in work organizations – involve some degree of power acknowledgement and response. Some individuals walk away from struggles for power, particularly if they know they will not win. Others feel the obligation to dent the power of others in some small way (Dutton, 2008; Gill et al., 2008; Haslam et al., 2011; Kimura, 2008).

Women and men at work know that they have to respond or negotiate around the rules set by the senior members of the company. Some individuals, however, are more personally powerful than others, a fact noted several years ago by social psychologists (French and Raven, 1959). They identified different forms of power – those that come with the job, that is being the senior manager, power that comes with individual charisma, power connected with specific forms of knowledge and power associated with experience of particular situations.

There is a tension in social science perspectives on gender–power relations between the 'objective' notion of power, where the focus is upon the fact that certain attributes are valued more highly than others. From this perspective, gender inequality is simply the result of social norms that are potentially changeable, as for example in the work of sex-role theorists such as Sandra Bem.

The 'subjective/interactive' perspective, on the other hand, involves unravelling the meaning of gendered interactions. It involves taking account of the *relationship* as well as the characteristics of men and women and their roles in society as in the work of Peter Leonard or Wendy Hollway.

Gender relations are the site for power struggles and power-based conflicts in work organizations as well as in the domestic sphere. Power remains firmly in the hands of (some) men, although not without resistance from other men and women.

Foucault argued that power and knowledge are equivalent, and the fact that men have traditionally been the ones to define what is and is not knowledge has ensured power stability (Burrell, 1988; Foucault, 1982). Patriarchal knowledge has defined women and men, femininity and masculinity, and as such has limited the discourses available through which to understand gender–power relations as distinct from the model whereby women are subordinate and men are superordinate (Leonard, 1984).

## Conclusions

Although things have changed for women so that even under patriarchy there have been more opportunities for economic independence and success, the price of attainment remains high. Women in their pursuit and achievement of power stand to lose their subjective sense of femininity, the sense of being a woman, their creative energy and peace of mind. Men continue to retain their advantages, although many do mentor women and openly support equal opportunities in a variety of ways. This has not, however, led to a real shift in the gender–power balance, but to some women gaining success.

Why do men appear to take up women's causes at work if in the end it might shift the power balance? Why do women persist in their attempts to enter the male bastions of power in the workplace when the cost is so great?

The answer lies in the relationship between women and men and the way in which power evolves and is managed. The decision to enter a profession, to distinguish herself in some way from other women, has ensured either a 'fight to the death' or opt out (which may in fact be the same thing).

Although power is constant, in that relationships are always between super-ordinate and subordinate individuals and groups, the form is fluid. Power relations are not inevitable, unchanging or unalterable (Faith, 1994).

## Notes

1 http://bbc.co.uk/news/entertainment-arts-22554217.
2 http://theguardian.com/commentisfree/2014/mar/14/ageism-sexism-workplace-ubiquitous-women-opportunities.
3 http://beautyredefined.net/anti-aging-and-symbolic-annihilation/.
4 http://washingtonpost.com/lifestyle/magazine/a-wrinkle-in-time-twenty-years-after-the-beauty-myth-naomi-wolf-addresses-the-aging-myth/2011/05/11/AGiEhvCH_story.html.
5 Horney believed that infants are aware of sex differences from the very start of life (see Sayers, 1986: 37).
6 This is a crude and far from complete account of the Oedipal crisis and the development of the superego. See Nicolson (2012) for a user-friendly version and references to more detailed perspectives.
7 Lacan (1977) argued that the 'sign' (the smallest unit of analysis in semiotics) is situated internally to the subject within the realm of thought. This means that the 'signifier' (material, phonic component) refers to any given 'signified' (conceptual component) through the mediation of a language with no fixed anchor point (cf. Saussure, 1974, who considered that there was a fixed core of language).

# 3

# GENDER AT WORK

## Introduction

In what follows I examine gender identity and gender role socialization to assess how:

- gendered behaviours and experiences are 'transferred' from the family to the workplace;
- gender-role 'spillover' is held together through biography, reflexivity and unconscious processes.

As proposed in Chapter 2, the intrapsychic and the material contexts of power relations are structured on clear gendered lines, so that there is an intrinsic link between gender and everyday experience. Men are more powerful than women in almost any context where power counts. Women and men, boys and girls gain implicit knowledge of how this works as they develop biologically, intellectually, emotionally and socially. This applies regardless of whether one takes a behaviourist, cognitive developmental, social constructionist or psychoanalytic perspective on the psychology of human development.

## Gender-role development

Despite the best efforts of feminist activists and scholars during the 1980s and 1990s, gender-role socialization and stereotypical role expectations remain an integral part of human experience from infancy, sexual intimacy, parenthood and in work organizations (Bleier, 1984; Capezza and Arriaga, 2008; Fox and Suzy, 2012; Lester, 2008; Loughrey, 2008; Niederle and Vesterlund, 2007). More striking, in the twenty-first century however, is just how far the rhetoric of cognitive-neuropsychology, particularly concerning the (so-called) hard wiring of the brain, reinforces discourses of gendered differences in behaviour and thinking across Western societies (Fine, 2011). One depressing outcome of this discursive context is the dearth of contemporary research into gender roles, stereotyping and socialization. It is as if the fascinating discoveries related to the human genome and technological developments in MRI scanning have destroyed any previous understandings about socialization, social learning and social pressures to conformity. While technology might eclipse other scientific tools, such as personality tests, observations and questionnaires, many scientists who engage in cognitive neuroscience are cautious about the 'truths' at their disposal (Ruigrok et al., 2014). The public and the media, it appears, are less so (Grabe and Kamhawi, 2006; Hyde, 2007).

While contemporary evidence from neuroscience pertaining to the gendered brain needs to be taken seriously, it is also crucial to hold in mind that John Archer (1989), observing studies of gender-role socialization for girls and boys stated that, 'The most striking feature is the separation of their social worlds, entailing two different cultures (1989: 367)'. If this is still the case, and why would it not be so, it is not surprising that women and men adopt different patterns of behaviours and enjoy differential sets of expertise (Cameron, 1992; Haslam et al., 2011). However, *difference* of this kind signifies the state of career achievement for gendered adults in work organizations and the power dynamic remains one that disadvantages women.

Boys/men appear to be more aggressive and less empathic than girls/women according to contemporary neuropsychology research (Gordon, 2003; Ruigrok et al., 2014). Archer and colleagues, however, have shown though that under different conditions girls may be just as aggressive as boys, findings which have implications for understanding gender and power relations (Archer and Coyne, 2005; Coyne and Archer, 2005). To understand the ways in which women and men operate at the organizational level it is therefore useful to examine the processes and practices surrounding gender-role socialization and the differences between the experiences and expectations of girls and boys.

Archer (1986, 1989) made the case that gender-role development is not simply the result of differential socialization. The basis of femininity and masculinity underlying the socialization process is qualitatively different. Boys, from an early age, are under pressure to conform to their gender roles, which contrasts markedly with the experience of girls. Boys are also pressured to maintain a sharp distinction between their interaction with other boys and with girls, limiting their relationships with the latter.

How does this work? There appear to be two main sources of pressure: the punishment of femininity in boys, and the elevation of masculinity, and thus other boys, as manifesting a superior form of development.

### Different pathways

> Masculinity is like a club, entry to which boys can gain in different degrees. The general requirements for entry centre on not being a sissy and on being tough.
>
> *(Archer, 1989: 368)*

> Femininity, the dark continent or semiotic underside, the cyclical, fertile, messy, unpredictable, all-too-uncertain, all-too-sensual, all-too-human, incoherent (inconstant) inconsistency that reflects the ambiguities of feeling more than the abstruse convictions of logical thought. Masculinities have fed hungrily off this opposition, suppressing nature by science, emotion by thought, seeking modes of self-representation which bolster the certainty needed by those who feel born to rule, but are unsure of their right or capacity to do so.
>
> *(Frosh, 2002: 5)*

There is abundant evidence from studies of developmental psychology that boys are more likely to be punished if they exhibit 'feminine' behaviour, while little attention is given to girls' transgressions of this type. As Frosh asserts, masculinity depends on being different from the (apparently) irrational and dangerous femininity and to an important extent masculinity itself is repressive to boys and men. Girls, for example, are indulged or ignored if they wear cowboy or spacemen suits but boys are not indulged if they wear make-up or high-heeled shoes – far from it (Bee, 1981; Nicolson, 2014). There appears to be more anxiety about the possibility of a boy being a 'sissy' than of girls behaving like 'tomboys' with the former being seen as so uncomfortable that it has been identified in the United States as a 'child-hood gender disturbance' (Archer, 1986, 1989).

Masculinity then, or indeed masculin*ities*, which Archer argues is both more complex and contradictory than femininity, is characterized by rigid role requirements in childhood. By this he meant that more is expected of boys/men at any one time in childhood, but in particular they learn to avoid the feminine. During this time, girls are relatively free. The female role, however, becomes less flexible in adolescence, which 'can be viewed as a way of marking out both the subordination of women and their value as a sexual and reproductive commodity for men (Archer, 1989: 369)'. Across the life span, however, particularly because of childbirth and motherhood, females experience a far greater degree of change than do males (Archer, 1986; Archer and Lloyd, 2000; Nicolson, 2014).

Archer illustrates this through popular culture, citing, for instance, the *Beano* (children's comic), which depicts the different range of expectations permissible for girls and the limits to those for boys.

> 'Minnie the Minx' is a positive character who climbs trees and plays masculine sports, Softy Walter (in 'Dennis the Menace') is an object of ridicule who associates with girls, has feminine interests such as dolls and musical boxes, lack toughness, and cries.
>
> *(1989: 368)*

In Enid Blyton's *Famous Five*, 'George' (really Georgina) claims she can do anything that her companions Dick and Julian can do, and her behaviour is contrasted with the more traditionally feminine cousin Anne. As Archer points out, being a tomboy may give a girl enhanced status.

This situation for girls is not as clear-cut as Archer maintains though, and although there is a limited status before adolescence for the tomboy, there are increasing sanctions as the girl reaches puberty. Even for young girls the role models of George and Minnie as tomboys do not have the autonomy and power of real boys. The 'problems' of femininity become apparent well before and beyond adolescence (see Nicolson, 2014).

A more contemporary variation on this theme is the portrayal of Meg Griffin in television cartoon *Family Guy*. She has an older brother and a baby brother, both of whom are exploited by (and who sometimes exploit) the dysfunctional parents. However, only Meg is routinely put down for being sexless, which for a girl, and this one in particular, means she is seen as dull, fat and ugly, and simply doesn't count in the family. The cartoon draw-ings do not necessarily reflect this image, and neither of her brothers has been drawn to be attractive. The baby has a misshapen head and her older brother is extremely overweight and positively 'thick'. But he is a boy and wants to avoid any connection with his sister at home or in school.

### Gender boundaries

As boys become socialized into masculinity they gradually become segregated from their female peers (Coyne and Archer, 2005; Gough, 2006; Gough and Edwards, 1998). 'Boys' games' emerge, which exclude sisters and former friends, and these games coincide with the distinction of masculinity from 'other' behaviours (Coplan et al., 2001). Richmal Crompton's *Just William* books again provide good illustrations of this. William and his friends, the 'Outlaws', have sisters and know girls from school, but a constant theme is the fear of being made to play with girls. At certain times one member of the Outlaws may have a secretly good experience or feeling about being with a particular girl, but they always find a way to overcome this, and return to the 'real' world of boys. One of their worst fears is spending time with Violet Elizabeth Bott, the ultra-feminine child who uses her femininity ('I'll scream and I'll scream until I'm sick' – said with a lisp!) to persuade them to allow her to join them. While she wants to play with *them*, their project is to avoid her – they would never want to manipulate their way into joining girls.

However, this does not coincide fully with the empirical work that suggests that boys 'spoil' girls' games. In the *Just William* books, for example, they tend to avoid girls.

There is far greater emphasis on gender equality among boys and girls in some of the twenty-first-century equivalents such as the *Harry Potter* and *Hunger Games* series for example. Girls there, while feminine in character, are equally portrayed with a sense of adventure, strength and logical intelligence. But this it seems may not be enough to challenge gender boundaries and stereotyping in contemporary adolescence and adulthood. Thorne (1986), cited by Archer, suggested that gendered play is like a contest and includes 'pollution rituals' where one side or the other is able to contaminate the rivals. Thorne observed that girls tend to be more likely to be invaded/polluted by boys, which leads to girls having defensive tactics such as chasing boys away or telling adults (or screaming till they are sick). It also means that even though they may have shown toughness and bravery in the end they themselves are polluted by patriarchy (if not individual boys) and become submissive. Femininity is seen as dangerous when masculinity is threatened by being outshone on its own terms or seduced into a relationship with a woman.

There is, if nothing else, ambivalence on the part of pre-adolescent boys towards their female peers. Archer concludes that this is because of the social importance placed on the masculine role, and although the emphasis varies during the course of childhood/adolescent development, flexibility for boys is only permissible once the masculine role has been clearly transmitted (Cameron, 1992; Haslam et al., 2011). Recent research on play in childhood has focused on girls' and boys' interest in computer and other electronic games suggesting there remain differences in gendered interests with boys being technical and girls social (Beasley and Collins Standley, 2002; Cherney and London, 2006).

### *Reproduction of mothering*

Discourses of masculinity, then, are about independence and autonomy (Addis and Mahalik, 2003; Hearn, 2004; Seidler, 2004), while femininity is still about engaging in co-operative behaviours, nurturance and dependence (Auster and Ohm, 2000; Broverman et al., 1970). Archer's analysis of the development of gender roles assumed cultural transmission though a system of direct reward, and punishment for violation, at various stages of development. This occurs through the traditional channels of socialization – the family, peer group, school (Weitzman, 1979) – and, as Archer points out, upholds the privileging of masculinity and boys/men.

It is the mother, though, who is most often the primary agent of childhood development/socialization within the family. This fact reiterates complex questions about how the subordination of women and the supremacy of masculinity and the male role are reproduced in the family and consequently in the workplace reminiscent of Freud's view discussed and outlined above in Chapter 2.

Chodorow (1978), the American sociologist/psychoanalyst, has been influential in explaining this apparent paradox, although not without challenge. She asserts that as it is *women* who *mother*, a responsibility with which they are charged based on their abilities to give birth, lactate and thus feed infants, their influence, particularly on an unconscious level, is paramount.

As a sociologist, Chodorow, who also is a practising psychoanalyst, argues that women's role as a mother became high profile as a consequence of economic development and the resulting division of labour in Western capitalist societies. Mothering has 'ceased to be embedded in a range of other activities and human relations. It stands out in its emotional intensity and meaning, and its centrality for women's lives and social definition' (Chodorow, 1978: 6). Even prior to industrialization and the genesis of the bourgeois family, though, there was little to persuade the observer that child-care was the province of men, or even a shared role. So why do women continue to take the primary child-care responsibility? And in so doing do they continue to reproduce the traditional mothering role in the next generation?

It is as a psychoanalyst rather than sociologist that Chodorow (2000) makes her theoretical contribution to the debate on the reproduction of mothering. According to Chodorow, within the context of patriarchy, women's mothering is causally related to the way child-care and the division of labour have evolved. Contemporary mothering is about concern for others, nurturance, vigilance and dependence on a breadwinner. It is, however, *not* about ambition, intellect and competitiveness. The psychological capacities that underlie gendered child-rearing tasks are thus reproduced both consciously and unconsciously from generation to generation.

> Women as mothers, produce daughters with mothering capacities and the desire to mother. These capacities and needs are built into and grow out of the mother-daughter relationship itself. By contrast, women as mothers (and men as not-mothers) produce sons whose nurturant capacities and needs have been systematically curtailed and suppressed.
>
> *(Chodorow, 1978: 7)*

But how does this happen? By definition, patriarchal culture oppresses women, particularly through the motherhood role, when they experience loss of self/autonomy to an extreme extent. Chodorow, aware of the contradictions inherent in the practice of selfless mothering, suggests that part of women's/mothers' behaviour is to try to meet needs that cannot be met through relationships with adult men and women, through their relationship with the infant/child. This is different in relation to sons than it is for daughters. Mothers demand different things from different-sex children – sons are expected to be substitute husbands, while daughters are treated as substitute mothers. Masculinity/independence is fostered in sons who feel pressure to separate psychologically from their mothers, and who thus emerge from their pre-Oedipal attachment with the desire to assert their masculinity through the domination of women (Chodorow, 2000). There is less conflict for girls, and femininity/nurturance is encouraged and sustained in daughters (Chodorow, 1978: 212).

Sayers (1982) suggests that in effect Chodorow is saying that gender identity equates with personality 'style'. Sayers also shows that Chodorow's work has been used politically to reinforce the centrality of mothering to child-care, letting men off the hook of domestic drudgery so they can engage in more important things. Crucial to this discussion of the emergence of gendered behaviours and emotions is the strength of *emotional segregation* between women and men encapsulated in both Archer's and Chodorow's work, despite coming from very different perspectives.

## Femininity at work

How, then, may we understand these aspects of gendered behaviour as they play out at work? Debates about biological essentialism versus socialization/behavioural learning, psychoanalysis and the meaning of the gendered body versus liberal feminism have neither been resolved nor have they evaporated. What is clear from consideration of the literature on femininity, masculinity and gender roles is that biology, social context, ideology and experience of being a gendered person all contribute towards understanding professional socialization and the culture of organizations. Women have babies, they tend towards 'passivity', irrationality and socially oriented behaviours rather than action, aggression and logical decision-making. Thus it is to be expected that they will not make the best leaders and top-ranking professionals in the private-sector workplace or in public life.

### Sex-role spill-over

Sex-role spill-over, that is behaving in work organizations, as in family and private life, seems inescapable for many women regardless of their seniority. This process occurs in two ways: first, where the skills, expectations and behaviours that women employ in managing their domestic/family lives are also used at work (Eagly and Carli, 2003; Fletcher, 2004; Mandell and Pherwani, 2003; Potts, 2005); and, second, when professional women have to deal with the strains of managing their dual roles (Gill et al., 2008; Rees and Monrouxe, 2010).

As Davidson and Cooper (1992) outlined, all managers have home and work roles and responsibilities, but women report more stress than do men. This is true at all stages of the life cycle, regardless of marriage and parenthood; as in fact female managers are less likely to have children than male managers (Foster, 2001; Sharp et al., 2012). Whereas for a man marriage and a family is experienced as an asset ensuring stability, for a woman it is a potential burden because it comes with responsibilities for the health and welfare of the wider family (see Cinamon and Rich, 2002; Davidson and Cooper, 1992).

Underlying these gender differences in experience are the assumptions about the roles of 'wife' and 'mother'. For men they indicate the provision of comfort and support, but for women they mean two sets of overlapping responsibilities. As the domestic roles of women often circumscribe their characteristic repertoires, this role overlap has major implications for the way they manage the competing aspects of their lives. Illustration of how this may operate on a fundamental level can be seen through looking at the motherhood role.

Women are socialized into motherhood within the traditional feminine role, which does not simply mean that they desire to be mothers. It means that they desire to become mothers *in a particular way*: they want to become 'perfect' mothers.

A prevalent and popular theme in psychology/psychoanalysis over many recent years has reinforced the view that mothers, through their inability to fulfil total infant/family needs, are to blame for psychological problems in the next generation (see Sayers, 1992). This view is both potentially misogynist, but also indicative of a sense of omnipotence on the part of the women/mothers who accept this charge and feel so responsible. Thus:

> mothers are totally responsible for the outcomes of their mothering, even if their behaviour in turn is shaped by male-dominant society. Belief in the all-powerful mother spawns a recurrent tendency to blame the mother on the one hand, and a fantasy of maternal perfectibility on the other.
>
> *(Chodorow and Contratto, 1982: 55)*

From this, Chodorow and Contratto extrapolated that women come to see themselves as responsible for everything from men's bad behaviour to the unmet needs of all children. This theme of the perfect mother comes to provide a template for women's behaviour, emotionality, and for the standards they set themselves in the public sphere. If we take from both the sex-role learning perspective of John Archer and the psychoanalytic framework employed by Nancy Chodorow, it is clear that while femininity has potentially fluid boundaries at early stages of girls' development, it is soon constrained by motherhood practices: both in that women who work are likely to become mothers, and that women are not expected to engage in the kinds of behaviours that would in any way be deemed 'unmotherly'.

As girls are socialized into expecting to be mothers on the conscious level, they anticipate their role so that it is assured of becoming integral to their repertoire. On the unconscious level, girls identify with their own mothers and women in general, and thus mothering has become incorporated into expectations and beliefs about women's 'styles' and work-related roles.

### Academic women

At a workshop run by feminist psychologists almost two decades ago (Woollett et al., 1995) attended (incidentally) exclusively by women, and set up to explore women's experiences as academic psychologists, the following became clear, supporting the view that women engaged in sex-role spill-over.

First, women had *expectations of themselves* corresponding to some extent with traditional female/mother roles but that are inappropriate in patriarchal settings. Interactions with students made this clear. Women academics have to *teach themselves* not to be responsible for their students' potential misery or failures, which is not the same as the negligence of student needs operationalised by some colleagues.

I recalled an example of my relationship with a female postgraduate who was completing her PhD – a typically stressful experience for both parties. She had requested to see me to discuss an aspect of the final draft that was worrying her, and we met for around one and a half hours. The following week the same student phoned to say that although she had appreciated my willingness to discuss her work, she had been too anxious to concentrate fully so asked whether we could meet again. I agreed, as I liked her and was keen that she should finish her thesis, which had great promise. However I felt extremely resentful as soon as I had agreed to do this.

The second meeting we had, as with the previous one, seemed to me to be effective, but did not diffuse her worries. This left me feeling that my skills as a supervisor were somehow inadequate, but I was angry with myself for feeling that way, as I knew it was based on something about me (intrapsychically) and the material context (student and supervisor in a high-pressured university setting) rather than some objective reality. I was also angry with her for not seeming to value my time on either occasion, while also appearing to devalue the high quality of attention she had had from me over the preceding years.

The problem here lay with the interaction and expectations that both took for granted, which need now to be re-examined. I chose my graduate students on the basis that I liked them and was interested in their work. I felt omnipotent enough to reserve the option to turn down those applicants who did not match these criteria. This corresponds with female academic behaviours observed by Maaret Wager (1995) in which women academics describe their work almost as a hobby. It also corresponds with the behaviour of mothers who freely give time and attention to their children, which is fine when the mother is feeling strong, able and willing to give – which may be much of the time. However, it is impossible for the child/student to recognize times when these conditions do not apply, which brings about a serious mismatch. This leads to a failure – in the case of the student the failure on my part (mother/teacher/supervisor) was to set adequate boundaries in advance. The failure on hers was not to question or reflect upon her expectation of the boundaries of support and individual attention she was entitled to receive.

Second, also arising from thinking about this workshop was a sense that these *expectations of 'woman as mother' are reciprocated* by colleagues and students who expected female academics to be 'motherly'. This is the case, I think, in the example I have just given, but arose in the workshop in relation to teaching undergraduates. Students appeared to find it easier to knock on the door of the female academic for advice or material, rather than approach a male staff member. Several female colleagues reported, for instance, that a common excuse students give for disturbing *them* was, 'I need to get in touch with Dr X [male colleague] but as he is so busy, perhaps I could ask you . . .'.

Third, ambitious behaviour in relation to women's academic careers is seen as less acceptable than it is for a man. Think about Reggie's approach to me, described in the Introduction, where he fully expected me to stand aside in the promotion round in favour of a young male colleague and was rather shocked that I found this unpalatable. This is characteristic of the experience of many female professionals, and an important issue in the management/negotiation of the professional role. An assertive, forthright woman is seen as 'aggressive' or 'over the top', which is not the case for men exhibiting the same behaviour. Again, recall the young male health-service manager also discussed in the Introduction who felt it was the right thing to tell his seniors that he could do the job better than the present incumbent. Such behaviour and attitudes are not acceptable in *mothering* but they fit with masculinity and *leadership*.

Typical of women in many academic departments is that they either becomes positioned as the aggressive harridans, or they keep their heads down and get on with their work. If they are invisible they are (more or less) acceptable even in the academy. If they do achieve, then jokes may be made about their use of sexuality to gain favours from senior men (see Chapter 5), but rarely is a woman academic seen to have achieved on the basis of her work.

Fourth, women academics seem to have an overdeveloped *sense of responsibility* in relation to their work which resonates with the fantasy of the perfect mother described above – they set out to achieve the impossible in relation to the quality and quantity of their research and their teaching.

In contemporary cases, where pay equality in academic organizations is now regularly disputed, some of these gendered characteristics persist. Liz Schafer, a professor of drama and theatre studies in a British university, engaged in a battle for pay parity with other professors, most of whom were male, between 2007 and 2011. She declared she was not normally bothered about money, a potentially non-competitive statement. However having once seen an article demonstrating a pay gap of £9,000 between male and female professors at her institution, she took up arms. She mounted a campaign with other women in similar positions: 'We were polite, and we were ignored' (Schafer, 2011: 33). She also realized that once she was provided with detailed figures of male comparators that she was 'being treated like a fool' (p. 34). The next step she and her colleagues took was to identify these 'comparators'. Their investigations revealed that the male comparators and other male colleagues had applied for other jobs (some of whom had not even been shortlisted) and others had simply received 'hunter-gatherer' emails tempting them to apply for another post. This flimsy evidence of greater value than their peers presented to the senior management had, it seemed, been enough for these men to get a significant salary hike.

Throughout the piece in *The Times Higher Education* Schafer describes a journey of *difference* between the ways that men and women professors tackled their organizations to gain greater pay increases. Men seemed to engage in opaque processes (perhaps over a social drink) while women, who were thought to be less mobile, went through the official channels for promotion and compensation. Women were seen as 'loyal servants who will stay put' (p. 37) Schafer proposes.

Despite the student/lecturer power relationship having the clear child/mother potential, and women being less aware of how to jostle for more pay, women in the academic context are still not 'typically' feminine in any sense. Scholarship and research are not seen as typical of stereotyped female behaviour. Since the 1990s when women comprised only 3 per cent of professors in the UK, with similar numbers in Europe, Canada and the USA (Wager, 1995), there has been a significant increase in numbers (see Introduction). Even so, the pay gaps are significant as Schafer's case demonstrated and *perceptions* of gendered behaviours and the actual behaviours of women and men in relation to competition remain serious barriers to pay parity.

## The culture trap

> It is obvious that a great deal of sex role learning takes place among women during the early phases of their lives, and that this can translate itself into an attitude of mind that creates difficulties later in worklife generally. This we have called 'the culture trap'.
>
> *(Davidson and Cooper, 1992: 56)*

What is 'normal' feminine behaviour in organizations? For women in the professions and management there are still relatively few same-sex role models for them to learn from, and there are clear problems in trying to emulate men. An enduring debate among feminists has centred around the idea of *essential* femininity, and Carol Gilligan's (1982) work on female morality has been correctly criticized for failing to problematize the distinction she found between female and male 'styles' (Faludi, 1992) (Reay and Ball, 2000). Similarly, much has been said in favour of women managers and female management style, relying on the assumption that it is fairer and more democratic than is male style. However, while gender differences must not be ignored, they have to be understood in *context*, if inequality is to be recognized and key changes made. It needs to be acknowledged that in the world of business and the professions typical female behaviour is not valued by those with power. Nor is it seen as effective in terms of organizational and professional goals (McDowell, 2001; Reay and Ball, 2000; Smithson and Stokoe, 2005; Van Vianen and Fischer, 2002).

Flanders (1994) argued that 'Whereas male managers tend to have one role – that of the traditional stereotyped manager – there are many different roles that women can adopt' (p. 68). This echoes John Archer's thesis about gender-role development and the lack of clarity about femininity. This makes it more difficult for a woman to enter a man's world because not only has she not had socialization into 'masculinity', which arguably corresponds with what is expected of managers and senior professionals, but she may be unclear about her own sense of 'femininity' as she is not primarily a mother while in the professional context.

Flanders indicates that many women thus adopt inappropriate roles that resemble stereotypical female ones, which in themselves may prove problematic in other contexts.

These include 'the mother confessor'. In such a role the senior woman offers a shoulder to cry on. This is time consuming and emotionally tiring, and may lead to conflict in carrying out the executive role (Cassell and Walsh, 1991).

Another possibility is the 'departmental mascot', a fate that often befalls a token woman (see Davidson and Cooper, 1992). This includes: the 'departmental tea lady' who is asked to take minutes at meetings in the secretary's absence, or literally make tea; the 'bridesmaid' who acts in relation to her senior manager as if she were a personal assistant and thus indispensable; the 'seductress' who engages in a mild flirtation in order to get noticed or because this is the major pattern she has developed to relate to men; and finally 'the feminist' who is seen as strident, aggressive and anti-male.

However, most professional women have been made, or made themselves, aware of these obvious pitfalls. Many of the female doctors I interviewed in the early 1990s commented how they were initially expected to do the equivalent of make tea on the wards, but that they soon made it clear that they were not prepared to do this. Many senior women managers never revealed their ability to type, despite its obvious use in a variety of contexts.

The message that might be construed from such a list of potential pitfalls, that is to avoid making these mistakes, is not an easy one to respond to. Women who are ambitious wish to be both visible and indistinguishable from male colleagues with whom they want to compete on the basis of professional merit alone.

## Women at the top: has anything changed?

Kate McKenzie Davey (1993) did an interview study with women graduates early in their management careers to examine how they coped with issues of femininity. She found ambivalence and conflict in the interview material, although the overt message was positive. Much of her data revealed the differences between women's and men's perceptions of good practice in management. Women see men's styles as different from and less acceptable than their own. 'They, men, seem to be terrific backbiters . . . back-stabbers is perhaps a better word and I come across it where a man has tried to stab me in the back and I think, but why?' (McKenzie Davey, 1993: 9). Another of her respondents reinforced this point. 'I don't want to be like them, I don't want to play the game like they do' (ibid.).

In our study of leadership in the NHS (Nicolson et al., 2011) it was clear that the rhetoric of gender and leadership/management had evolved but the challenges are much the same as they were in the 1990s. The women in senior roles, despite their frequent denials of their difference, saw themselves as being able to develop teams and that they were reasonably good at relationships. The men, on the whole, saw there was a job to be done and that they had to push their ideas and plans through (in some cases) no matter what. Among the female managers there was an emphasis on what is best for the patients while among the men there was a tendency to focus on organizational efficiency. I saw this as a generalization but not without some clear and striking evidence.

There was a difference in how women and men identified good leadership qualities in others. So, for example, this woman identified such qualities in another:

> Yep, I think Fanny (not her real name) who is our head of [a non-clinical department] . . . I think she is a very good example of what I'm talking about in terms of her job. And her role relies a lot on other people. Erm so as a personality she is a very responsible person, she gets on with everybody and you can really see how that works for her because when she needs somebody to do something or she needs people to listen, they are going to because they have got a good relationship with her and she has taken time to build relationships even when it is perhaps not necessary.

These are very much relational qualities that a woman admires in a female leader. On the other hand, a male clinical leader talked about his frustrations in working in his organization where he was in charge of reorganizing a clinical service:

A: I was forced upon them . . .
Q: That's what I was going to ask. So presumably there was a lot of resentment I guess?
A: Yes.
Q: And how does it manifest itself?
A: Erm, non-cooperation, making life difficult for you sometimes, people talking about erm . . . sort of criticising you behind your back and erm playing silly games behind your back that makes management of other people more and more difficult. Erm you know, and yet we sort of have to fight another battle to win hearts and minds, when we, you know, don't really have the time to do that, we have got to have our focus on doing what we are meant to do, which is to manage patients and to manage our beds properly.

This extract from the interview with someone whose role it is to lead change is revealing. The respondent recognizes that he is not taking people with him and, in his view, the followers appear to eschew co-operation. He also believes they are mocking him and that that mockery is contagious. He does not appear to countenance the possibility of consulting the workforce and trying to find a pathway between efficiency and the experiences of the workforce. Also using the world 'we' implies that he sees himself as representing authority.

Women managers, however, are not complacent nor do they necessarily stick to their mother/carer traditional roles as part of their management style. Women in these positions expect something different from themselves. Many find that although they might reject traditional female roles, they are able to save something of their femininity by adapting it to the management context (Fairhurst, 2009; Nicolson et al., 2011).

Geraldine McCool, the solicitor interviewed by me for an article in the *Independent* newspaper, said she ran her department in a way that differed from male management style. She told me that she was still able to draw on lessons from her early years which enabled her to employ emotional intelligence as the only means of ensuring commitment from others. She told me:

> Although I often responded to my gut reactions I never took irrevocable action until I had spoken to everyone whose opinion was relevant. This gave me the confidence of knowing that my decisions were well informed.

She believed in transparency at all levels and that teamwork and joint decision-making were vital ingredients to effective leadership and organizational strength: 'Even if you come to a decision they do not agree with, at least they will know why something has occurred' (Nicolson, 1995c: 30).

On the other side of the coin are senior women who try to be like men or at least avoid taking a woman-oriented position. My research with female academics and clinical consultants (Nicolson and Welsh, 1994) revealed little empathy for the day-to-day discrimination that juniors had to face. One female consultant, for instance, talking of sexual harassment, said: 'Men are in the main responsible for sexual harassment. There are large numbers of women working in less powerful positions in the health service. They need to be encouraged to object to such behaviour' (female, 41, paediatrics). This comment showed little awareness of her own position of authority and potential influence, ignoring the cost to a junior woman of complaining about a senior colleague in a hierarchical profession when personal recommendation in appointments and promotion counts for a great deal. Another, again talking of sexual harassment, confirmed her own capabilities and inferred the inadequacies of those who could not handle this kind of male behaviour.

> A professor of a surgical department made a stupid (but nasty) remark in an otherwise serious meeting, designed to put me down and prevent me arguing for a particular option. Pointless, silly, off-putting, no sexual approach intended, but simply to put me off my stride. It didn't.
>
> *(Female clinical academic in her forties)*

Senior women in the research sample overall, tended to demonstrate similar attitudes when they claimed an awareness of harassment and discrimination. The junior women and men looked for support from those in authority to stop discrimination. The senior women considered it had to be handled (in some neutral way) and that it was not serious.

McKenzie Davey's sample of younger women graduates in management, however, suggested more reflexivity about the dominance of men and how to cope with it. One engineer said that she had 'become one of the lads and that can be quite easy because again you . . . drink a pint or two you talk laddish things and . . . that's the only way that some men can relate to women' (McKenzie Davey, 1993: 10).

Two other women actively acknowledged the need to play by men's rules in order to survive, but unlike the older medical women neither was happy with this. One said, 'I'm not saying it's the best way, but I've got to look at it that way' (p. 11), and the other, 'Perhaps I'm learning these men's rules . . . I don't know . . . but I haven't got confidence in them' (ibid.).

Jane McLoughlin's businesswomen were also aware of the tension between men's and women's rules. Some demonstrated this by competing with men and not women.

> At the start of my career, I felt very competitive with men. I felt I did the work as well as they did. I still feel more competitive with men than with women. I felt proud at beating men, and that was an incentive to keep pushing forward.
>
> *(McLoughlin, 1992: 112)*

This was also true for women bosses:

> I've always got along well with the women who work for me, but I handle them by saying, 'Watch me and do as I do'. I've never thrown my weight around except with men, because men challenged me much more. I've never felt competition with people below me, but I've had desperately hard times competing with men above me.
>
> *(McLoughlin, 1992: 112)*

This is reminiscent of the work of Thorne (1986) in relation to girls' defensive behaviour towards boys who try to disrupt their play. As the traditional adversary, boys/men are fair game and the habits of early development die hard.

Women know how to be women, and how to work with women like themselves. But being a woman at present remains marginal to the commercial and professional world – a successful woman has to be more than herself. Women's lives, circumscribed by gender roles and power relations, mean that women bring different sets of experiences to their work. Patriarchal cultures tend to overlook the strengths women's life experiences potentially bring to business and professional life (Smith, 1978). The culture trap is not only about the 'limitations' of women's attitudes and behaviour, but is about the way these are positioned as marginal to a patriarchal context.

### Women in pursuit of power: organizational roles

What is typical of the successful woman? Is it someone who pretends to be a man or at least attempts to behave as if she were gender free like the senior doctors? That there are few role models or precedents is generally seen to disadvantage women climbing the career ladder. How does a feminine but ambitious woman behave? Can a woman work happily with men and avoid the pitfalls mentioned by Flanders above?

Not all successful women see the absence of predecessors as a problem. In an article called 'The vice chancellors' about women as university vice-chancellors (published originally in *Times Higher Educational Supplement* on 28 July 1995 but now online[1]), newly appointed women discussed their plans in the context of the male-dominated context of university life at that time.

Janet Finch, now a dame, interviewed prior to taking over as the vice-chancellor at the University of Keele in the autumn of 1995, proposed:

> 'Because there isn't a role model of a woman manager in universities, in many ways you can define the role yourself. That creates opportunities . . . I am clear about what I want to do, I am straightforward, so it is easy for people to disagree with me. It has brought me into conflict with people, most of whom are men.' Her advice to women contemplating a management career is 'not to be put off by the lack of other women', but try to find mentors, and make contact with women in similar positions of seniority.

Elizabeth Esteve-Coll, who as a contemporary of Finch and vice-chancellor of the University of East Anglia, challenged the view that women operated along gendered lines:

It is a generally held view that women rule by emotion, which is pejorative, or that they rule by intuition which is intended as praise, but nobody can manage a large complex organisation, the size of a small town in some cases, with responsibility for many millions of pounds on the basis of intuition.

As a woman and vice-chancellor in the mid-1990s, Christine King identified an excitement and expectation of culture change at her university. She declared her commitment to teamwork and doing things differently. As an 'outsider' she believed that a woman might be able to identify possibilities and new approaches to bring about change. She declared:

I would favour training schemes giving opportunities to women and a woman-only staff monitoring scheme, but I am not in favour of quotas. There is nothing worse than the wrong woman in the wrong job, everybody suffers when that happens.

Each of these women had taken a slightly different position on the issue of gender, but each of them clearly believes that women who achieve senior status deserve to do so. None appears to feel that power and influence is detrimental to their femininity, but all feel they are being assessed as senior *women* rather than as vice-chancellors per se.

## Masculinity at work

A critical analysis of men and masculinities is particularly important in the study of work, organizations and management. Yet an examination of the available literature reveals a recurring paradox. The categories of men and masculinity are frequently central to the analyses, yet they remain taken for granted, hidden and unexamined.

*(Collinson and Hearn, 1994: 3)*

Since the executive role is usually perceived by both men and women as fundamentally a male role, any individual woman manager is unlikely to be seen as adequately fitting or meeting the role requirements.

*(Davidson and Cooper, 1992: 81)*

Analysis of professional socialization and patriarchal culture has traditionally relied upon feminist critique (e.g. Smith, 1978; Witz, 1992). Masculinity as an organizational issue is both ignored and taken for granted in the literature on management. As Collinson and Hearn (1994) assert, 'manager' and 'leader' equal man unproblematically.

As a consequence of this invisible masculinity 'most organisations are saturated with masculine values' (Burton, 1991: 3, cited in Collinson and Hearn, 1994). Thus, as Dorothy Smith declared,

> women have been largely excluded from the work of producing the forms of thought and the images and symbols in which thought is expressed and ordered. There is a circle effect. Men attend to and treat as significant only what men say.
>
> *(1991: 281)*

The result is that masculine aspects of professional culture are taken for granted, and socialization into this context enables men but disables women.

Hence, the notion of the lifetime career and full-time work are part of a man's expectation, which is one of the reasons that unemployment and redundancy, and frequently retirement as well, appear to be so destructive of men's mental health (Archer and Rhodes, 1993). Connected with this is the relationship between masculine identity and the role of the breadwinner/ provider (Ehrenreich, 1983). Although there were changes in emphasis over time, a crucial aspect of masculine identity is that a man could support a wife and children. In order to do this, he has to be in paid employment, and if work is the key to his masculinity, work organizations are also likely to be a major site on which masculinity is rehearsed and confirmed.

Confirmation of masculinity occurs at a number of levels: the practical, discursive and the unconscious (Giddens, 2003).

### Practical masculinity

This involves the process of simply 'being a man' in an unreflexive way, taking masculine ways of behaving and values for granted.[2] Such active confirmations of masculinity are unfamiliar to women who are made to feel uncomfortable when subjected to 'laddish' behaviour. It frequently takes the form of sexual innuendo, and occurs in common rooms, during lunch time or at after-hours social gatherings. It frequently occurs in formal meetings also, where jokes about sexual habits and *double entendres* are repeatedly employed to 'lighten the mood'. Many women find that they choose to quietly exclude themselves from the repartee, take a full part, or disapprove at the risk of being censured for their lack of fun (see Cockburn, 1993).

Examples of this are common in medical education. Many young women find that in anatomy classes, it is considered acceptable to cut off a female breast and throw it in the waste bin, while penises and testicles are routinely treated with great reverence. Many making this observation are ridiculed by anatomy demonstrators, most of whom are recently qualified junior doctors. This practice debases the female body, while the treatment of students' protests interpreted as such ensures that young women's public acknowledgement of this debasement is curtailed and may lead them to the recognition that they should be quiet about such matters.

Another germane example, which led to a female student making a successful complaint resulting in a minor disciplinary action, arose when a lecturer discussing obesity used the final 10 minutes of the lecture to show slides of an extremely fat woman in a bikini, exhibiting a number of 'provocative' poses. When a female student complained that this was both gratuitous in that it contributed nothing to the lecture content, and sexist in that it devalued women, the male lecturer publicly humiliated her in front of more than 100 students by accusing her of being humourless.

This behaviour occurs in other professions as well of course. Cynthia Cockburn provides an example of a presentation given to a mixed-sex group of managers from a high street retail company's computer division:

> The middle and senior staff of the Division had gone away together at company expense for a weekend's conference in a hotel. The occasion was intended to review the Division's work and build esprit de corps. The first morning's business opened with a presentation by a senior manager. He had prepared a 'visual aid' in the form of a life-sized photograph of a bare-breasted model. In the photo she appeared leaning against a rock with a hole in it. In this space the senior manager had superimposed a second photo, of the divisional director's face. He opened the talk as follows. 'We are lucky to have [the director] with us this morning. He's just risen from a sick bed. [pause for effect]. His secretary has flu.' This drew a laugh – not only from the audience but from the director — and from his secretary who was also present at the time. There followed other sexual allusions and jokes from this and subsequent speakers.
>
> *(1993: 153–154)*

This kind of behaviour, which appears to span the professions, emphasizes woman as 'other'. They are either 'just' secretaries so 'justifiably' the objects of sexual innuendo, or they are kill-joys. What women are not, it seems, is part of the establishment, the foreground of professional organizations and culture. If they were, then this form of masculinity would be positioned as problematic rather than the reactions of the women.

### Discursive masculinity

Men, like women, actively construct their identities/subjectivities through reflexivity, developing their biographies over the course of time (see Chapter 1).

Career progression, as central to cultural notions of masculinity, becomes a key element in the construction of biography and subjectivity. Careers thus confer a meaning to subjective experiences of masculinity (see Collinson and Hearn, 1994).

Working with women who are in a subordinate position coheres with the operation of discursive consciousness and masculine subjectivity. Relationships with female juniors, secretaries, nurses or wives strengthen the conflation of masculinity and career within the patriarchal framework within which most lives are organized. The traditional superordinate/subordinate pattern evolves from the time of a man's entry into the professional organization to his achievement of senior status: son, brother, husband/boss. The brother/sister relationship is best accomplished while the man is still at the aspirational level where it remains possible, as with young children, to 'play' together. However, the young man/boy expects to be chosen as the 'heir'. Working alongside or in a junior capacity, once he has outgrown the possibility that the woman is 'mother', is a deeply humiliating experience for some men.

In one example, a senior female manager in the health-care service acted as mentor to a management trainee. She took an active interest in his career development and singled him out for involvement with some complex but high-status projects, ensuring that where possible his role was made visible to the relevant members of the hierarchy. Like most people, his work was not always perfect, and on a few occasions she had to get him to rewrite reports, or was critical of the way he had handled a particular situation. He took the criticism seriously, and far from appearing resentful, he asked for as much feedback as she was willing to provide.

He left after completing the required training period, and three years later returned in a senior role, where the two of them were working together again but this time at the same level, although she was the more experienced person and actively looking for promotion. At first, he tried to seek her support in the way he had before, and was taken aback when she also came to him for advice and support. She had recognized their implicit equality, while he was still seeking the mother/son relationship. As the months passed, however, he gradually distanced himself from her, and in fact shortly before she left to take up a promoted post elsewhere, she realized that far from being her ally, he had made strong connections with colleagues she considered to be her enemies.

### Unconscious masculinity

Working with women as equals disrupts masculine subjectivity in complex ways, then – they might choose the patriarch or older brother role or, like the man in the example above, the son to his mentor mother. That working with women is problematic for men is not to say that all men are misogynist. One of the findings from my study of doctors, lecturers and medical students was the way that senior men's perspectives on gender discrimination were polarized. Some were deeply concerned and supportive of equal opportunities and angry about sexual harassment of women by men: 'Sexual harassment can certainly have serious consequences for some individuals, and should be opposed whenever it occurs – especially in an academic establishment' (man in his fifties); 'Intentional harassment can harm (psychologically) individuals and if they are not secure, cause long-term problems' (man in his forties). Others saw sexual harassment and the pursuit of equal opportunities as trivial or a joke: 'It's not the duty of medical educators' (man in his fifties); 'Sexual harassment is not a problem in my opinion' (man in his twenties); 'Life is too short and there are more pressing problems and needs of the student' (anonymous); 'Does it exist?' (man in his thirties).

Other men in the study were careless about equal opportunities issues, revealing underlying prejudice in the expression of their views. As one man said: 'Medical school starts with bias against males – by taking equal ratios of males and females. Many more males apply for medical school than females, and so the chance of a male being offered a place is less than a female' (anonymous male hospital consultant and honorary lecturer attached to a medical school); or another: 'Sensible women will want to have a family and this is more compatible with some specialties than others' (anonymous male hospital consultant and honorary lecturer attached to a medical school).

That particular view has been aired once again in June 2014 by a television celebrity, Kirstie Allsopp, who proposed that young women should find a man and have babies before going to university or they might fall victim to their biological clocks.[3] This assertion caused a media storm on both sides of the argument but indicates that even while in 2014 women may be entering the professions and public life in greater numbers, attitudes towards their continued success subtly work against them.

It is difficult for men to *experience* women/other as equal or the same, and pressure to recognize women as equals and/or superiors caused by both policy and the characteristics of ambitious and capable women precipitates anxiety, guilt and envy in the men.

## Envy and anxiety

Freud theorized penis envy as a pathological female characteristic. Women wanted what they could never have – the penis and the phallus, the symbol of power. Other psychoanalytic writers, such as Erikson, have suggested that men may envy women their ability to bear children. What has not been suggested is that men might experience an equivalent to penis envy in their relationships with women.

Jane Ussher (1995) in her paper 'Masculinity as masquerade' suggested that men experience a fantasy or hope that their penis is in fact a phallus. She asserts that men are in fact condemned by the phallic illusion because the real organ and the real man never/rarely match up to the symbol. Ussher's paper focuses upon male sexual dysfunction and the representation of the penis/phallus in lesbian pornography. However, parallels may also be drawn in relation to professional culture. Men experience masculine subjectivity/ identity through their relation to woman as 'other', and their superordinate relation to the women in their lives at various stages of their biographies. Even if they themselves do not achieve the professional accolade and success they desire, they see others like them doing so. This echoes Freud's idea of identification with the father/men as resolution to the Oedipal crisis.

In patriarchal organizations women on the whole are not in the higher echelons of power, so all is well. However, men are continuing to witness increased numbers of women entering their professional lives, and these women are refusing to go away. Many seem keen to achieve, some are managing to do so. Some senior men are beginning to take more notice of these women than they are of equivalent men. There are affirmative action programmes which may be seen to make things easier for women than for themselves. There is apparent turmoil and the possibility of seeing women with power. This seeming chaos and disturbance in the patriarchal order creates extreme anxiety and envy in many men and women. In the short term this may stimulate greater productivity through a sense of competitiveness, but if anxiety and envy are the basis of motivation, the final achievements will be pathological and damaging to health.

But what is envy in this context? Envy is a destructive and uncomfortable emotional state, and was brought to the fore in the psychoanalytic work of Melanie Klein. As Julia Segal writes in her account of Klein's contribution to psychoanalysis: 'Envy is spoiling and damaging in nature, neatly expressed in "throwing shit" at someone or something' (Segal, 1992: 54).

Here, I want to examine the role of envy in the creation of an organizational culture that is damaging to women and to men, and to do that I briefly examine the work of Melanie Klein and the object-relations school of psychoanalysis.

## Melanie Klein, anxiety and envy

Melanie Klein specialized in working psychoanalytically with infants and young children. She began her career within a Freudian framework, but departed from his theories to develop her own controversial perspectives. The main source of contention between Freud and Klein was her perspective on the Oedipus complex and the development of the superego (see discussion of this in Chapter 2). In contrast to Freud, she believed that major psychic developments took place in the first six months of life. Klein argued that the first relationship an infant has is with the mother's breast, not as Freud believed with itself alone or, later, the mother as a whole person. This object, and the relationship the infant has with it, influences all subsequent ones. This fantasy 'breast', however, was an object endowed with meaning that went beyond that of a mammary gland producing milk. Klein found that fantasies about the breast included the breast as a source of comfort, love, hope, babies, peace and serenity. Babies fantasized about taking this breast into itself and fusing with it. There were, conversely, fantasies about being eaten by it, torn apart or threatened, of the breast being damaged or dangerous inside and outside of the baby. These primitive fantasies Klein hypothesized belonged to the *paranoid-schizoid position* (Segal, 1992: 41).

As the baby grows, it realizes that the breast does not have a life of its own, but is part of the mother and not the baby herself. This development takes place under the influence of the more mature *depressive position* (ibid.).

The depressive position is not comfortable, and under stress the child or adult may attempt to get rid of the new awareness that it brings. The individual splits the object into the 'good' and the 'bad'. This creates what Klein called 'part-objects' as a defence against persecutory fantasies, which includes the defence mechanism of 'idealization'. It may be illustrated thus:

A small girl's own envy and jealousy of her mother is painful reality: in her attempts to get rid of this she creates Cinderella's envious stepmother, a persecutory fantasy. The fairy-godmother and Cinderella, as a helpless innocent victim, are both idealisations which then defend the girl from the phantasy woman.

*(Segal, 1992: 42)*

## Anxiety

Where the paranoid-schizoid position deals in part-objects, the infant under the influence of the depressive position becomes much more aware of whole objects, in which characteristics felt to be loved and good co-exist with those felt to be bad and dangerous. At the same time the child/adult feels more integrated/whole/human sharing good and bad characteristics and conflicts with others (Bolden and Gosling, 2006).

Anxiety, according to Klein, following Freud, relates to aggressive/ destructive instincts (e.g. 'death instinct'), which exists from the start of life in opposition to the 'life instinct'. The child has early fears about her own aggressive impulses, and fears attacks from a revengeful mother/breast which the child has taken into her own body. This fear Klein called 'persecutory anxiety' which is part of the paranoid-schizoid position.

Klein distinguished this from anxiety in the depressive position in which the fears are for the safety of the mother/breast. This anxiety is qualitatively different from persecutory anxiety and more bearable.

Anxiety is important in Klein's theorizing and clinical work because seeking the source of a present anxiety can bring relief. Anxiety can also prevent or motivate change. For instance, reflecting upon anxiety may lead to re-organizing style of work, changing organization or career. Under the pressure of persecutory anxieties 'splitting', 'disintegration' and 'denial' take place which prevents change and avoids facing external processes. Under the burden of depressive anxieties integration and acceptance of reality may occur (Segal, 1992: 53).

## Envy

Envy is the angry feeling that another person possesses and enjoys something desirable – the envious impulse being to take it away or to spoil it. Moreover, envy implies the subject's relation to one person only and goes back to the earliest exclusive relation with the mother. Jealousy is based on envy, but involves a relation to at least two people; it is mainly

> concerned with love that the subject feels is his due and has been taken
> away, or is in danger of being taken away, from him by his rival.
>
> *(Klein, 1975/1993: 181)*

Envy originates from the paranoid-schizoid position and jealousy from the depressive. Klein believed that envy, arising in the earliest stage of infancy, was the source of many adult difficulties. Envy destroys pleasure in the self and others, so that the envious parts of the mind may prevent happiness, creativity and success for everyone (Segal, 1992: 54).

## Defences against anxiety and gender relations

Dividing feelings into good and bad, which enables children/adults to gain relief from internal conflicts, is called *splitting*. This process is often accompanied by *projection*, which involves locating the feelings in others rather than oneself. Thus, unpleasant qualities such as slyness, dishonesty, stupidity and so on are seen only as the attributes of the other.

In relationships it may be possible for the other person, unconsciously, to experience the feelings that are being projected into them. This process is called *projective identification*. The state of mind whereby other people's feelings are experienced as one's own is called *countertransference*. Projective identification often leads to recipients acting out the countertransference derived from the projected feelings. These processes often occur in organizations under threat whereby managers might experience distress and depression projected by staff under notice of redundancy (Halton, 1994).

Projective identification as a defence against anxiety and envy in gender relations provides key insights into interpersonal life. This may be the case particularly in professions and organizations where women are increasing in number. Women entering business, management, academia or the traditional professions, even if they are not specifically ambitious, do not neatly fit the feminine stereotype as I have argued. This may precipitate a sense of chaos and threat to those in established roles.

In some contexts this perceived absence of feminine qualities in these women might be extremely distressing for the men they work alongside or who are being managed directly by them. Nursing, social work, psychotherapy and academia – particularly in the 'softer' subjects, certain aspects of the law (e.g. marital work) or medicine (e.g. public health medicine, family planning) – may be seen as areas that are more accessible to women, and therefore men's sense of masculinity and potency are under greater threat than, say, in finance or engineering.

The following example will illustrate what I mean. A well-qualified woman academic (Janet) was appointed as a lecturer to a university English literature department. She had been an academic for years and published widely although, like many academics experiencing a career log-jam, had not gained a promoted post. She moved institutions to what was perceived as a more prestigious department, in order to effect a career move. Her male colleague (John), with a similar specialization who was to share the teaching of a course with her, seemed at interview to be pleasant, relaxed and welcoming. John had a respectable publishing record, but did not have Janet's high profile, which she had achieved through international interest in her work on women in literature. He, like her, was hoping for a promotion before too long, as they were both at the top of the lecturer pay scale. When she arrived to take up her post, however, she found him changed. He would not spare her the time for a chat or to show her the library, nor would he introduce her to anyone, despite her request to meet a few key people. This made her feel vulnerable and isolated, particularly because she was in a new town, and her family had remained behind to sell their house. This feeling of isolation was made even worse when she set about the task of meeting people off her own bat, and they told her how pleasant John was and how pleased he had been at her appointment. She was perplexed.

As time passed, she became confident in her own networks, but it remained a problem not to have a comfortable working relationship with the closest colleague, particularly when their part of the English department came under threat of a move to a less suitable building, far away from the lecture theatres and library. She kept stressing to John that they could best fight the threat by working together and sharing information (something he had not done before). She noticed that under stress he would come to see her and talk. It would start with him saying he was worried about a certain development, and Janet would reciprocate with her attempt at empathy and analysis and expression of her own feeling. Were they going to man-age a working relationship at last? She began to notice that any attempt by her at sharing her anxieties with him resulted in his leaving her office. She was left feeling anxious and even more isolated than before he had entered the room, feeling as if she had misunderstood the politics or practicalities of the developing crisis over accommodation. Eventually, she had a physical collapse following a panic attack. She noted that he avoided her for several weeks following her panic attack, while she coped and received adequate sympathy from others. One day, a colleague with whom she had become friendly said to Janet how amazing it was that John had remained so relaxed all through the (now resolved) accommodation crisis. Janet suddenly realized what had been going on.

John, who valued his relaxed, friendly style, had been threatened by the arrival of the high-profile, hard-working and energetic Janet. She would move quickly and impatiently around the department, and within a few months of taking up the post had made some interesting and important friends at the university. This had made John particularly worried that she would gain the edge and get her promotion before him.

However, Janet was also insecure. John had played upon her isolation and vulnerability as a new person by not supporting her, and also on her need for social contacts and co-operation under the threat of the office move by enabling her to express fears that he saw were as strong as his own. Instead of enabling her to alleviate some of her anxieties and share their worries as she had done for him, he would cut off and leave.

John, who despised manifestations of anxiety in others, was overwhelmed by his own internal persecutory anxiety that had its origins in unresolved situations from infancy/childhood. He therefore split it off and projected it into other people, so he was then able to see himself as ultra-relaxed and others as tense. In this case Janet was an ideal target for his projections. She was vulnerable and made anxious by (mainly) outside factors such as being new and having the threat of the office-move crisis looming. He envied her abilities and high profile and the fact that she had gained attention from people who regarded him as pleasant, but insignificant. By projecting his despised anxiety onto Janet, he was able to dismiss her in his own mind.

*He* could not cope otherwise with his anxiety or his envy. The more stressed *she* became, the more she accepted the countertransference, eventually becoming so anxious that she collapsed. Not until she realized what was happening could she observe his behaviour dispassionately.

John, unaware of her insight, continued to try and re-kindle the anxieties and insecurities in Janet, but to no avail as she had both gained understanding of their relationship, and the external crises had gone away. She had been reacting to outside threats initially, but through the process of projective identification had taken in John's anxiety (which was internal to him, although fuelled by Janet's arrival and by the accommodation issue).

Her anxiety was resolved, but his situation became more acute because he was unable to project onto Janet anymore. Even when he did get his promotion before she did, he did not feel released from his internal persecutors.

This example involved a woman and a man, but why is it generalisable to gender at work? Janet and John worked in a patriarchal context, and although John eventually was promoted and Janet was not, John was not a 'success' in his own eyes. His subject area was not traditionally masculine, and whereas other men in his field had moved up the hierarchy to management or built international reputations, constantly flying from one conference to another, he was 'just' a lecturer. Janet, on the other hand, was well known, and as a woman had achieved more than many other women by gaining a permanent post in a prestigious department. Also, as a woman,[4] she was used to being sociable and sharing with colleagues, especially under threat. She was also able to relate without difficulty to senior male colleagues. John found this difficult because it reinforced his junior status in relation to them. Janet had a sense of personal responsibility for the future welfare of their branch of literature in the department and university, and for those reasons she found it impossible to detach herself from the accommodation crisis issue, and in order to be effective she knew she needed John's co-operation. John would have been aware of that need/expectation. His feelings about Janet overshadowed his concern and sense of responsibility towards his work. He wanted to exploit and destroy her because her presence humiliated him, as did the presence of other successful women. What made Janet special, however, was her comparability – age, career stage and subject area. Given her starting point he knew that she was likely to outstrip him, and that this would be a public and unbearable humiliation.

This pattern whereby the woman is better qualified than the man is likely to become increasingly common. It echoes the cliché that a woman has to be twice as good as a man to achieve the same recognition, but the point here is that there are double problems for women as men realize this and see female colleagues as a threat.

In the following Chapter I outline the way that these unconscious processes/defence mechanisms occur on an institution-wide basis.

## Conclusions

Understanding gender relations at work cannot be achieved through traditional, 'objective' means alone. Psychometric measurement and the facts and figures representing the changing structures of organizations and professional groups do provide important clues about trends. For instance, without statistics on the numbers of women in senior management posts, the influence on organizations of equal opportunities policies, wider demographic and educational trends would not be available. Surveys may also provide strong evidence of the existence, scope, location and style of, for example, sexual harassment. However, quantification is only half the story. Women and men engage in power politics in conscious and unconscious ways, on both a grand and small scale. Patriarchal organizations value men and patriarchy more than they value women and their accomplishments. Many women are not only being forced to fail, but also are suffering ill health as a consequence. Through employing a feminist analysis of organizational culture, it is possible to construct and deconstruct biographies to reveal power struggles that are pervasive and damaging to equality, which ultimately disclose more about power and gender politics than do statistics.

## Notes

1 www.timeshighereducation.co.uk/news/the-vice-chancellors/94683.article.
2 I am not implying any biological aspect, but referring to the ideas developed earlier.
3 http://telegraph.co.uk/women/womens-life/10870063/Kirstie-Allsopps-right.-Dont-miss-the-baby-boat.html.
4 This is not intended to be a crude gender stereotype, but relates to issues raised earlier in this chapter that indicate although women do not have innate social propensity, nevertheless for a variety of structural/historical reasons they have different interactional styles and expectations.

# 4

# STILL IN THE SHADOW OF THE GLASS CEILING?

## Introduction

In this chapter I extend the analysis of the individual and interpersonal aspects of gender at work to an examination of women in organizational life.

To do this I examine the material and discursive contexts in particular to explore:

- the systemic practices that subordinate women in professional life;
- ways in which women's achievements continue to take place in patriarchal, and often toxic, contexts which continue to uphold and display male success and female failure;
- discursive practices around the way women and others realize and explain their achievements;
- then, with more emphasis on the intra-psychic, how women and men negotiate their relationships in the context of their biographies and within patriarchal culture.

One well-rehearsed discourse of women's continued lack of visibility and power is the concept of the *glass ceiling*. The idea of a glass ceiling suggests that while women might see a potential pathway to the top of their profession, there comes a point when they crash into this hitherto invisible barrier and their progress is halted (Arulampalam et al., 2007; Cotter et al., 2001; Evans and Adams, 2007; Smith et al., 2011). Despite talk of sticky doors by Nemat Shafik of the Bank of England, and shattering glass from Hillary Clinton, the rhetoric of the minority of very powerful women, for most of us the glass ceiling, made of toughened glass, remains in place. This is something that has remained somewhat fixed despite long-established legislation in Western industrial democracies, such as the Equal Pay Act in the United States[1] and similarly in Britain the Equal Pay Act[2] and Sexual Discrimination Act of 1975.[3] Such legislation was promoted to ensure that those who had the abilities to reach the top could do so and that women in all walks of professional and working life would be paid the same as a man doing the same work. That legal changes have on the whole not changed the balance of women to men in roles in public life suggests other forces at work – psychosocial and systemic structural/material ones – favour the status quo.

In 1990 the Hansard Society's report *Women at the Top*, focusing on British government and public decision-making roles in particular, concluded that the state of women's representation at the top of government, business and the professions in Britain was wholly unacceptable.

> Many women are blocked in their attempts to gain access to the higher reaches of public and professional life. They remain clustered in positions that fail to make full use of their qualifications and abilities. Over 70% of women work in lower-level clerical and service sector jobs; over 40% of women work in jobs where they have no male colleagues . . . For too many there is a glass ceiling over their aspirations – it allows them to see where they might go, but stops them getting there. In any given occupation and in any given public position, the higher the rank, prestige or power, the smaller the proportion of women.
>
> *(Hansard, 1990: 15)*

Much has been written about the glass ceiling over the intervening years since the 1990 Hansard report (Arulampalam et al., 2007; Davidson and Cooper, 1992; Evans and Adams, 2007b; Evans and David, 2007; Flanders, 1994; Smith et al., 2011). However, in their joint report of 2013 with the Hansard Society, in conjunction with the Fawcett Society and others, the authors claimed that relatively little had changed since 1990.[4] This is particularly shocking given the post-feminist rhetoric underlining a belief that women have equal chances of success as do men, in all professional spheres at least, and numerous claims that the glass ceiling has been shattered.

Women *do* break through the glass ceiling and achieve senior positions of course, but the more senior a woman becomes, the more isolated she is from other women. Some writers now take a more optimistic position on women leading in politics and public life, though, than the Hansard authors. Genovese and Steckenrider (2013), for example, indicate their belief that more women are at the heads of government; however, their fascinating edited volume, including chapters on each of Golda Meir, Indira Gandhi and Benazir Bhutto, takes a cross-section from the twentieth and twenty-first centuries rather than a contemporary analysis. Furthermore, women at the top frequently experience highly dangerous and distressing events including assassination (Bhutto was murdered by a bomb and gunfire in 2007) and 'political' stabs in the back. Julia Gillard, the Labour Prime Minister of Australia between 2010 and 2013, was given a very hard time for not being married or a mother, and judging from examination of press coverage throughout her period of office, it is clear that she was being undermined from within as well as outside her party. In 2012 she gave a speech, which became known as 'the misogyny speech', in which she stated that she refused to be lectured on sexism by a man she considered to be a misogynist.[5] She lost the leadership of her party to Kevin Rudd, a former prime minister, in 2013 at least partly as a result of the back stabs.

What is at issue here are the psychological and physical costs to women of success and how far the fact of some women's success has the potential to break the glass ceiling for others.

At the end of Chapter 3, I outlined the threats to men and patriarchal culture imposed by women's rise up organizational hierarchies. Here I want to explore further the *implications* of male success for *women's experiences*; particularly their management of self-esteem, relationships with other women, assessment of their own career potential and their emotional/mental health.

To effect this, I focus first on how far the patriarchal organizational structures and the systems of professions constrain the lives of the women within them. Second, I focus on the psychological consequences of this. Third, I identify the factors that hinder change and those which encourage it.

## Organizational structures and professional women's lives

The statistics outlined in the Introduction to this book provide clear evidence that male bastions of power in the professions and in the domestic sphere have remained firmly in place over recent generations. These dual areas of subordination doubly disadvantage professional women striving for and achieving success in senior posts.

Evidence from *Sex and Power* (2013) further demonstrates a serious under-representation of women in all positions of social, professional and political influence. In the British House of Commons, which is at the bottom of the league table of modern democracies, only around 6.3 per cent of members are women. Similarly in the House of Lords only 13 per cent of life peers are women, although the commission suggest that 'even this is better than the dismal representation of women in the Commons' (Hansard Society, 1990: 4). In public office women's appointments remain low despite active measures to recruit women to government posts. Less than one-fifth of all honours go to women. Similarly the judiciary, civil service, legal profession, senior management, company board-room directors, academia, media and trade unions all have too few women in senior influential positions.

## What do these patterns reveal?

It is clear that 'unofficial' discrimination is endemic, has taken place over a number of years and continues to do so. In the medical profession, for example, 40–50 per cent of medical school entrants have been women for getting on for 20 years, but the proportion of women represented at the higher echelons of clinical practice suggests that there must be insurmountable barriers (Health Trends, 1991; Riska, 2001).

In the broadcast and print media women are scarcely found in upper management in the newspaper and magazine world, despite the preponderance of women readers, especially of magazines (Hansard, 1990, 2013). Similarly, the upper ranks of the television industry demonstrate a marked absence of women in influential roles. In publishing in the UK, 75 per cent of employees in editorial departments are women, but few get to the ranks above editor. Men are typically more than twice as likely to become managers in publishing (see Hansard, 1990).

The fact that there have been some initiatives to change this state of affairs, such as equal opportunities programmes of various kinds including Opportunity 2000 in the UK National Health Service, WIST (Women in Surgical Training) and part-time training programmes set up by the Royal College of Obstetricians and Gynaecologists, and that they have met with only limited success, further serves to indicate the strength of institutionalized prejudice. Recent studies by the University of Exeter into women's surgical careers can be downloaded.[6] The team is looking at women's career choices and their pathways to achieving (or failing to achieve) their goals.

Constraints on women's lives in patriarchal organizations are character-ized by various forms of discrimination that take an invisible toll on their health (emotional and physical). Women are still the 'other' or marginal to the main organizational objectives, even when successful. Women who are successful are isolated from other women by definition.

## Processes of discrimination

Widespread discrimination still occurs, despite legislation and post-feminist beliefs that have consequences for all women and men. Women who break through the traditional career barriers are no less subject to these processes than those who do not, as with Julia Gillard.

There are three kinds of discriminatory processes that are increasingly well documented and that keep the patriarchal structures and systems in place. These are:

- the socio-material context in which the overt structural barriers such as lack of child-care facilities, lack of female or women-friendly role models or mentors discriminates against women;
- the discursive, and to some extent, intra-psychic, covert barriers to women's advancement and support in organizations, such as prejudiced attitudes, beliefs and male-defined exclusionary behaviour;
- the unconscious psychological, or intrapsychic, impact of patriarchal organizations upon women's motivation and self-esteem, combined with the reflexive relationship between biographical context and knowledge. This is often hidden from the women themselves in that the impact of patriarchal culture seeps into the discourses women employ to achieve a reflexive self-evaluation.

## Overt structural barriers to women's careers: motherhood

> the amount of support women receive from their partners is limited . . . traditional role models are usually maintained.
>
> *(Simpson, 1990: 120)*

This is still the case although there is evidence that increasingly many women do get support from their partners, which in turn enhances their work experience and career success (Paustian-Underdahl et al., 2013). It also increases women's motivation and expectations that their abilities will be recognized and suitably rewarded. Despite the increased support that many women receive now, they still continue to be charged with domestic and child-care responsibilities to a far greater extent than men (Apter, 1993; Nicolson, 2003). Few organizations have day-care facilities, and long working hours continue to discriminate against those with primary child-care responsibilities, particularly the low-waged and middle-income women. The child-blind organizational context supports the habit of early morning and evening meetings that eat into 'out of hours'/domestic time which potentially makes attendance difficult for women, or makes their lack of attendance potentially embarrassing.

It is also clear now that far more women from all sections of society experience being victims of domestic violence and abuse, which militates against career success in a number of important ways (Dryden et al., 2009; Nicolson, 1998, 2010).

As Carolyn Kagan and Sue Lewis argued in their account of working as academic psychologists:

> No allowances have been made because we have families, and no formal or informal offers of reorganising responsibilities or timetables have been forthcoming. It is not only women who have had families. However, all the men with families have had wives who stopped working for various lengths of time when their children were born.
>
> *(1990: 21)*

Despite greater flexibility including both maternity and paternity leave arrangements it remains difficult in many professions for women either to make up for career gaps or to work flexibly in ways that allow for the kinds of achievements that augment their organizational successes. Those for whom motherhood and child-care responsibilities do not hold back their career aspirations and success are the exceptions that make the headlines.

The disproportionate relationship between gender and domestic/child-care responsibility also disadvantages women because they cannot expect to have their meals cooked and children cared for ready for their return from work. As White et al. (1992: 189) observed in their summary of the literature, even full-time career women perform the overwhelming majority of domestic and child-care tasks. Successful women, as with men, have to give up time with their children for the sake of their careers, but unlike men, women's role in relation to parenting is constantly being discussed in the media and at various interpersonal levels. Therefore, even if a woman has chosen to be child-free or employ professional full-time child-care, she is in constant danger of reproach or having to justify her choice, from colleagues, friends and family.

## Mentors

Another observable barrier to women's achievement has been the lack of female role models and mentors (Hiller et al., 2006). Studies have shown that same-sex mentors are beneficial, which puts women at a disadvantage because of limited choice (Bettinger and Long, 2005; Lockwood, 2006; Richey et al., 1988). White and colleagues (1992) had indicated in their 'profile' of the successful career woman that she was likely to have identified an individual who had been influential in her career and acted to raise confidence in her own abilities. They found that mentors also gave practical help, but did not particularly act as role models. The modest number of very senior female figures in commerce, industry and the professions suggests that if a woman has a mentor, he is likely to be a man. While male mentors might be effective in the medium term, there are problems with long-term relationships between senior men and up-and-coming women. Issues of sexuality and power are likely to inhibit the quality of the relationship (see Chapter 5 for a fuller discussion).

In order to overcome the lack of potential mentors, especially for women and other minority groups, some formal mentoring schemes have been introduced. There are, however, interesting differences between formal mentoring schemes and informal mentoring.

One clinical psychology training scheme, for example, graduate trainees meet with allocated mentors at least three times a year during the 3 years of their professional training, the aim being to consider clinical issues and to enable the trainee to discuss their anxieties and the pleasures they achieve from their work. These include practical, clinical, ethical, career and interpersonal work-related issues but not academic work. This relationship continues for the first year following the completion of the training (thus four years in total). The mentor is normally a trained and experienced clinical psychologist, and generally there is no element of personal choice in the relationship. This scheme has been generally positive in that clinical psychology trainees feel they have gained support and knowledge through these relationships. However, such a scheme potentially lacks the emotional ties that bind the partnerships where the mentor/mentee choose each other.

One example, illustrative of how choice in the mentoring relationship can result in a long-term, mutually beneficial commitment, was an effective informal association among a group of three male academics. Professor A, in his late fifties when the relationship started, was a pro-vice chancellor,[7] and had taken an interest in the career of Professor B, recently appointed to a chair in the same subject area, supported by Professor A. Dr C, appointed to Professor B's department, was included in their social round, and Professor B brought him to the attention of Professor A. When a new chair was created, four years after Dr C's appointment, Professor A, who had had several opportunities to meet and encourage Dr C., urged him to apply. Professor B helped Dr C. to 'polish up' his CV, and Professor A was a member of the board who duly appointed Dr C to the chair.

There is no sense in which I am suggesting that Dr C. was not an ideal and probably even the best candidate for the post. Even so the process through which he was groomed and encouraged may have made all the difference to his securing the post. All three members of this network took the fact of their relationships for granted and the senior ones had had their own similar experiences earlier in their careers. They all benefited from supporting each other, even though all three were at different career stages. The older men achieved a stake in the future, but were still active on committees to which eventually all three were involved and offered mutual support – in public and in private.

This informal model is more effective in terms of career advancement and motivation than any formal system could ever be because of the emotional investment. The system cannot work for women in the same way, because there is not the long-term continuity or the number of women to make this possible, and neither is there a tradition of such practice. It is difficult for cross-sex long-term relationships to work effectively because they are likely to give rise to sexual gossip and speculation (Davidson and Cooper, 1992; Hearn and Parkin, 1987; see also Chapter 5).

## Overt sexist attitudes

> Blatant sex discrimination includes those discriminatory actions directed against women that are quite obvious to most observers and are highly visible.
>
> *(Benokraitis and Feagin, 1995: 59)*

These range from sexist remarks and jokes in meetings or public spaces at work, to violent and abusive behaviour from sexual harassment, to rape (Anderson et al., 1993). These actions have negative implications for women at all levels of the organization. Seniority is no barrier to sexism. My own relatively recent experience included two such scenes. As a senior member of staff I found myself frequently in all-male company at meetings, which as a rule presented no overt difficulty; in fact it was often fun. However when a senior, and to my eyes misogynist, man headed up and chaired those meetings, my male colleagues failed to notice how I was being treated, or at least the *impact* of that treatment on my ability to be effective in that context.

One of the two occasions took place on a warm summer day, the atmosphere in the meeting was relaxed and there was laughter at various stages. But at one point I had felt a little chilly and put my jacket, which had been on the back of my chair, over my shoulders. I was almost unaware of doing so. However the chair of the meeting suddenly turned and addressed a remark to me of something along the lines of, 'Well, if you are cold I suggest you hang upside down on the chandelier and pedal'. My colleagues all laughed – they thought the man a little crazy anyway, but even so he was in a powerful position in the organization we worked in. Because I knew that this represented an attack that would not have been made to anyone else (all male) in the room, I experienced this as extremely undermining and, although I see myself as tough enough to ignore such behaviours, reflecting at length over subsequent years I realized that I had felt humiliated both by the image conjured up and the intention to shift the discussion from the substantive content to the hostile and personal attack on my dignity.

The second example involved another senior male chair of a meeting who, while waiting for everyone to arrive, started talking about the physical appearance of a particular female singer. The others joined in joking about her. One of my colleagues, a gay man, looked at me, lifted his eyebrows but then joined in with the others. I felt unable to say anything, including complain about the discussion, as the others all seemed to treat it as a bonding experience with the more senior man.

Anti-women remarks and behaviours occur in formal situations such as these committee meetings, appointment or promotion boards. Sexist remarks in general make it difficult for women committee members. Should they object every time something sexist is said or wait until there are potentially serious consequences that may influence a promotion or appointment panel? They risk making dangerous and permanent enemies, being further labelled as outsiders, accused of lack of humour and being excluded from such panels in future because they cause trouble.

A woman being assessed by an appointment panel is still at risk of being asked questions about her domestic commitments, even in this second decade of the twenty-first century or, if she is unmarried, facing questions or innuendo about her sexuality. This continues to happen despite legislation aimed to prevent such remarks and behaviours. They are under the surface. I felt, for example, that if I had told my colleagues about how I experienced the meetings I outlined above, they would have suggested that I had overreacted. They might have apologized on behalf of men, as one actually did when I reported to him that the head of the institution complained there were too many middle-aged women in administrative roles. But that, no doubt unintentionally, is dismissive of the complaint. That not every man would be overtly or covertly sexist does not mean that sexism can be defeated. It sometimes means, as in this case, that it is ignored because, although women may feel put down, they recognize that many men ignore sexist remarks since they themselves disapprove. A strange but common paradoxical dilemma!

However, it is not only men who hold sexist attitudes. One survey of accountants, civil engineers, surveyors, bankers, lawyers, architects, computer managers and insurers in the UK made it clear that 'Women would rather work with men than with other women . . . Four times as many professional women would prefer to be surrounded by men at work, than by women' (MORI, 1994: 7).

Also around 25 per cent of the women surveyed said they would prefer a male to a female boss, despite reported experiences of discrimination. Only 4 per cent of men said they wanted a female boss, a view that suggests that female bosses will have poor quality day-to-day relationships at work if most colleagues view them so disapprovingly.

Sadly, in 2013 a similar survey in the USA came to the clear conclusion that most men and women would prefer a male to female boss because women were seen as micro-managers or passive aggressive.[8]

A Gallup Survey confirmed this showing that, in 1954, when Gallup first asked the question, 66 per cent of Americans clamed to prefer a male boss, in 2013, 35 per cent of the workforce still felt the same. This was at a time when there were more women than ever in positions of management and consequently more members of the workforce being exposed to working for women. There was light at the end of the tunnel, though, because it appeared that among those who did work for a female boss claimed to prefer working for a woman than working for a man.[9]

## Sexual harassment

Sexual harassment, which includes anything from drawing attention to a woman's body to causing embarrassment and demanding sexual favours, is a powerful discriminatory factor and may occur to women at any stage of their career (Bendelow and Williams, 1998; Brown et al., 1996; Kath, 2004;

Nicolson and Welsh, 1993; Robbins et al., 1997; Stockdale et al., 2008). The remarks may be apparently approving of a woman's body, as is frequently the case with junior staff and students. For older more senior women, it is more likely to be derogatory. This male behaviour seems commonplace according to numerous workplace surveys and I found that around 25 per cent of medical students reported being aware of sexual harassment taking place at university (Nicolson and Welsh, 1992). This corresponded to other university surveys (e.g. SUSU, 1992). The consequences of unchallenged sexual harassment are to poison the organizational culture, both in the long term and on a daily basis (Campbell et al., 1994).

## Backlash: covert barriers to women's success: complaining

Policies to combat overt sexism are limited in their effectiveness as they require the victim to report the perpetrator's behaviour (Campbell et al., 1994). One example of this is the NHS action plan for the implementation and monitoring of Opportunity 2000. The intent to combat sexist behaviour was clear, but sanctions for transgression stated in the documentation are obscure. A brief reference to complaints procedures is as follows: 'Any woman who wants to complain about not being treated fairly under these procedures should put her complaints in writing to her general manager/chief executive with a copy to the non-executive director with specific responsibility for women's issues' (NHS Management Executive, 1992: 5). This blanket procedure, intended to apply to women doctors as well as other health-service employees, is bizarre. There is an abundance of anecdotal data and an increase in empirical research-based data to suggest that this individualistic response is tricky and is unlikely to happen, except in severe cases, where a person's life becomes intolerable[10] (Aitkenhead and Liff, 1990). Women making complaints of sexual harassment and discrimination are routinely humiliated and their working environment is often hostile.

While it seems impossible for effective complaints to be made against senior men, complaints against senior women are numerous and well publicized. Such complaints have themselves been perceived as a form of discrimination. Wendy Savage, a senior lecturer and honorary consultant in obstetrics and gynaecology, was suspended during the mid-1980s for professional misconduct. She was cleared of all charges by the inquiry. Her subsequent analysis of events leading up to and following this affair made explicit the role of gender–power relations in the clinical establishment (Savage, 1986). Savage attributed her suspension and criticisms made of her clinical practice directly to the patriarchal structure of medicine and its operation within her speciality of obstetrics and gynaecology in particular, as well as inherent misogyny operating on a personal level in her health authority. Her account detailed discriminatory processes at several levels – the interpersonal, the organizational and the cultural. There seemed no individual, or structure within the hospital, health authority or Royal College that was not inherently biased in favour of the male-dominated status quo. Thus, her defence was supported largely by friends, lawyers and patients rather than from within the obstetrics and gynaecology hierarchy.

## Patriarchal culture

The patriarchal culture in all professions and business organizations is widespread and integral to most systems (Campbell et al., 1995). Women are still largely invisible, and what they do is second-best compared with what men do. Covert barriers to women's career progression represent the 'backlash' to the perceived threat of the rise of women's power in organizations.

The patriarchal culture of professional organizations, paradoxically, is both clearly visible and hidden during the socialization processes that occur when young women and men enter the system (Brown et al., 1996; Byers and Fitzgerald, 2002; Callaghan and Thompson, 2002; Gay, 1995; Schwarz, 1990).

At medical school, for example, where socialization begins as an undergraduate, the deep-rooted value system in relation to who is going to be a successful (as opposed to a 'good') doctor is transmitted to medical students of both sexes; for example that men make better hospital consultants and women make better general practitioners (Nicolson and Welsh, 1992). There is continued evidence that this happens across the NHS for both clinicians and managers although in the twenty-first century there are efforts to deny such attitudes (Nicolson et al., 2011).

In clinical psychology, the path to qualification and promotion is more complex: acceptance on the postgraduate training course is dependent upon a good first-degree result, and sometimes a PhD, and a selection interview. Because up to 90 per cent of psychology undergraduates are women (Morris et al., 1990), there is hidden pressure to reduce the proportion of women at each of these stages to enable men to achieve places on the clinical psychology courses. Thus it is more difficult for women to get to the first rung of the ladder. Women doctors have an advantage because they don't have to compete to get to this stage, and there are only 50 per cent at the point of entry so fear of them appears to be not so great – but it is increasing!

One example of covert discrimination reported by Wendy Savage was the Royal College of Obstetricians and Gynaecologists, where male members are invited to join clubs for which membership is limited to selected men alone and women seem unable or unwilling to contest this either by seeking membership or forming parallel associations.

> Excluded from the cosy male get-togethers where, it is rumoured, all the consultant posts are 'fixed', women have formed their own club but it does not seem to be an effective pressure group for women, either as obstetricians or as patients. The incongruity of a speciality devoted to women being almost totally controlled by men has always struck me forcefully.
>
> *(Savage, 1986: 59)*

The level at which policy and practice are organized and the speciality is regulated has an effect that penetrates post-graduate medical education and cannot be eradicated by the introduction of part-time training posts and the acceptance of career breaks.

Women it seems are evaluated on criteria other than those used to evaluate men. There are recent examples where this is blatantly clear. For example, Helena Daly was sacked from a consultant post in 1993 for 'personal misconduct' when it was alleged she had been rude to secretaries and nurses. A letter in the *British Medical Journal*, on behalf of the Medical Women's Federation in support of her, made it clear that she had been judged as a *woman* rather than a doctor and that this was a relatively common occurrence.

These echo issues that social scientists have known about for many years, and yet they are as alive today as ever. It is that there is a mismatch between the image of the valued, successful senior professional and the image of the 'normal' woman (cf. Broverman et al., 1970). Dorothy Smith argued several decades ago now that:

> Men attend to and treat as significant only what men say. The circle of men whose writing and talk was significant to each other extends backwards in time as far as our records reach. What men were doing was relevant to men, was written by men about men for men. Men listened and listen to what one another said.
>
> *(1978: 281)*

A few years earlier than that it had been made quite clear that women in the professions are excluded *because they are not men*.

Women have a 'servant' image, and the origin of this is 'the assumption that women innately, instinctively, or hormonally are adept at nurturing, sacrificing, and caring for others' (Prather, 1971: 17). Further, as a servant 'American society implies women are better qualified than men for nurturant occupations, which are usually paid less and are of lower status than other professions . . . employers can feel justified . . . avoiding promoting women into positions of leadership' (ibid.).

So the identification and challenging of patriarchal bias is not new, yet it is persistent and underpins the formal processes through which promotions are achieved and power is distributed. However, it appears that the more patriarchy is challenged, the more energy is given to the backlash (Faludi, 1992).

## Old-boy networks

What makes those in power so aware of women, especially powerful women, as different from themselves? Men, groomed for power, often find themselves in formal and informal decision-making contexts with men they have known at school, university or in a previous career posts. Loyalty to such peers is frequently referred to as the 'old-boy network' and reinforced through membership of formal or informal groups such as elite golf clubs, membership of gentlemen's clubs, after hours drinking, rugby clubs and similar activities from which women are either by definition excluded, such as the Masons, or made to feel uncomfortable by being there, such as all-male after-hours social events (Benokraitis and Feagin, 1995; Campbell et al., 1995; Davidson and Cooper, 1992; Flanders, 1994). As one woman in Davidson and Cooper's study said:

> I felt very isolated. They would all go to all-male clubs at lunch time and that, of course, is where a lot of the real business goes on. Of course, I was therefore totally excluded from that. That was a big source of prejudice by them. It would have been much easier for me if there had been another woman in my position.
>
> *(1992: 88)*

Such networks, however, are not only about excluding non-members, but are concerned with the socialization of younger professionals, and information giving. Women therefore are unable to learn expected ways of behaving. The 'old-boy network' is the continuation of the socialization into masculinity discussed in Chapter 2 and, as argued in that chapter, masculinity is equivalent to senior management behaviour. It has thus been estimated that over

50 per cent of all jobs in management came through personal contacts of these kinds (Davidson and Cooper, 1992: 88). This reinforces the notion that the senior woman had further to climb to reach the top than her male peers.

## Patronage

The issue of patronage is closely linked to 'old-boy networks', as well as to mentoring, in that senior men will often choose to assist the career of some-one similar to themselves or to the people they admire. Patronage is overt in the medical profession, and there have been several examples in academic life when a postgraduate student of the professor has obtained an academic post in that department despite strong competition from outside. The Brit-ish Medical Association has expressed concern about this system, aware of the way minority groups (i.e. those not reflected among the current senior echelons of the profession) are disadvantaged:

> patrons will relate best to those who follow their own image . . . this means that already disadvantaged groups such as women, overseas doc-tors and doctors of ethnic minority origin, are least likely to benefit from the system, even though they are in most need of support.
>
> *(BMA, 1993: 1)*

Wendy Savage, in her powerful account of her own experiences, is well aware of the issues of patronage and reproduction of values through recruit-ment, citing examples from decision-making processes about appointments. In one case, a male professor

> weighed in with a vote for 'the chap we know'. It was then that one of the panel mounted an amazing attack on the Australian woman, repeating gossip that she was a difficult woman to work with, con-tinuing innuendo about her personal life which it would be wrong to repeat. I was disgusted by this behaviour and so angry that I could hardly express my disapproval. I left the room abruptly.
>
> *(Savage, 1986: 24)*

Many women who move up the career ladder are rejected, often under similar circumstances. They themselves, like Savage, might wish to publicize the behaviour of the senior men who actively and blatantly discriminate. However, it appears that, far from assisting change, such publicity reduces other women's motivation (Benokritis and Feagin, 1995).

## Bad behaviour?

But is anger and disapproval the way to tackle patronage or any other displays of prejudice that comprise the glass ceiling? The cost to women for expressing such unfeminine behaviour may be high. Women have to cope with a dual assessment – as professionals in competition with men, and as female professionals. As the latter, they have to be both *better* than men professionally, and feminine both socially and professionally. It is a crucial dilemma.

It can be no coincidence that, apart from Wendy Savage and Helena Daly, mentioned above, well-publicized professional and personal misconduct cases in the medical profession during the 1990s had women, such as Marietta Higgs or Carole Starkey, at their centre, and part of the case against them is that colleagues were 'afraid' to tell them that their practices appeared to be inadequate (see Nicolson, 1993b), implying that they were neither good doctors nor good women. In these cases their professional colleagues fail either to train, correct or socialize these women, but leave them exposed. During interviews in 2010 with senior women we were told frequently of the sleeplessness and anxiety that went hand in hand with their senior position. Does this mean that women really are difficult to work with and will not respond to criticism, or are there organizational factors that expose the mistakes of women rather than those of men? 'The bad behaviour of some doctors is accepted as the norm in a stressful environment. It may even be rewarded with respect and sometimes affection. How different the response if that doctor is a woman' (Markham, 1993: 686).

The problem for women is that they are almost exclusively isolated from other women when they reach senior positions. Although some may welcome this (MORI, 1994), this female misogyny arises because of the complex way that patriarchal culture is embedded in our perceptions of organizational life. Women frequently use time and energy in their early careers discovering the exclusionary force of patriarchal culture. They once, perhaps, believed themselves to be the exceptions to the stereotypical woman they so despised. However, there is little comfort in being the Queen Bee, when the wolves are baying for the blood of a scapegoat. It is the woman who is dispensable.

## Unconscious barriers: identifying the boundaries

How far are members of organizations aware of the implications of their own behaviour? The young female professional or manager attending the board meeting for the first time only experiences her own strangeness and terror with the situation. She is noticeable in the minority as a woman; the men know each other and are like each other; men are familiar with the routine and assist newcomers. How can she know why some board members fear her presence? She sees herself as new and inexperienced. Some of them know from her qualifications and background and that she is on the 'fast track'. They may feel unable to welcome her as she represents a threat. Thus, they behave as if she is invisible and a burden. But why is she perceived as such a threat? There is no evidence that women are going to take over companies or professional groups in any large numbers.

The male head of a division finds it difficult to cope when he knows that the new female recruit is better qualified for *his* job than he is himself. As time passes she wonders what more on earth she has to do to get his attention and praise. He is terrified that his incompetencies will be exposed and does what he (legitimately) can to hinder her finding out, and thus obstructs her progress.

In Chapter 3, I discussed the concepts of envy and anxiety as applied to men and women working in organizations. There, I suggested that instead of taking the traditional Freudian framework whereby women (unconsciously) envied men their power and success (i.e. envied their having a penis), it was increasingly the case that some men (unconsciously) envied women their skills and achievements. This was made more acute by the wider interest taken by feminist activists and academics, management scientists and politicians in women's progress. Here I want to examine these aspects of the unconscious as they relate to organizational processes.

## The unconscious at work

Just as individuals operate defence mechanisms to protect themselves against anxiety, so do groups and organizations (Bion, 1961; de Board, 1978; Freud, 1921; Jaques, 1955).

> Like individuals, institutions develop defences against difficult emotions which are too threatening or too painful to acknowledge. These emotions may be a response to external threats such as government policy or social change. They may arise from internal conflicts between management and employees or between groups and departments in competition for resources.
>
> *(Halton, 1994: 12)*

In organizations the unconscious operates at the level of the individual as well as the group/organization itself. Unconscious processes are sources of energy, creativity and motivation at both of these levels, but unconscious defences against the overwhelming feelings of anxiety and envy frequently block energy, which may result in poor emotional and/or physical health for all.

The implementation of equal opportunities policies or the appointment of a female senior executive may arouse group emotional responses that appear to have no basis in the changes that the policy or the appointment has actually precipitated. The large-scale defection of Church of England clergy to the Roman Catholic Church on the recognition of women priests and later women bishops is an example of this. Major anxieties were aroused by their fear of women having equal power and opportunities in the Church, but the Bible, God and personal conscience issues were produced as reasons for these defections. This process was really a large-scale denial of inherent misogyny in the organization and those who ran it.

Organizations that comprise an increasing number of aspiring junior and middle-ranking women are at crisis point. Men and women appear to have extensive fantasies and fears about changes that female management might bring that will increase the problems in their daily working lives, and in their sense of subjectivity/identity.

## Men's fantasies and fears

Accounts of men's concerns about women entering the higher echelons of their organizations and professions are (stereo)typically couched in 'logic'. Thus, the infamous paper by Crawford (1989) about the state of the profession of clinical psychology in the UK written at the time a major review was being carried out:

> Almost all current trainees are female. The trend towards an increasingly female intake was first commented on in an article by Humphrey and Haward (1981) in which they said, 'if this trend were to continue there may well be cause for concern'. The trend has indeed continued and I believe there is cause for concern. First, there is the practical problem of a nearly all-female profession providing services for men. If the situation were reversed I am sure there would be numerous letters of complaint from women and quite rightly so. However, the problems of a female dominated profession are not just the mirror image of a male-dominated one. Whilst the BPS [British Psychological Society] adheres to a non-sexist policy, the world at large is not necessarily so enlightened. National pay rates for women are

significantly below those for men. Predominantly the female professions are lower in status and pay than predominantly male professions. Compare a nurse, teacher or occupational therapist with a surgeon, accountant or barrister.

As pay and status in clinical psychology have fallen, so men are no longer being attracted into the profession but as the profession becomes increasingly all female, so it will become harder to persuade general managers, mostly male, to improve pay and status: a downward spiral of a declining profession.

*(Crawford, 1989: 30)*

In fact Crawford's overt fears were unfounded. Clinical psychologists' salary scales were upgraded to the satisfaction of all those within the profession. Women and men continued to enter the profession and compete for the senior and top positions, which are still mainly held by men. However, this is by no means exclusively so, and the trend towards women in powerful positions in clinical psychology is likely to continue.

What is interesting in this extract is the misogyny and anxiety couched in concern for standards. First, the writer, it seems, believes in equality, but is anxious that the 'outside world' of managers and other policy-makers is not so enlightened, and thus salaries might fall compared with other groups. Second, there is the fear that a male patient might have to receive clinical treatment from a female psychologist. And third, there is the unstated fear that women might be promoted over the heads of men.

The denied anxiety in these 'logical' male fantasies seems to be about the subordination of men: that subordinated men are less than men — they have experienced the ultimate catastrophe, (metaphorical) castration. As in childhood, this anxiety is too much to bear and men need to find a variety of ways to defend themselves against this anxiety.

## The psychological consequences of barriers to women's careers

Some institutional defences are healthy, in the sense that they enable the staff to cope with stress and develop through their work in the organisations. But some institutional defences, like some individual defences, can obstruct contact with reality and in this way damage the staff and hinder the organisation in fulfilling its tasks and in adapting to changing circumstances. Central among these defences is denial, which involves pushing certain thoughts, feelings and experiences out of conscious awareness because they have become too anxiety provoking.

*(Halton, 1994: 12)*

Barriers to women's career progress, essentially conscious and deliberate on the part of *some* men, go largely unnoticed because they are about maintaining the status quo. However, they *do* have an unconscious negative influence on women that reduces their motivation and has a derogatory influence on self-esteem.

Some women early in their careers *might* see sexist behaviour as a challenge, or believe that some women specifically attract such comments and behaviours, and they are the exceptions. However, most women will come eventually to realize the constraints of patriarchy on their own careers as they make attempts to move up the hierarchy.

## Conclusions

Professional life, particularly for senior women in a patriarchal context, is stressful. Professional actions and decisions require expert knowledge and skilful execution, and thus daily life is characterized by a sense of responsibility that is likely at times to give rise to anxiety (see de Board, 1978). Men, particularly those who perceive threats from women or an individual woman, are also in danger of being overwhelmed.

Women witness the ease by which ordinary men achieve what they themselves are struggling to reach and this brings about envious reactions, particularly in the isolated and battle weary. Men in senior positions watch better-qualified, highly motivated women climbing the ladder towards them with unmitigated terror.

## Notes

1 http://eeoc.gov/laws/statutes/epa.cfm.
2 http://legislation.gov.uk/ukpga/1970/41.
3 http://legislation.gov.uk/ukpga/1975/65.
4 http://fawcettsociety.org.uk/wp-content/uploads/2013/02/Sex-and-Power-2013-FINAL-REPORT.pdf.
5 http://abc.net.au/news/2012–10–09/julia-gillard-attacks-abbott-of-hypocrisy/4303634.
6 http://surgicalcareers.rcseng.ac.uk/wins/research-and-stats.

7 A senior academic/administrative post. Pro-vice-chancellors chair policy and resources type of committees and, normally, with the vice-chancellor (or CEO) take part in all key policy decisions.

8 http://edition.cnn.com/2013/11/13/living/identity-gallup-male-boss-female-boss/.

9 http://gallup.com/poll/165791/americans-prefer-male-boss.aspx.

10 This is similar to Bruno Bettelheim's observation in *The Informed Heart* (1979) that victims will only fight their oppressors when they intuitively feel there is nothing left to lose. When a person still feels they have career potential, they are likely to try to carry on despite the sexual harassment.

# 5

# SEXUALITY, POWER AND ORGANIZATION

## Introduction

In this chapter, I:

- re-examine the way the construction of femininity and masculinity 'sexes' organizational life and in so doing exacerbates the subordination of women to male desire;
- identify the processes whereby men and patriarchy exert power over women through both verbal and physical sexual harassment, while imposing constraints on women's *own* sexual desire and behaviour in the context of the sexed organizational hierarchy.

'Women work as "women"' (MacKinnon, 1979: 9). As such they are not equally valued members of an organization, but positioned as objects of male desire and male derision. The *fact* of gender at work, and the ways in which gender–power relations are conducted within patriarchal cultures overall, makes sexuality a crucial component of these power relations (Chrisler and Ferguson, 2006; Jones, 2006; Lim and Cortina, 2005). Male heterosexuality underlies the patriarchal culture of professional and organizational life as

Laurie Penny writing in the *New Statesman*, in an article about sexual bully-ing in the Westminster Parliament, proposes:

> Workplaces where the groping of women by high-status men goes unchecked are environments whose vectors of power are clear. Sexual harassment in general is not just about having your bottom pinched or your boobs squeezed on the sly. It is about having your bottom pinched and your boobs squeezed and being unable to say anything about it because the groper is an important man – and if you speak up, or reject his advances too loudly, it's you who risks being called a lying slut and stonewalled out of the party. It is about a culture of silence that proves who has the power.[1]

Sexuality and power become abusive when the internal dynamics are opaque in such a way that patriarchal power relations are maintained and strengthened – perhaps there are more informal groupings of senior men and 'old-boy networks' become more active. This might be as a response to the threat to patriarchal structures posed by a more confident female senior workforce. But these patterns that maintain and reproduce abuse and discrimination are not in the best interests of organizational productivity and eventually if unchecked the system may lose any flexibility around its boundaries resulting in sterility and failure to respond to the demands of the exterior world (Baillien and de Witte, 2009; Stouten et al., 2010).

## Constructing sexuality at work

While ambitious and influential heterosexual men (and in a slightly different way gay men) may gain credibility from visible sexual activity while positioning themselves as active/potent/creative, professional women are assumed to have to choose between being the bimbo/whore or the asexual serious professional woman. It is no coincidence that sexual relations at work directly resemble sexual relations outside. This arrangement that conflates power, influence and sexuality not only privileges men and heterosexuality, but devalues women's working experiences through the threat, or reality, of harassment and forfeiture of their own sexuality and expressions of desire. As Jane Ussher asserts:

> whilst men were positioned as the active driving force, the 'naturally' sexual beings, women were seen to be playing a key role in arousing male desire. Women's sexuality was therefore both fatal and flawed – paradoxically framed either as absent, within the archetype of the

asexual pure Madonna, or as the all-encompassing and dangerously omnipotent, an image represented most clearly by the witch or the whore.

*(1993: 10–11)*

Men have power in organizations and professional life, while women, even powerful ones, are on the whole in subordinate positions as we have seen in earlier chapters. Women, as both subordinates and the objects of male desire, may be seen by men as one of the 'benefits' of their position. The master/servant relationship whereby the woman/secretary will make coffee, buy cigarettes or cater to the male boss's emotional or sexual needs is the subject of myth, fiction and reality. Many men frequently behave as if women in these subordinate roles in the office are also available sexually (MacKinnon, 1979; Morris, 1994). They might likewise assume that other men see women in that way. Examples of this type of abusive power have been uncovered among political elites in Western societies. In the USA, female interns, for instance, have been exploited, and their lives and reputations attacked and in some cases destroyed. The Bill Clinton/Monica Lewinsky case is one of the more public examples. The story came to light in 1998 when Clinton, president at the time, denied having sexual relations with Lewinsky, who was 22 years old when the scandal broke.

In the UK too, high-profile female politicians and aides have asserted that they have been witnesses and victims of sexism and sexual harassment, which are commonplace in such a male dominated hierarchy.[2]

The sexual exploitation of women by men occurs when men have direct power over women's conditions of work, their hiring and firing, as in the case of secretaries, shop-floor factory workers, waitresses and domestic staff. These workers tend to have little power, in that their lack of formal qualifications and skill makes them easily replaceable.

As MacKinnon depicted:

> In such jobs a woman is employed as a woman. She is also, apparently, treated like a woman, with one aspect of this being specifically sexual. Specifically, if part of the reason a woman is hired is to be pleasing to the male boss, whose notion of a qualified worker merges with a sexist notion of the proper role of women, it is hardly surprising that sexual intimacy, forced when necessary, would be considered part of her duties and his privileges.

*(MacKinnon, 1979: 18)*

As Naomi Wolf (1991) observed, the rules that governed employment in what had been specifically 'display professions', such as fashion modelling, actresses, night-club hostesses and so on, where beauty had been a requirement, appear to have been extended. 'What is happening today is that all the professions into which women are making strides are being rapidly reclassified – so far as the women are concerned – as display professions' (Wolf, 1990: 27).

Thus female bank managers, lawyers and head teachers of schools all have to look both powerful and sexy. The appearance of Marcia Clark, the female prosecution lawyer in the O.J. Simpson murder trial in the early 1990s, which was televized throughout the world, was the subject of direct discussion. Television programmes, news and comment in the media focused on the length of her skirts and manner of clothing. This reached a crescendo when she changed her hairstyle. More noticeably the appearance and sexual currency of women in the media spotlight, such as news presenters and actors, are constantly being publicly dissected because of apparent flaws or changes in their appearance. Ashley Judd, an actor, wrote a piece for the *Daily Beast* (online) where she stated that conversations about women's bodies are used to define and control us – whether they are in the mass media or in small private groups. 'Our worth ascertained and ascribed based on the reduction of personhood to simple physical objectification. Our voices, our personhood, our potential, and our accomplishments are regularly minimized and muted.'[3]

Why should this be the case? Marcia Clark's legal skills, clearly on display, were deemed by the media to be less relevant to the proceedings than her sexual appeal. Her colleagues and the defence lawyers (mostly men) were discussed in a variety of ways, but it was only with her that appearance was on the agenda. Women as professionals have to tread a tightrope between visibility and invisibility *because of this positioning as sexual*; and dress style, gestures and language are part of this (Fox and Lituchy, 2012; Sheppard, 1989).

Some occupations for women are seen as almost equivalent to mistress/sex object/whore. Secretaries, waitresses and nurses, for instance, have traditionally been positioned in this way by the men who work in a superordinate rank (Robbins et al., 1997). MacKinnon quotes an example of one secretarial college attempting to help their graduates ensure employment. The advice was to 'sell' themselves. To do this they are made into a 'Pretty package' (MacKinnon, 1979: 21).

One of the most blatant contexts for women being seen as sex objects by men, while they are seeing themselves as potential professionals, is the university (Butler and Landells, 1995). There some male academics/

lecturers who appear to judge all female students by appearance, and see them as potential, usually heterosexual, partners, regardless of whether they themselves or the students are married or with partners (Campbell-Breen, 2006; Paludi et al., 2006). Indeed, the practice of married lecturers having serial sexual encounters with female students is so embedded in the cultural mores of academic life that it could almost be positioned as a 'privilege' of the occupation (see, for instance, Bradbury's *The History Man*) (Hill and Silva, 2005).

During selection and assessment procedures (for staff as well as students it seems) there are numerous accounts of men making remarks about an applicant's body. As Kagan and Lewis's (1990a) reports of conversations in a psychology department in the UK demonstrated:

> (At interview)
> *female staff*: are you ready to interview another prospective student yet?
> *male colleague*: Yes. What have you got there? I don't want just anyone –
> give me another of those pretty little girls.
> *female staff*: Have you got the rest of the application forms there?
> *male colleague*: You don't need to see them. All we need to know is if
> they've got long blonde hair and big boobs.
> (At assessment)
> *female staff*: I'm not sure which student hasn't handed in her essays yet.
> *male colleague*: You must know. Brown hair. So ugly you wouldn't even
> want to mug her.

Male American university staff appeared to have similar expectations about the raison d'être of female students, which comes as a shock to the young women involved. As Carter and Jeffs (1995) alluded to, one American study revealed that 26 per cent of male academics admitted to sexual involvement with female students (Carter and Jeffs, 1995: 17).

One woman recounted the following:

> My whole feeling about surviving in a large university was to get to know my faculty members, so that when they were grading the papers, they were dealing with a person. So I'd always try to meet the people who were teaching my courses. When I went about doing that, one of my professors made an appointment for me to come to his office in the evening. I didn't think anything was weird about it. It wasn't convenient, but everybody had busy schedules. But when I got down there, it was quite clear that he has something else in mind. And it was

very hard to figure out how to react. He kissed me, and I didn't know what to do at first. I got slightly involved, and then I thought, wait a minute: this is really weird. And I found a way to get out of the office and back to my dormitory. Clearly if I'd been willing, we'd have had sex right there on the floor of his office.

*(Majorie Carroll, in Morris (ed.) 1994: 65)*

A woman, ambitious and serious about her university education and future career, was seen by the lecturer in the framework of *his* needs, and thus as offering herself sexually. He was incapable, it seemed, of treating a woman as a peer or potential peer, only as a sex object.

Lesbian women are often doubly at risk. Although they themselves may never feel tempted to begin a relationship with a man at work, their sexuality is no protection against men's advances. Lesbians are further in jeopardy of harassment and ridicule from their both male and female colleagues if knowledge of their sexuality becomes publicly available (Cortina et al., 1998; Kitzinger, 1994). However, their experience of prejudice and censure may depend on the level in the hierarchy they have achieved. Single marital status (even if they are not actually without a long-term partner) had for some lesbian women been perceived by their superiors as indicators of flexibility as they were free of the trammels of heterosexual lifestyles. One woman in a study of lesbians in management felt that because she was perceived as more masculine she was sometimes given more stimulating and challenging tasks (Hall, 1989).

## Consensual sex

To find wanted sexual attention, you have to give and receive a certain amount of unwanted sexual attention. Clearly, the truth is that if no one was ever allowed to risk offering unsolicited sexual attention, we would all be solitary creatures.

*(Roiphe, 1993)*

Roiphe's aim in writing this was to challenge what she saw as the feminist prescription of asexuality implicit in anti-date-rape and sexual harassment campaigns. Her analysis, however, is limited by what must be her lack of experience of gender relations on campus. While there is little doubt that certain anti-sexual harassment procedures such as detailed checking by men as to whether they are causing offence to women in everyday conversation is insulting to most people, there is a danger, by emphasizing the extremes of political correctness, that the power of male sexuality is being reduced in its importance. One example from some years ago, told to me by a male friend who was head of a university department, demonstrated that predatory men knew exactly what they were doing. My friend was worried that a married male professor on his staff, well known for seducing young female students, had given him a box of recorded tapes to 'prove' that all the relationships he had had were consensual. My friend did not want to listen to these tapes. They had been given to him for safe keeping just in case someone might make a complaint against the predatory professor. Both he and I were horrified, but at the time there was no particular rule against that professor's behaviour other than he had to declare an interest to avoid bias during an assessment board!

However, to make the simplistic point that many men see women as sex-objects may obscure the complexity of sexuality and gendered relationships. Just because women are seen by some men within the framework of patriarchal culture in this way does not mean that men do not fall in love or that women themselves do not have sexual desire. Nor does it mean that some women are not prepared to take advantage of these processes, or find the idea of sex with a powerful man, per se, exciting.

It would not be uncommon for a heterosexual female student to express the view that her lecturers are more exciting and interesting intellectually than the young men who are fellow students. She may also feel that she is singled out and special because of her relationship with the lecturer. The dilemma is that the male senior man/lecturer–female junior woman/student sexual liaison is often not based on mutual understanding of why each party is involved.

> When you're in a relationship where there's a significant disparity of power, the weaker person is drawn by the attention. In a university situation, of course, the excitement that comes from an intellectual relationship combines with the excitement of a potential sexual relationship. For me it was enormously confusing, and I didn't know what to do with it.
>
> *(Majorie Carroll, in Morris (ed.) 1994: 65)*

The confusion occurs because the relationship takes place within a structure that, in itself, is more constraining to the parties involved than are the mores of patriarchy. In everyday life, when people meet outside the workplace, it is likely that a woman will have a relationship with a man who is in a senior position to her own, that he will wield more power at work than she will and that he will earn more (Church and Summerfield, 1995). Men reach the top quicker than women in all spheres of professional life.

However, if the individuals concerned are in the same organization each participant will know of the other's power-position in relation to themselves. This applies whether or not they are in the same department. Working together makes a sexual relationship even more intriguing, risky, exciting and potentially dangerous. The man, by virtue of being in a senior position will also *know* more than the woman does about how the organization works, both structurally and formally and in terms of the informal interpersonal level, at least for those involved at the top of the hierarchy. He may also have more experience, specialized knowledge of their profession. He will move in social and professional circles with others who are senior to her. She therefore has much to gain informally from such a sexual liaison.

It is frequently suggested that women who have sexual relationships with male bosses have an advantage over other women and their male peers (MacKinnon, 1979). Some men see women as gaining an unfair advantage. In our medical student research, for instance, in answer to the question about whether female students had advantages over men, we often gained the response that middle-aged consultants were likely to give pretty young women priority in selection to junior house officer jobs and in some cases better marks (Nicolson and Welsh, 1992). However, if this is the case, their advantage is relatively short lived:

> Despite the indications that few benefits redound to the woman who accedes, much folklore exists about the woman who 'slept her way to the top' or the academic professional woman who 'got her degree on her back'. These aphorisms suggest that women who are not qualified for their jobs or promotions acquire them instead by sexual means.
> . . . Since so few women get to the top at all, it cannot be very common.
>
> *(MacKinnon, 1979: 37–38)*

In fact women who do engage in sexual relationships at work with senior men rarely achieve in this way (Hearn and Parkin, 1987). When the relationship ends, it is the woman who loses her job and/or her power (Gutek, 1989).

If a woman is having a relationship with a senior man, or lecturer in the case of a student, she is unlikely to experience a sense of privilege in her everyday life. Indeed, she is likely to have to negotiate greater obstacles than she would if she were not in the relationship. Celia Morris (1994) clarifies this point from her interviews with professional women:

The trap many women fall into is the belief that giving themselves sexually makes them safer. Behind the romantic folderol attached to sex lies the conviction that it is finally what a man wants and needs from a woman, and that when she has allowed herself to be most vulnerable, he will protect her. In this way, sex becomes the most precious thing a woman has and her ultimate weapon in a precarious world.

*(1994: 85)*

However, this, as Morris goes on to demonstrate, happens only rarely. Usually at the end of a relationship a woman is 'unceremoniously dumped' (ibid.).

Some women believe the myth themselves. One woman, an American working as a lecturer in a prestigious medical school who was seen and saw herself on the 'fast track', actually started an affair with a man she suspected would get the post of chair in her department.

I knew he'd get the chairmanship. So whether my motivation for developing an affair with him was based on just my sexual friskiness or on the fact that I thought I'd have an advantage in a very cut-throat system, I can't really tell. I'm ambitious enough that if I'd thought that sex would get me anywhere, I'd probably have done it.

*(Pamela Cutrer in Morris, 1994: 91)*

However, when she wanted the affair to end, he did not, and she was forced to have sex with him in order to gain promotion. She said, 'We had sex and I got the raise' (p. 91).

She continued to have sex with him when he demanded it, and this lasted for nearly three years. Then she was able to re-organize her working life so she did not need to have contact with him. Only then could the relationship stop.

Sexual or sexualized romance in organizations stimulates emotion, not only in the two participants, but in the potential audience. Colleagues who are aware of an affair at work may believe it distorts communication, trust and power relationships. As Carter and Jeffs propose, sexual relationships in university departments pollute the social context by creating tensions of various kinds: 'As one mature [female] student put it: "I could not believe what was going on. I gave up a good job to come here for training. I was shocked to find lecturers regularly using their power to seduce students"' (1995: 16). The complications of illicit relationships in a university context are numerous. Do colleagues who find out 'blow the whistle'? Carter and

Jeffs interviewed someone who saw their head of department out with a student miles away from the university town. Although they had not said anything, s/he contemplated resignation because of the feeling that the head of department had since become difficult to work with and, it seemed, waiting to catch his witness out.

Lecturer/student liaisons also rouse an element of envy from other students through expectations that the woman will be given privileges over them because of her relationship. Other members of staff who may have wanted a relationship with the same student, or who themselves do not behave in that way, but secretly would like to do so may also feel envious or resentful. Fellow students of both sexes are made to feel uncomfortable in seminars when the tutor and his girlfriend are present.

## Boys will be boys

It seems that despite both women and men being sexual beings, it is only men who are able to reap the benefits from sex at work. Women who achieve at work frequently are seen as having 'used' their sexuality, while men are seen as being 'natural' or as having been 'used' by the woman (Gutek, 1989).

Lynne Segal (1994) argues that recognition of women's equality in every sphere of life can only occur as a consequence of the demolition of '[hetero]"sexuality" as confirmation of "manhood" . . . Its discursive displacement is central to the battle against the hierarchical gender relations which it serves to symbolise' (Segal, 1994: 317).

The pervasive notion that male equals activity/potency and female equals passivity/responsiveness lends weight to the 'normality' of sexual exploitation at work where boys will be boys for whom sex is part of their legitimate pursuit.

Purkiss (1994), re-examining the concept of the 'lecherous professor', draws attention to the university as a site for male academic sexual exploitation of female students. It is not only the ethical interpersonal issues that are at stake.

Frequently, the man's worth/ability is set directly against the wrongs afflicted on the woman who complains of sexual exploitation. Majorie Carroll, mentioned above, found this out the hard way, when she went to complain about the sexualized behaviour of her lecturer who had tried to have sexual intercourse with her:

> four of us went to see the head resident, who was a graduate student living in the dormitory, and explained . . . he told us not to say anything because this faculty member was up for tenure and we could get

him into trouble! This was an area in which I'd intended to major, and I ended up shifting my field of study because I knew I couldn't deal with this and didn't want to have to. So as I result, I changed what I was concentrating on as an undergraduate. And he got tenure.

*(Majorie Carroll, in Morris (ed.), 1994: 65)*

Two accounts in the UK *Times Higher Education Supplement*, now rebranded as the *THE*, raised similar issues:

One Equal Opportunities officer who spoke to a vice-chancellor about a professor who had been involved with a string of students was informed he was a leader in his field, an asset the university could not afford to lose. It was then made abundantly clear that she was employed to calm the students and not upset the professor in the process.

*(Carter and Jeffs, 1995: 16–17)*

I was extremely reluctant to bring a complaint against the tutor. I did so only because I could not face any more tutorials with him, and yet I had to if I were to pass that paper . . . I did complain. And here I was very lucky. [A female tutor] took it seriously.

*(Sanders, 1995: 16–17)*

## Blue stocking, virgin or executive tart?

Searching for a desire of their own – free from entanglement with male-centred myths and meanings – led some heterosexual feminists to abandon longings for physical and emotional intimacy with men.

*(Segal, 1994: 214)*

Experiencing feminism and heterosexuality as contradictory, many women have opted for a separation between their public life – as strong feminists, as women who work with other women – and their personal life. A feminist might be very attached to a man who is not without his faults . . . Once I practically had to force a woman I worked with for years to introduce me to the man whom I knew was her partner.

*(Valverde, 1985)*

Women traditionally, were not only assumed to be asexual socially, but also biologically and psychologically, in that they neither desired nor experienced pleasurable sensations through sexual behaviours. Sex and the pursuit of sex, was for the man's pleasure and for reproduction.

*(Nicolson, 1994)*

What are the costs to a professional woman in avoiding being the object of male desire? Is it possible for a woman to be seen as having a choice about how to conduct her sexuality? The paradoxes surrounding female sexuality and its representation have been well documented frequently by feminist writers (Jeffreys, 1990; Ussher, 1989). Women as a group are seen under patriarchy as either the virgin/Madonna figure or the loose woman/whore. These images, however, have had to be 'updated' to apply to professional women who do not fit easily into either category. Because they work in the intellectual/active world of men they cannot be the virginal/Madonna figure perched on her pedestal, and are unlikely to be taken seriously for long if they are seen as the whore. There is a problem in expressing any sexuality at all, as may be seen from the preceding sections of this chapter. As Ehrenreich and English (1979) explained several years ago, traditionally the more competent a women was intellectually, the less likely she was to be seen as fecund. This potential for sterility was considered to be socially dangerous.

Thus, in the late twentieth and early twenty-first century, as women began to achieve in their professions or rise up the management hierarchy, they made themselves sexually 'invisible'. Women who were in senior positions consciously try not to be identified as or mistaken for a secretary, the universally sexual being, where the 'boss–secretary relation should be seen as an important nodal point for the organization of sexuality and pleasure' (Pringle, 1989: 162).

Consequently, women needed to desexualize themselves while not being seen as 'men'. This occurs through careful attention to dress, on the one hand, and, equally important, in relation to verbal and non-verbal communication. Women in this position have to avoid both flirting and gestures that imply subordination, but neither must they appear aggressive.

Sheppard (1989) summarizes some of the 'advice' literature thus. Women's clothing has to avoid drawing attention to her body, but must not look too much like the male business suit either. She must not be seen leaving a business meeting to use the toilet, nor should she be seen purchasing a sanitary towel from the women's toilets as this reminds witnesses that she may have menstrually related moods, she should be careful that the language she uses is not about bodies, and she should be aware of the kinds of pictures she uses in her office. 'A painting of a cavalry charge or a steam locomotive would probably be too masculine: a watercolour of a meadow with a lot of pastels might be too feminine. Hang only neuter art' (Sheppard, 1989: 150).

However, if a powerful woman, despite careful attention to all these details, transgresses a major patriarchal rule and compromises a man in some way, she is 'put down' via her sexuality. The example of the journalist Ginny Dougary makes this point.

As she recounts in her book *The Executive Tart and Other Myths* (1994), she interviewed Norman Lamont, the former British Chancellor of the Exchequer, for *The Times* newspaper. Lamont was indiscreet about the Prime Minister John Major, which Dougary duly reported. She was astonished to read the accounts of herself as the journalist, which seemed to overtake media and public concern about the comments of the former Chancellor about the Prime Minister. She was described as

> a 'flame haired', 'alluring' temptress who had enticed poor, helpless Norman into a 'tender trap' using those shameless, age-old feminine wiles. Dougary had even, or so I read [of herself], 'won Norman's heart'. Ah, of course, that must be why she got a good interview.
>
> *(Dougary, 1994: 242)*

She describes as how the weeks passed the Lamont affair became known as 'Lunchgate', and that David Mellor (an ex-Tory Minister, sacked for sexual transgressions) made a vitriolic attack on her (and other women journalists) in a piece in the *Guardian* called 'Who needs old harridans?', where he compares Lynn Barber, whom he refers to as '"a sabre-toothed old harridan who by the look of her has lived a bit, and none too wisely either", to Ginny Dougary "the sorceress's apprentice . . . Quite what it is in Ms Dougary's CV that qualifies her for all this advanced superciliousness is beyond me. But I'm steering clear of her, and I suspect after this, even old Norman will too"' (Dougary, 1994: 242–243).

## Sexual harassment

> Sexual harassment, most broadly defined, refers to the unwanted imposition of sexual requirements in the context of a relationship of unequal power.
>
> *(MacKinnon, 1979: 1)*

> Sexual harassment is the 'unsolicited non reciprocal male behaviour that asserts a woman's sex role over her function as a worker'.
>
> *(Benokraitis and Feagin, 1994: 31, with reference to Singleton, 1990)*

> Sexual harassment is any unsolicited and unwelcome sexual advance, request for sexual favours, comment or physical contact when such a contact has the purpose or effect of unreasonably interfering with an individual's work or academic performance or of creating an intimidatory, hostile or offensive working or academic environment.
>
> *(Nicolson and Welsh, 1992[4])*

Sexual harassment, verbal, physical and visual, poisons the atmosphere of any organization. Sexist calendars, jokes, personal remarks about women's bodies, groping and rape all occur in organizations and have been well documented (Brant and Too, 1994; Charney and Russell, 1994).

All organizations throughout their hierarchies, containing men from all social class groups, are hosts to acts of sexual harassment, and despite its long-standing identification as being 'against the rules', complaints procedures are invariably problematic (see, for example, MacKinnon, 1979; see also Chapter 4 and this chapter above).

The first legislation against sexual harassment at work appeared in the United States in the second half of the 1970s (European Parliament, Working Paper, 1994) and many of the early cases have been outlined by MacKinnon (1979). The European Community is taking legislation about sexual harassment seriously and aims to ensure that all member countries have adequate legislation and complaints procedures (European Parliament, Working Paper, 1994).

There is, however, no doubt that the behaviour and motivation of the perpetrators and the experiences of the victims are complex, traumatic and long-lasting, not least because of the ramifications of making a complaint, resulting in continued harassment or the compulsion to change jobs if the victim does not complain but finds the situation intolerable.

Even those women who have the motivation and stamina to bring a complaint to court have to endure similar ordeals to victims of rape, although in sexual harassment cases their identities, details of their sexual histories and current lifestyle are made public, which is humiliating. This is compounded if the victim loses her case as with Anita Hill versus Judge Clarence Thomas. However, despite her experience of losing, having her reputation challenged and threat of public humiliation, Anita Hill inspired and provided comfort to a great many women both in the USA and the rest of the world (Morris, 1994).

Sexual harassment is a serious offence. It is akin to threat and intimidation as the hundreds of case studies recorded now testify (see Brant and Too, 1994; MacKinnon, 1979; Morris, 1994; Wise and Stanley, 1987).

Not all feminist writers agree, however. Roiphe (1993) states that:

> Our female professors and high-ranking executives, our congress-women and editors, are every bit as strong as their male counterparts. They have earned their position of authority. To declare that their authority is vulnerable to a dirty joke from someone of inferior status just because that person happens to be a man is to undermine their position. Female authority is not (and should not be seen as) so fragile that it shatters at the first sign of male sexuality. Any rules saying otherwise strip women, in the public eye, of their hard-earned authority.
>
> *(Roiphe, 1993: 90)*

But as I set out in this book, life is more complex. The constant exposure to sexism is an overriding reason why more women are not in authority, and those that do reach senior positions often sacrifice their feminine identity and relations with other women to do so. Men ensure that junior men are protected from the threat of a challenge from women and feminism in general. But if we take Roiphe seriously, then women who achieve seniority will continue to take the role of Queen Bee with no regard for the health and welfare of those who follow or her female peers.

Shirley Williams, a member of the British House of Lords, ex-MP and someone who had been perceived publicly to be a champion of fairness and a role model for women came out with surprising attitudes to sexual harassment underlining some of these complexities in 2014. Lord Rennard, of the Liberal Democratic Party (the same party as Williams), had been accused by several women party workers of inappropriate behaviours including touching them sexually. The women had over several months refused to back down from their claims against Rennard, reporting how humiliating and stressful their experiences had been. Indeed, they were risking their own reputations by their strong endeavours. Shirley Williams, though, far from supporting these women, said that the whole thing had been blown up and that his behaviour was part of Rennard's private life.[5] Williams also made it clear in this article that women should expect to have a difficult time in public life and tolerate men taking advantage of them!

## Sexual abuse, gender at work and the caring professions

If sexual harassment is treated as a 'normal' part of working life, and greater concern is offered to the accused whose career might suffer than to the victim, there is little chance that sexual abuse at work will ever be taken seriously.

The female body remains a generalized object of sexual pleasure for men (Snitow et al., 1984; Ussher, 1989), and the persistent portrayal of erotic images has its influence on, and is influenced by, symbolic meanings that are culturally pervasive (Martin, 1990).

It is sometimes difficult to distinguish between sexual abuse and sexual harassment. Both are about exploitation of (usually) women by (usually) men in a context where the man has power over the woman's work or life. Examples of sexual harassment at work have ranged from pictures of naked women on office walls to multiple rape (see Anderson et al., 1993). So is there a difference?

One example was provided by a group of women doctors at a seminar I ran for Women in Medicine on sexual harassment. One woman told me that when she had been a junior doctor attached to a gynaecological team, one male gynaecologist was known to fondle and abuse the bodies of women undergoing surgery. He would remark on their shape, the tautness or otherwise of their vaginas, and play with their breasts. He would also leave them uncovered when this was not necessary. On one occasion, he used the patient's vagina gratuitously as a 'container' for a surgical instrument. He made a joke and the doctor telling me the story was so angry that she had told him his behaviour was totally unacceptable. He ignored her comments, but 10 minutes later made a general remark to the team that most of them needed a consultant's reference for their next job if they seriously wanted a career. I was the only person at the seminar who was shocked by this story. The other women doctors present were able to confirm that they had witnessed similar behaviours by male surgeons in relation to anaesthetized female bodies on several occasions.

But what motivated this man and other abusers like him? The intent on the part of the perpetrator seems to be to gain and maintain sexual and political power over (and possibly have sex with) the victim. Neither abuse nor harassment can be about mutual affection, although in cases of both, some perpetrators have declared their love (see Morris, 1994).

One distinction is that harassment happens to women who are in a context where the men concerned may be in senior roles, but they only have power over the working life of that woman. Abuse occurs to girls/women when the perpetrator has a major influence over the victim's life and physical/emotional well-being (Raitt, 1994). Thus a parent or parent-figure, such as a school-teacher, is a potential sexual abuser.

The health professional, psychotherapist or social worker who exploits their access to and power over adult women's bodies and minds also may perpetrate abuse.

Sue Llewellyn (1992), in her review of the literature on the sexual abuse of clients by therapists, found that the majority of abuse was from men to women with around 10 per cent of male therapists admitting to having sex with patients, and up to 80 per cent of these repeating their behaviour. Intimacies between physicians and patients occur regularly despite professional ruling against such behaviours and the risk of being debarred from practice (Gartrell et al., 1986; Kardener, 1974).

Health and social work professions are among those with high numbers of women aspiring to and achieving senior positions. The fact of sexual abuse raises dilemmas for professional women in these perverse patriarchal organizations.

## Whistle blowing

Rosemary, a clinical psychologist, had been friendly with Jeremy, her colleague for several years. In fact he had been instrumental in helping her get appointed to the clinic, and supported and encouraged her through two promotions. She was also friendly with his wife.

She inadvertently discovered him one evening in an embarrassing and clearly sexual embrace with a female client, and faced the dilemma of how to handle her discovery. He was clearly abusing his client, by taking advantage of his privileged knowledge of her vulnerabilities, the power of his role in relation to her, and also presumably deceiving colleagues and his wife. Rosemary, as a health professional, was deeply concerned for the welfare of the patients in the care of psychologists in general, and her clinic in particular, as well as being shocked by the inappropriate and unprofessional conduct of her friend. After much discussion and soul searching she told Jeremy that she had no option other than to report his behaviour, and he became very angry with her, trying to tell her that the relationship with the patient was really one between equals and thus none of Rosemary's business. She, however, did tell their boss, who reprimanded Jeremy, who promised that he would not behave that way again. In the meantime, though, Rosemary received an angry telephone call from her friend, Jeremy's wife (whom she had not wanted to hear about these events). Jeremy's wife accused Rosemary of being a busybody and of jealousy. When she repeated her story at a discussion about sexual abuse in therapy, she was wondering whether she had been right to report Jeremy, but no one at the conference left her in any doubt she had been right. Rosemary, however, still believes that she suffered more from the censure of being labelled as 'disloyal' to a colleague than Jeremy did from being reprimanded for abuse.

## The toxic context

The problems faced by professional women (such as hospital doctors, lawyers, academics) in dealing with sexual harassment, abuse and discrimination, include the following.

First, the behaviours that constitute sexual harassment may be masked or appear less serious than those experienced by women in lower-status occupations. Professional organizations (e.g. hospitals, universities, legal practices, professional associations, schools) tend to have norms of behaviour that prohibit overt and violent actions, as has been reported in relation to the police, fire service and so on.

On the whole, for professional women, sexual harassment is likely to be verbal and low key. Thus the victim's plight is likely to be invisible, and the overall ethos of 'not rocking the boat' will be applied against anyone who complains about harassing behaviour that on the surface is not impinging on the environment. Thus as with Anita Hill, there was a public demonstration of ambivalence towards the female victim (Morris, 1994). Frances Conley, a neurosurgeon at Stanford University medical school, who resigned in protest against a persistent sexual harasser being appointed to head her department, is quoted as saying:

> What women put up with in the medical field is more subtle. But it can be just as devastating because it happens far more frequently, it's pervasive, and it's a cultural thing. It's like a ton of feathers. We all get hit daily by a feather of verbal abuse dropping on us.
>
> *(Conley in Morris, 1994: 111)*

Second, and clearly related, is that women correctly believe their careers will suffer if they complain, and thus despite being privileged over the part-time semi-skilled workers in material ways, they have potentially more to lose and so keep quiet or at least take anonymous action. An account in the *British Medical Journal* in October 1992 (Anonymous, 1992) where a female doctor recalled a meeting with an older colleague who grabbed her bottom, another one who would brush against junior women, enter colleagues' rooms at night and offer to swap duties for sex. Her complaints that some lecturers' slides or comments were sexist and gratuitous were dismissed which, to her, made it clear that the medical establishment was saturated with sexism and sexual harassment, but that there was little support to enable anyone to complain overtly.

Clarence Thomas's staff declared Anita Hill to be a 'very hard, arrogant, opinionated' woman who 'looked after herself' (see Morris, 1994: 22).

Third, women in the professions, by virtue of their numbers and the organizational/professional ethos, are unlikely to get support from a peer group.

It is therefore important to acknowledge both that personal assertiveness and organizational mechanisms for dealing with sexual harassment are not adequate for combating the problem; indeed, they may result in a culture that dismisses its existence, 'because if it happened we would know about it wouldn't we?'

## Conclusions

Sexuality is part of everyday life and professional organizations are far from being 'safe havens'. Indeed, it may be argued that work organizations are among the most sexually explicit social contexts (Hearn and Parkin, 1987). It is, however, difficult to disentangle sexuality from gender and power relations, and although there is no attempt to assume universal heterosexuality by that observation, there is little doubt that heterosexual men set the sexual and power agendas in professional life.

## Notes

1  http://newstatesman.com/2014/01/casual-bullying-women-shows-westminster-is-dangerously-out-of-step.
2  http://telegraph.co.uk/news/politics/10763038/Predatory-male-sex-assaults-culture-thrives-in-Parliament.html.
3  http://thedailybeast.com/articles/2012/04/09/ashley-judd-slaps-media-in-the-face-for-speculation-over-her-puffy-appearance.html.
4  The operational definition used in our survey is adapted from the University of Sheffield guidelines.
5  http://theguardian.com/politics/2013/may/09/lady-shirley-williams-lord-rennard.

# 6

# GENDER, POWER AND LEADERSHIP

## Introduction

In this chapter I explore:

- the intrapsychic contexts of gender and power for women and men at the top of their professions and organizations, particularly related to the use of relationships and emotion;
- the discursive construction of leadership and the rhetoric of gender within relevant discourses;
- systemic thinking and how it contributes to making sense of gender, organization and leadership in twenty-first-century organizations.

Leadership has become a buzz-word and a panacea for twenty-first-century organizational success or failure, so that the 'lack of leadership' seems to have become the preferred means of accounting for failure of universities, banks, hospitals, the BBC, schools, political parties and any other organization (Haslam et al., 2011; Thoms, 2008; Tourish and Vatcha, 2005). Most evidence suggests that men are more likely to be appointed to leadership positions than are women (Collinson, 2005; Eagly and Carli, 2003; Ernst, 2003;

Fletcher, 2004; Ford, 2006; Potts, 2005; Schnurr, 2008) and consequently it is mostly those men who have become members of the newsworthy list of 'failed' leaders. So what is leadership and how is it gendered?

Research on leadership per se has been abundant for several decades but despite so many attempts to identify the characteristics necessary for effective leadership (Western, 2013), robust evidence remains scarce (Alban-Metcalfe and Alimo-Metcalfe, 2009; Fairhurst and Grant, 2010; Ford, 2010; Gray et al., 2010; Haslam et al., 2011; Nicolson et al., 2011; Western, 2013). This could well be because leadership is context specific and a *process* rather than a set of characteristics found in one person. However, it is also possible that the selection of leaders is frequently conducted by those (mostly men) who are in leadership positions themselves seeking out clones (whether consciously or unconsciously) (Fairhurst, 2009; Fairhurst and Grant, 2010).

Alimo-Metcalfe et al. (2007), in their comprehensive review of the literature on leadership, showed that formal studies of leadership date back (at least) to the beginning of the twentieth century. They propose that, despite changes in the way leadership has been studied and the underlying epistemological stance taken by the researchers, 'in all cases, the emphasis has been on identifying those factors that make certain individuals particularly effective in influencing the behaviour of other individuals or groups and in making things happen that would not otherwise occur or preventing undesired outcomes' (p. 2). As 'many have pointed out, that in spite of the plethora of studies, we still seem to know little about the defining characteristics of effective leadership' (Higgs, 2002: 3).

Scholarly and thoughtful intervention such as this has not appeared to quell the appetite for pursuing an ideal of leadership, perhaps impelled by the changing demands across public-sector institutions such as the NHS and the BBC and the private sector, particularly banking and industry. The tantalizing questions remain about what those factors that produce successful and inspired leadership might actually be and the significance of the context to understanding how certain characteristics might be more or less relevant or effective in particular organizations (Fairhurst, 2009; Liden and Antonakis, 2009; Uhl-Bien, 2006).

One important set of findings suggests that leadership does have an effect on organizational performance – for good and for ill (Currie et al., 2009; Schilling, 2009). A good leader may not necessarily be doing 'good' for the organization he or she is leading but their leadership qualities may be outstanding. Stalin and Hitler, charismatic and murderous dictators, changed the face of Europe and beyond through their evil intentions and actions. Paul Flowers' poor leadership and personal flaws led to huge losses for the

Co-op Bank in the UK even though his intentions were not ruthless. Gordon Brown's apparent bullying style of leadership led to the loss of the 2010 general election for the British Labour Party despite his somewhat inflexible manner. But in addition, or conversely, the context, culture, climate and/or structure of an organization each has an impact on the performance of the people who lead in it (Carroll et al., 2008; Goodwin, 2000; Michie and West, 2004).

Focusing on the relationship(s) between 'leadership' and context has revitalized contemporary research in this area, particularly through the development of qualitative research, discursive and social constructionist epistemologies (Grint, 2005; Uhl-Bien, 2006) although it is unclear at this stage how far a connection might be developed between this research and its applications (Fambrough and Hart, 2008).

But what of gender? There are undeniably visible differences between women and men's expectations, attitudes and behaviour in relation to leading in work organizations, and these distinctions solidify as individuals rise up the organizational hierarchy. Men, it is proposed, either push for attaining career success and seniority, or they come to terms with having underachieved or deviated from social expectations. Women's experience is more complex. Socialization into femininity, as we have seen, is not as clear-cut as socialization into masculinity so that women do not have expectations of certain success but some are prepared to have a go (Niederle and Vesterlund, 2007)! There have been some important changes to the demographics of leadership over the past decade (Nicolson, 2003; Nicolson et al., 2011) and also to the expectations that leaders will be more 'relational', building networks and enhancing communication (Genovese and Steckenrider, 2013; Iles and Preece, 2006; Morrell and Hartley, 2006). There has also been an increased emphasis on the value of emotional intelligence in effective leadership of complex organizations (Dasborough, 2006; Fambrough and Hart, 2008; Lopes et al., 2006; Riggio and Reichard, 2008; Sy et al., 2006). It might therefore be argued that leadership that seeks to build relationships and is emotionally intelligent is just as likely to be accomplished by a talented woman as a man.

## Where have all the women gone?

How do women and men negotiate boundaries between self, other, organization, family and culture in order to sustain themselves in an effective leadership role? Women in a patriarchal context need to be able to distinguish between their sense of subjectivity/self, cultural and interpersonal expectations and the meaning given to their organizational contribution by others *because they are women*. It is difficult to have control over the latter but it is vital to recognize through the process of reflexivity that those meanings exist, and also that boundaries are dynamic and shift from occasion to occasion.

The demographics may have changed, providing women with expectations of success in organizations and organizations having expectations of women as potential leaders. However, as we have seen, there are still relatively few high-profile women at the top of industry, finance and public-sector organizations. Women who find the going too tough may resign from the organization, or at least drop out of the fast track, doing so with fewer regrets than might men (see Marshall, 1994) or perhaps indicate that they have other interests and opportunities that attract them. In 2013, for example, Victoria Barnsley left her role as CEO of the publisher Harper-Collins after 13 years, making the comment that she had not been very good at 'managing up'.[1] The British Army's most senior woman, Brigadier Nicky Moffat, resigned in 2012, apparently angered and feeling despondent about the cuts made to the service.[2] Were these women really experiencing problems with their own capabilities or were they experiencing unconscious stresses as a result of exclusion from decisions that they themselves could take some responsibility for? To be able to have one's contribution valued provides a sense of personal worth and a degree of power in an organization where you have responsibilities. The accounts by these women sound as if, despite their obvious talents and career success, they have been rendered powerless.

There have been several other high-profile women who have chosen to leave top jobs for something less stressful or to set up their own business. In May 2014 the website Workforce[3] reported that women leave top jobs for different reasons to men. Men will on the whole enter another role or training for change while women cite domestic responsibilities in 44 per cent of cases. It is perhaps debatable whether women who have achieved top jobs then leave for family reasons or whether they become frustrated and stressed through lack of power. Perhaps the going is tougher for women isolated at the top of their organization than it might be for men supported by colleagues and mentors who have similar personal characteristics and histories of working together.

There is increasing evidence that women who do succeed in management or the professions are more likely to *increase* the problems and stress in their lives than if they opt out (Davidson and Cooper, 1983), and the more senior a woman becomes the more likely she is to be stressed at work than a man of equivalent seniority (Cushway, 1992; Fairhurst, 2005, 2009). There are good social reasons why women find the high-flying life difficult, particularly if they are mothers (Cooper and Lewis, 1993; Nicolson, 2003).

However, there are additional difficulties for senior women particularly in relation to the management of *psychological boundaries* between self, social context and in particular their sense of gendered subjectivity. To be doing 'male' things in patriarchal organizations and wanting to achieve in this arena does not preclude the desire to be feminine, enjoy being a woman and being seen as a woman with a sexual, intellectual and emotional presence that is feminine.

It is important to reiterate that while not subscribing to an essentialist perspective on gender differences and gendered behaviours, it is clear that women and men give different meanings to their bodies and experience differential socialization in such a way that it becomes difficult to disentangle what women do because they are born female, and what they do because of complicated cultural processes.

## The discursive construction of gender-deference

> The first psychological demand that flows from a woman's social role is that she must defer to others, follow their lead, articulate her needs only in relation to theirs. In essence, she is not to be the main actor in her own life. As a result of this social requirement, women come to believe they are not important in themselves for themselves. Women come to feel they are unworthy, undeserving and unentitled. Women are frequently self-deprecating and hesitant about their own initiatives. They feel reluctant to speak for themselves, to voice their own thoughts and ideas, to act on their own behalf. Being pushed to defer to others means that they come to undervalue and feel insecure about themselves, their wants and their opinions. A recognition of a woman's own needs can therefore be complicated and a process occurs in which women come to hide their desires from themselves.
>
> *(Eichenbaum and Orbach, 1982: 29)*

The women described above, and in preceding chapters, would not at first glance seem to fit into the social-role requirements outlined above. However, closer inspection, and indeed introspection, indicates that much of what Eichenbaum and Orbach say still resounds with twenty-first-century reality. These writers are providing a psychological baseline onto which women's career socialization, reflexivity and biography have become inscribed despite the rhetoric of gender equality.

There is no persuasive evidence of essential, immutable female characteristics that make deference a prerequisite for women's biographical development. However, as Bell and Newby noted so many years ago now, sexual stratification is about 'the relationships between the sexes rather than the attributes of one sex or the other' (1976: 152). While Bell and Newby focused their attention on husbands and wives, a similar perspective is crucial for understanding the relationships between the sexes in organizations, where people frequently spend years co-existing, competing, supporting and forming relationships with others who just happen to work together rather than choosing to share their lives. Bell and Newby identify the 'relational and normative means by which men (particularly husbands) maintain their traditional authority over women (wives), and . . . the necessary strategies they employ in attempting to ensure the stability of their power' (1976: 152). They argued that many wives believe their husbands have and ought to have more power than they do, and legitimation of this in traditional values leads to the hierarchical nature of the relationship between husband and wife as seeming natural and immutable. This position reverberates with studies of women and men in management and the professions, particularly some of the boss/secretary, student/lecturer relationships described above.

The continued existence of a tradition whereby men hold professional power serves to legitimate it, and for many women this implies and becomes manifest in their deference to a senior manager/professional who is also a man. Individual women who achieve power in their own right have challenged this, but their challenge does not deprive men of apparent legitimate authority in the eyes of both the men and other women. Many women, even senior and aspiring women, still exhibit non-assured, deferential qualities. Indeed, it is alarming to observe how far professional women's accounts of their subjectivity in organizational life concurs with this image. Tanton, discussing a workshop series on developing women's presence in senior management, said:

> Some other reasons were given as to why we need to develop women's presence. These referred to particular characteristics which women needed or lacked, for example, assertiveness, aggression, self-esteem, confidence, and so on. For example they said 'women are less aggressive', 'women lack self-esteem'. The focus of the group was on woman as 'other' to the characteristics of the male norm. This could

be interpreted as pragmatic given that they worked in what they described as 'male-dominated' organizational cultures.

Alternatively it could be seen as a measure of the depth of the entrenched values within society that even this group of women concentrating their attention on the issue of women's development approached it from the perspective of the 'centred male'.

*(1994: 9)*

So even senior and aspiring women recognize, in certain contexts at least, that they are outside the central arena for organizational action, either by virtue of deliberate exclusion or because they 'lack' the necessary qualities. This reinforces the potential at least for women's deference. But why is this still the case even for women who appear to overcome the socialization process of the patriarchal organizational culture and achieve success?

Women display deference because of ongoing patterns of subordination of women/girls to men/boys, which is part of a relationship pattern based on power dynamics in the family, socialization and cultural belief systems that are inescapable without taking on the mantle of outcast (Nicolson, 2003). It is not difficult to see or reflect upon the way that being seen and treated as subordinate and gaining recognition through deference may set up a template for social relations, both in the family and in professional organizations. If women feel insecure about their talents and abilities because of their socialization and gender–power relations inherent in the dominant culture, they will develop a range of coping/survival strategies to deal with this insecurity (see Cassell and Walsh, 1991; Marshall, 1984). This involves them attempting to negotiate their subjectivity and interpersonal relationships as though they were *other* than women. However, despite the claims of many women interviewed in studies of managers and businesswomen, this position has social and consequently psychological difficulties. This is in part because

The second requirement of woman's social role is that she must always be connected to others and shape her life according to a man. A woman's status will derive from that of her mate. Indeed her very sense of self and well-being may rely on their connection.

*(Eichenbaum and Orbach, 1982: 29)*

A woman not connected with a man, presenting herself as independent, is treated with suspicion whether that independence be at home or at work. In Chapter 5, there was evidence that some women are connected to men who are their seniors in sexualized ways, whether emotionally, through sexual harassment, exploitation or even when they believe themselves to be exploiting their heterosexuality in an organizational context. The sexualized nature of the work relationship carries over from this heterosexual connectedness where women identify with their immediate bosses or senior men. However, the connectedness is often the means of acting out a deferential relationship because the man is the superordinate one (Nicolson, 2012).

## Self, subjectivity and others

Eichenbaum and Orbach (1982) suggested that deference and connectedness to others naturally leads on *to* 'another psychological concomitant of women's social role: that of having emotional antennae. A woman must learn to anticipate others' needs' (1982: 29). Subjectivity for women appears to contain far greater complexity than subjectivity for men, and for women in senior management and in the professions this complexity is exaggerated by the apparent stepping outside the boundaries of feminine behaviour.

Socially and psychically men are separated from their mothers, and identify not specifically with individual fathers but with all men (Chodorow, 1978; Freud, 1922). Masculine identity is treated more seriously, and greater efforts are made by agents of socialization to ensure that boys do not step outside the boundaries of 'natural' masculine behaviour (Archer, 1989). On the other hand, women remain connected to their mothers and fathers in different ways, and feel guilt and anxiety about asserting their own needs. This process relates to women's professional roles too.

Much has been written about the differences in masculine and feminine leadership style. Frequent assertions are made about the benefits women as managers provide for their colleagues and junior staff especially because of their ability to focus on and deal with emotional issues (Collinson, 2005; Fletcher, 2004; Ford, 2006; Potts, 2005; Schnurr, 2008). This still does not mean that women are *valued* for their feminine qualities, nor is there much effort to understand the pressures of both having emotional antennae and coping with patriarchal organizations (Tanton, 1994).

## Boundaries and connectedness

A secure sense of boundary between 'self' and 'other' in effect means that an individual is able to enter relationships, connect appropriately with the other person/people, engage with the organization and remain subjectively secure, while having contributed to and benefited from the social/emotional exchange. Almost everyone experiences a degree of ego vulnerability at certain times, although some do so far more than others. Those people who feel empty unless they are in love (such as John, discussed in Chapter 4, who project all their unacceptable feelings outwards) are examples of those who have fragile egos and a fluid sense of boundaries between themselves and others, as well as the good and bad feelings in themselves. Poor boundary definition means that the individual is in constant danger of becoming overwhelmed by the feelings and actions of both their own and others. For many, particularly women, reflexive about their organizational role, there is evidence of struggles to identify the boundaries between home and work, self and organization, self and gender role, being a senior corporate executive and a feminist and so on. Boundary issues are important for everyone, and the process of reflexivity along with notions of biography and different levels of consciousness all point to the centrality of *conscious self-awareness* in the process of psychological survival.

Object relations theory in psychoanalysis, which refers to the work of Melanie Klein, Fairbairn, Guntrip and Winnicott, was particularly useful in identifying the importance of psychological/emotional boundaries in ego development. Simply stated, the infant, initially connected with her/his mother, fails to perceive separation. This develops gradually with the strength and maturity of the ego. The adult understands themselves to be separate as an individual, but this does not always translate itself into an emotional awareness. The social nature of subjectivity additionally suggests that the 'person' is also connected socially and culturally to others (Henriques et al., 1984/1998). However, there seems to be an important gender difference in the management of boundaries at work. There is an interesting tension between boundary management and 'barrier' management – with senior men and some women more skilled at the latter than discursively aware of the former.

In discussions with various male friends and colleagues in senior management positions, two characteristics emerged for what they believed made a good leader. First, the deliberate effort (usually successful) to ignore the needs of individuals in order to achieve management goals was cited and, second, they expressed fascination with 'feminine' insights that were often asked for and best employed to provide 'commentary' on their constructions of the organization.

I conjecture that the former represents an ability to construct barriers between self and others (although reasonably effective managers are able to see over them!), which helped them to survive the interpersonal rigours of organizational life; and the latter, in a more complex way, ensures that women enable men to manage their own boundaries. This interaction is frequently practised by men to uphold their own ego strength when the barriers waver, and by women to gain access to power and information through attachment and connectedness.

There are many examples of this. A manager in a university department, excellent at identifying talent and as well able to support women he believed had the appropriate qualities for promotion, was surprised when his secretary resigned accusing him of insensitivity. Other junior academic staff, particularly women on short-term research contracts, also saw him as 'a brute'. He, however, had enough insight into his own management style to tell me that if he worried about such things then he would go under himself, so that he had become immune although he failed to see why the woman in question did not see the world as he did. His priority was to make the unit effective, while keeping staff motivated. He was selective about choosing whom to mentor, and they tended to be those who shared similar points of view with him. However, this did not prevent his curiosity about interpersonal life in the department, although this was merely 'interesting' rather than essential to his management role. When the junior staff left, he saw them as exploiting a career opportunity elsewhere, and never considered the possibility that he might have handled them better.

Another man, who had recently been appointed in a senior position in an insurance company with the specific purpose of increasing 'efficiency', told me with some pride that he was completely unable to recognize emotional responses in his staff and believed that was his strength. He did, however, complain to me that various people made a habit of 'winging'. For example, he had engineered a staff redeployment exercise involving a move to another site that was a long way from where many of the junior administrative and secretarial staff had worked before, and thus the other side of town from where they lived. He claimed to be inundated with trivial complaints about car-parking facilities and the late arrival of the internal mail. He told me in some detail how he had personally been to see those responsible for the mail circulation and found very little difference between the timing of deliveries in the previous or new building. 'Why do I have to listen to this garbage?' he asked. I suggested it might have more to do with how they *felt* they had been, and were continued to be, treated than the timing of the mail and the car parking. He was intrigued, claiming that such ideas had never occurred to him, and we had a discussion about this, which he appeared to find interesting. However, it did not change his behaviour, nor his evaluation of the issues involved. He clung to his original views that made him feel safe.

On reflection, I think that we had both been engaging in a complex interaction of power, deference and connectedness that at the time was to mutual benefit, but provided little in the way of long-term change in either of our opinions or, if we had been working in the same institution, power relations. I was flattered that such a senior and influential person appeared to value my opinion, which also gave me a sense of connectedness to him and to power. He found my insights interesting and my attention emotionally supportive. But while I thought that I was having an influence on the decisions he might make, or how he might handle some of his staff, he was simply intrigued. He was achieving confirmation of his power – not taking my information/advice at face value.

This behaviour is also typical of managers and professionals working in the same organization. The senior man survives through defending himself from emotional onslaughts by denying their significance in the organizational goals. When there are occasions that some of these feelings might be overwhelming, he seeks to talk to a woman he trusts. This enables the woman to employ connectedness and emotional/nurturing skills and gain access and insights into senior management, possibly not available to her in the formal hierarchical structure. The man, however, continues to develop high-status strategic ideas with his male friends and colleagues, and sees the emotional contact as secondary to the real purpose of management.

This means that the woman gains some of her ambitions – access to information and aspects of power – but the relationship rarely contributes to her career in terms of mentoring or role modelling because the man is taking 'time out' from the real concerns, while she believes she is sharing them.

It is not only psychoanalysis that helps understand or identify these processes. Conversation analysis and the interpretation of gestures provides clues on interaction and meaning. Deborah Tannen, in her work on gender and language, drew attention to disparities in meanings that women and men assume are shared. For instance a man is likely to engage in the world 'as an individual in a hierarchical social order in which he was either one-up or one-down. In this world conversations are negotiations in which people try to achieve and maintain the upper hand if they can, and protect themselves from others' attempts to put them down and push them around' (Tannen, 1993/2007: 24–25). She argues that men's lives are about maintaining independence and avoiding failure. Thus, they are able to exploit necessary resources, including their female friends and colleagues, and believe others to be doing the same.

A woman, on the other hand, Tannen argues, approaches the world 'as an individual in a network of connections. In this world conversations are negotiations for closeness in which people try to seek and give confirmation and support, and to reach consensus' (Tannen, 1993/2007: 25). This does not mean that women do not have other goals, such as protecting themselves, but while men protect themselves from challenge, women protect themselves from others' attempts to exclude them and avoid isolation.

There are no essential biological gender differences involved here – this is part of differential socialization and expectations. There are rewards for both the men and women involved in these exchanges based on friendship, mutual respect and probably sexuality in many cases.

If psychoanalysts, from Freud, Chodorow and Horney to Orbach and Eichenbaum, are correct, then women experience a greater fluidity in their sense of subjectivity and their boundaries with other people than do men. To be emotionally *aware* and *need* connection with others, for many women, is part of being human. They see the world in terms of social relationships, and it is only because of the widespread acceptance that male dominated, patriarchal knowledge has the 'real' value that some women deny such understandings. So phenomena such as 'instinct' and 'female intuition' are ridiculed or downplayed, seen as unsound, unscientific knowledge, when in fact there is much anecdotal evidence to suggest that intuition pays off in the management of people and understanding organizational life, as frequently as any more 'objective' understanding of human interactions.

## Emotion

Maintaining ego strength is not simply a routine and intellectual project. To make sense of your self in a paradoxical context (that is one you wish to belong to, but one in which you are also marginal) is fraught with emotional pitfalls. Loneliness and isolation are emotionally laden experiences, and the desire for and achievement of independence and autonomy cannot compensate for lack of intimacy, support and connectedness. It is the latter that enable self-reflection and maintenance.

It is interesting that although a couple of decades have passed since academic attention has been paid to the role of emotion in organizations (Fineman, 1993) it is still difficult to have the importance of emotionally intelligent leadership widely acknowledged. It is no surprise to learn that women are seen as emotional and men as rational, and that rationality is valued over emotionality (Bolden and Gosling, 2006; Fambrough and Hart, 2008; Lewis, 2008; Riggio and Reichard, 2008). As a consequence, emotion is kept out of sight in the organizational world, and although some members are expected to exhibit emotion, they are the marginal, dispensable or inadequate staff. 'Emotion is to be expected in the less powerful such as interviewees and appraisees but the competent manager must herself remain unemotional' (Swan, 1994: 90).

It is clear that the category 'emotion' is a flexible one, however, and under certain circumstances emotion is seen as acceptable and even laudable. This is when it is associated with men, especially senior men. Thus the professor who choked back the tears on his retirement celebration was seen as 'human', and his distress and sadness at leaving his colleagues made up for past power struggles and previous contentions.

There are sometimes different emotions expressed by women and men as a response to the same event. On receiving the news that they had been passed over for promotion, Ian and Angela, two well-considered academics, met to express their outrage. Ian was furious and told his friend and colleague how he was undervalued, that he knew himself to be far more competent than colleagues who had already been promoted, and that he would immediately look for another post, at which time he would make his current university bid against their competitor to keep him. He was not prepared to experience such a rejection again. Angela, equally furious, said how she was also really upset, and felt that this rejection also made her feel undervalued. She kept thinking of how much more she needed to publish before next year's round of promotions, and wondered whether she was really up to that task. If her own university would not promote her, would she stand a chance of being appointed elsewhere? When they had finished their discussion she became even more gloomy, and downhearted, while Ian maintained his anger.

In this example, not only does the woman temper her anger with personal hurt and upset, but the failure to promote her is taken as an evaluation of her self-worth rather than an exercise in distributing limited rewards in a highly competitive situation. The hurt of rejection seeps through her ego boundary and influences her self-evaluation. This in turn leads her to be depressed and despondent. Ian, on the other hand, did not appear emotionally influenced by the board's decision. He also expressed genuine amazement that Angela, whom he admired, had made the interpretation that she did.

Men also do express emotion in organizations about professional matters, but in hidden ways. In engaging in sexual relationships, for example, men, particularly senior men, have the opportunity to expose and consider their vulnerabilities in a safe context (or at least one that is safe for the duration of the affair). Younger men are also able to turn to older women sometimes in ways that they could not turn to men, and even if the woman is their senior they are able to engage in an invisible emotional relationship. A senior male colleague of mine with whom I was working on a project once told me that meeting with me was like taking confession with a Catholic priest. He found himself telling me things about his feelings, and his understanding of his relationships with others in the university, almost against his will. He sometimes became angry and upset, and other times excited or amused, with the things he was relating. My motivation in this relationship was that I liked him, and would ask about the kinds of things that I would discuss with my women friends. It seems that these were clearly not on the agenda in the conversations he had with other people – or at least with male colleagues. The need for invisibility of his emotions outside the 'confessional' made him a difficult person to work with from my perspective. He would sometimes be impossible to contact, my messages with important queries about our work were only half answered, and every so often his secretary would phone to arrange an appointment that would have been unnecessary if he had responded to my written messages. He preferred to come to my office rather than meet in his own, and the pattern of our meetings would be some business and much emotional discussion. I clearly colluded with this pattern, but partly because, as in previous examples, my role gave me some influence, information and access to power. It was the secrecy of my role that perplexed me. There was no question of a sexual advance. It began to make sense once I began the thinking and the reading for this book. The work of Deborah Kolb and colleagues over many years has explored women's specific negotiation skills related to leadership and power in organizational relationships. Kolb and colleagues have identified ways in which gender relations and informal beliefs about the other sex have framed key power-related practices, some resembling my own experiences revealed above (Ely et al., 2011; Kolb, 2009).

## Hidden conflict and women's work

Sometimes women's informal role in the emotional life of an organization is called upon more directly. Deborah Kolb (1992) wrote:

> I often find myself drawn into conflicts at work. Colleagues come in, close the door, and then confide in me about some problem they have with a mutual associate or boss. I listen and, probably more often than is wise, agree to take the matter up with the other person(s). Sometimes I succeed in altering the situation and at other times I report back what I have learned. I often wonder why I get involved. Is it because I am accessible – my door is usually open – or because I relish good gossip or because people know of my interest in mediation or

because they think I will make a difference? Whatever the reasons for my own involvement, I have recently become aware of how pervasive this kind of informal peacemaking is.

*(Kolb, 1992: 63)*

As a result she conducted research on informal peacekeeping in organizations, a task that still seems to fall on senior or middle-ranking women. Kolb argues that whereas formal conflict resolution is well researched and a well-respected, vital role in an organization (although it may be the case that outside consultants are brought in to achieve these ends), informal peacemaking, particularly the kind she talks about, is almost forced to be invisible, and as such appears to hold no merit and has no value in the organizational culture. It is, however, for those who take that role, or have it put upon them, consuming of time and energy although, as Kolb herself accepts, it does have certain rewards. However, in her research she concluded that the women respondents 'seem to contribute to a gendered construction of their activities as unimportant and, ironically, to the reproduction of a gender-based system of relationships in organisations' (Kolb, 1992: 68).

Her respondents acted as go-betweens between senior managers and other senior or up-and-coming staff, sometimes but not always between men. Their shared characteristics were, first, that they were located in positions in the organization that enabled them to learn about emerging conflicts and problems. Second, they provided a sympathetic ear. They both appeared and felt non-threatening, easy to talk to and sensitive to interpersonal conflicts. The men perhaps believed that gender was important and that women were seen, and were able to take this peacekeeping role. Also the women in Kolb's study were in specific positions that gave them access to power. One was married to a senior manager, another shared an interest with the company president although was herself not in the management hierarchy, and the third, an academic, was one of the very few senior, tenured women at the university and known for taking women's issues seriously. They believed in their abilities and enjoyed that role.

## Isolation

Intimacy is a key in a world of connection where individuals negotiate complex networks of friendship, minimise differences, try to reach consensus, and avoid the appearance of superiority, which would highlight differences. In a world of status, independence is key, because a primary means of establishing status is to tell others what to do, and taking orders is a marker of low status. Though all humans need both intimacy and independence, women tend to focus on the first and men on the second.

*(Tannen, 1993/2007: 26)*

Even though it is unlikely that *all* women and *all* men's behaviour and needs may be always demarcated in such a way, there is increasing support for the view that psychological and social factors conspire to achieve these gender differences. The specific difficulty that this imposes upon the lives of senior professional women is that while they are likely to have developed skills that resemble those of male executives, there is something missing. There is no one with whom they are able to share intimacy. There are few opportunities for making the number of pragmatic relationships in corporate life of the same quality as men who relate to other men. While they are likely to have achieved the ability for independence there is nothing to moderate it, and instead of independent, they are lonely and isolated.

Sheppard found that female managers perceived themselves to be isolated in a variety of contexts, and much of this related to the way that organizational culture reflects male styles and interactional needs: 'Women can't take for granted with whom they can associate, as they perceive political consequences that may devolve from even the most casual or informal contacts' (1992: 156). They have to be careful of relationships with men which may be misconstrued as sexual (see Chapter 5), or that might be misconstrued as supportive instead of career-oriented friendships (see above in this chapter).

The female leaders and managers in Sheppard's research sample also stressed that they felt a lack of support from male colleagues and that there was a need for a network of women managers. More important in their sense of isolation was that by definition the women managers needed to detach themselves from being identified with women in clerical and secretarial posts, and well as those in junior roles in the organization. Thus, as Tanton (1994) concluded, the life of a female senior professional or manager is exceptionally cruel because she is both deprived and has to deprive herself of most opportunities for intimacy and connectedness.

Tanton continued by suggesting that the experience of isolation and loneliness may lead on to further uncomfortable issues operationalized by role descriptions. She summarizes some from earlier studies:

- *boundary-marker* (Marshall, 1984: Scase and Goffee, 1989) – 'where she treads the men may not wish to go', 'she represents the outside';
- *extra-visible manager* (Kantor, 1977; O'Leary and Johnson, 1991) – 'if she puts a foot wrong she will be noticed';

- *traitor* (O'Leary, 1988) – 'other women criticize my differentness [through promotion] from them';
- *martyr* – 'I have to go on and on or I'll let my women colleagues down';
- *one of the boys* (Marshall, 1984; Tanton, 1992) – 'I don't have any problems – I feel just like a man';
- *conformist* – 'conformity and the abandonment of critical conscious-ness are the prices of successful performance in the bureaucratic world' (Ferguson, 1984: 29);
- *unrecognized explorer* – I have to go where no other women have been but there's little recognition when I get there.

*(Tanton, 1994: 19–20)*

It is having to take on the mantle of outsider, stranger or marginal person in one of these guises that contributes to the stress levels of women managers and professionals (Bass et al., 2003; Gardiner and Tiggerman, 1999; David-son and Cooper, 1983; Marshall, 1994; Mick, 2006; Sharp, Franzway et al., 2012; Stordeur et al., 2001).

To cope with isolation and loneliness, barriers have to be erected. Men have opportunities of support from women to overcome the potential for desolation and emotional bleakness that strong barriers and the mainte-nance of power precipitate. Women do not have the same opportunities because they cannot afford to obtain support from junior women. This is partly because they need to be seen as different from the junior women, and partly because junior women's expectations of them are likely to weigh them down as much as support them.

To cope with being a woman in a man's world, women have to manage boundaries between themselves and other women, and themselves and men, and between themselves and the organizational culture that is patriarchal. Are they selling out? Are they losing their femininity? Are they exploiting their sexuality? Are they doing their job well? These issues have to be managed constantly if the woman professional is to survive in a form that she herself rec-ognizes and respects. She has constantly to redefine her own boundaries. Pro-motion and success mean personal growth, and that is the benefit of rewarded talent and ambition. However, for women, out of place in patriarchal organiza-tions, it is imperative that they reassess their relationship with themselves.

## Conclusions

In order to achieve leadership and senior management roles in their profes-sions, and negotiate successfully the intrigues of corporate life, men and women have adopted differential strategies for psychological survival. Men find attaching the attributes of their early sex-role socialization to be more attuned to this enterprise than do women who have more psychological work to do to fit their experiences to corporate life. Femininity, intellectual ability and competitiveness do not fit easily with beliefs about career success. In addition, women are women. That is, they have learned to be feminine, to negotiate the world in a feminine way, and have no reason not to value that. However, the predominant norms of organizational culture conflict with, or at least severely undervalue, the norms and expectations associated with being a woman. Thus women have to re-define themselves, both to negotiate organizational culture while maintaining their sense of femininity and as far as possible being true to their own subjective beliefs.

Women are frequently in close relationships with their male colleagues, but there is both anecdotal and research evidence to suggest that there are frequent misunderstandings of the function of these relationships, because of gender–power expectations and beliefs.

## Notes

1 http://theguardian.com/books/2013/jul/05/women-publishing-gail-rebuck-victoria-barnsley.
2 http://telegraph.co.uk/news/uknews/defence/9366975/Armys-most-senior-female-officer-quits-amid-cuts-anger.html.
3 http://workforce.com/articles/why-women-leave-top-jobs-and-the-toll-of-extreme-jobs.

# CONCLUSIONS

## Introduction

Many things have changed, some for the better, since the first edition of this book was published in 1996. The changes during the intervening 19 years, however, have disguised the continuing problems in gender–power relations across patriarchal organizations throughout the Western world. One way of concealing women's true everyday experience of life at work has been through the rise of motivational books and autobiographies of highly visible and successful women such as Sheryl Sandberg, with the implication being that women's time has come. Forget feminism – we can have it all if only we aspire to do so.

There is little doubt too that, as a previous US Secretary of State, Hillary Clinton has indeed smashed *a* glass ceiling – but one that belongs to her alone. Her success does not represent universal change for ambitious women. We wait to see whether she will make President yet.

Many of the other high-profile women I identified in the previous pages have also broken through tough barriers to achieve success and frequently fame. But focusing on their visibility and success alone does not do justice to the many other able women who struggle to reach the higher ranks of their organization or simply to maintain a sense of self and sanity in their everyday working lives.

The rhetoric of equal opportunities, or the legislation eschewing sexual harassment and gender discrimination in the workplace, combined with the image of pushing one's way through the sticky door, also serve to obscure the emotional and practical stress of being a woman aspiring to leadership, seniority and power. The emphasis of this new edition of *Gender, Power and Organization* therefore has been upon managing gender and the way that power is practised and frequently abused in a gendered way. This may frequently be at an unconscious level but is nonetheless problematic for women, men and organizations that are stifling talent.

Although I have attempted to reveal ongoing abuse of power by mostly male bosses and organizational leaders, I have also demonstrated how women might be able to support each other and learn important lessons from their male counterparts and competitors.

Since the first edition was published things have also changed for me. I became a professor five years after its initial publication, although the road to this advancement was hardly straightforward as I outlined above. The promotion meant taking on the role of head of a research group at my university followed four years later by an appointment to head of the department of Health and Social Care at Royal Holloway, University of London. That was a fascinating, if demanding, experience from which I learned much and which also increased my motivation to revisit this volume.

Following my three-year term as head I trained as an organizational consultant at the Tavistock and Portman NHS Foundation Trust after which I retired from my full-time academic post to work as an organizational consultant, coach and mediator to senior staff in universities, the NHS and social services departments. Discrimination and power-plays remain widespread in all these places of learning and care in subtle but compelling ways.

More research evidence about gender and power came my way since the first edition of the book too. As principal investigator for a four-year study of leadership in the NHS, our team uncovered detailed examples of gender–power relations, not only within the organizations studied but also in relationships between the young female researchers and male interviewees on more than one occasion. Similarly, power and gender played a key role in exacerbating stressful dynamics in an action project with senior social work staff that I consulted to. These, and other studies I have engaged with, provided immensely rich data on gender and power in organizations and how gender enters all elements of life at work.

Women and men still live different lives and have different careers. It frequently takes many years of trial and error before an individual woman is able to recognize this and identify the implications for her own working experience. As men hold the authority in all professional organizations, the burden falls on women to make sense of the culture and its constraints and develop suitable coping strategies. The result is that women commonly find individualized means of survival (Cassell and Walsh, 1993; Gill et al., 2008; Lester, 2008; Marshall, 1984; McKenzie Davey, 1993), which gives rise to both the myth and the reality of the Queen Bee or Female Barracuda (Morris, 1994; Ussher, 1990b). A self-fulfilling prophecy may be involved: to survive, a woman has to both fail other women and isolate her emotional self from men (Cooper, 1997; Sealy and Vinnicombe, 2013).

Power, by nature, is a rare commodity, and beyond the grasp of most women and men; but power is almost exclusively in the hands of men. As Celia Morris (1994: 233) proposed: 'It should come as no surprise that women have looked on other women as rivals in the competition for scarce resources — whether for men, positions or esteem — or that they've scapegoated those who try to do things differently.'

This is still as true as ever. But, as argued above, there is little future in being an isolated woman, however outstanding that makes an individual feel. There are fewer opportunities for connection, support or mentorship. These represent the only hope for denting patriarchy.

## Women and power

How far has a feminist consciousness seeped into the population of young career women since the mid-1990s? Perhaps not a great deal if you consider this depressing insight from Naomi Wolf written then but sadly still appropriate to twenty-first-century women — if not more so:

> If women are to take their rightful power, there will have to be a vast surge in organisational activities among us. The opposition says derisively that women can't work together; we react to this with terrific defensiveness but we know there is a grain of truth in the charge. Something unique to women often leads women-to-women organisations into failure.
>
> *(1994: 307)*

Women need other women, and thus have to support each other. There is no point in saying 'there are no other senior women in my organization' — that is the thin end of the wedge. Women in senior positions, to gain, maintain and to work effectively with power, need other women alongside them. To achieve this they need to do something about recruiting, training and promoting other women.

While corporate and political efforts have gone into persuading organizations of the need to do the latter, there is not much evidence that women have changed their views towards others. Senior women rarely called them-selves feminists in the 1990s (Kitch, 1994) and even fewer choose to do so in the twenty-first century. Thus, taking the male view of what is best about organizational behaviour and knowledge for granted actually pathologizes women's differences (Eagly and Carli, 2003; Sealy and Vinnicombe, 2013).

It is the overwhelming male view that women cannot work together. Wolf (1994) is right to say that many women have accepted that to be the case, giving rise to the predominant myth that a female boss is less good than a male one. But many men cannot work together either. Some senior and influential men refuse contact with an enemy or rival, others play dan-gerous games with the sole intention of damaging their adversary, with no mind to the corporate welfare. It is women's oppression, isolation and lack of experience that enables the continuation of the belief that women cannot co-operate with each other. If there were more women to choose from as allies, then this myth could be assuaged.

## Support and resistance

Feminists have grown up with the idea of various kinds of support groups, but for those for whom feminism is anathema, it is likely that such groups might seem just as repugnant as the idea of feminism itself. The first action necessary for the isolated female senior professional or executive is to recog-nize that she is not just a doctor, academic, manager or a lawyer, but whether she accepts it or not, she is a *woman* lawyer. It is clear from much of the research evidence cited above that that is how women are seen. The atti-tudes of Margaret Thatcher, the *woman* British Prime Minister who rejected feminist and women's concerns, led to a disgraceful waste of talent. This woman had the opportunity to make a difference but she chose not to do so. As time passes with no obvious female successors in British politics it can be argued that this is the legacy of the first female prime minister who chose not to bring others up behind.

Senior women, then, have to ensure they are succeeded by other women travelling in their wake. Men behave in that way as I have demonstrated. Men, however supportive of equal opportunities they might be, still see their prior commitment to carrying on the patriarchal tradition and, whether consciously or not, mentor, support and promote other men. Men see the future as taking root in those who reflect their own image – and women must learn to do the same. It is hard when there is no tradition, and there is no doubt a need to fight. But instead of fighting alone for promotion, having to work harder and shine brighter than male rivals, surely it makes ecological sense to put energy into supporting other women who in turn offer mutual benefits?

In the mid-1980s in the UK, a group of women psychologists, mainly in junior academic or postgraduate posts, decided to challenge the British Psychological Society's establishment and set up what later became the Psychology of Women Section (POWS) (for details see Burns, 1990). Through working co-operatively, having a common purpose, sharing the demanding tasks and empathy during defeats on the way to success, they benefited emotionally while also learning much about patriarchal organizations. That was beneficial in itself. However, working together and achieving the explicit aims also gave each member of the group self-confidence and the impetus to carry on working as feminist psychologists in contrast to Wolf's account above of women who fail to work together.

It was not a perfect group. There were various 'falling-outs'. However, none of the original group now remains in a junior post, a fact that did raise some criticisms from other feminist psychologists, suspecting that the whole endeavour might have been a 'career move'. However, POWS continues to thrive under a totally new group of young women, and whether this new group knows it or not, the opportunities they have now for influencing psychology are the result of women's achievement through challenging male power in a fight not only against the senior men in the establishment at the time, but sadly senior women who disparaged the aims of POWs and put the women activists down. July 2013 saw the 25th anniversary of the annual POWS conference with delegates from across the globe as well as the UK. The need and desire to work with other women for women has clearly produced sustainable results.

Women with career ambitions and others who have achieved seniority share a history, biology, culture and struggle. What has been both surprising and obvious in my experience of working alongside as well as supervising other women from similar and different professional backgrounds is that, whatever the starting point, the game turns out to be the same. It is about gender, power and patriarchy. It operates under different disguises, but women are always outside the main arena however far they have attempted to be part of the culture. That can only change if we recognize that men fear our strength not our isolated presence.

# REFERENCES

Acker, J. (1990) Hierarchies, jobs, bodies: A theory of gendered organizations. *Gender & society*, *4*(2), 139–158.

Ackerman, N. W. (1972) *The Psychodynamics of Family Life: Diagnosis and Treatment of Family Relationships*, New York: Basic Books, Inc.

Ackoff, R. L. (1998) A systemic view of transformational leadership. *Systemic Practice and Action Research*, *11*(1), 23–36.

Addis, M. E. and Mahalik, J. R. (2003) Men, masculinity, and the contexts of help seeking. *American Psychologist*, *58*(1), 5.

Afifi, M. (2007) Gender differences in mental health. *Singapore Medical Journal*, *48*(5), 385–391.

Ainsworth, M. D., Blehar, M. Waters, E. and Wall, S. (1978) *Patterns of Attachment: A Psychological Study of the Strange Situation*.

Aitkenhead, M. and Liff, S. (1990) The effectiveness of equal opportunities policies, in J. Firth-Cozens and M. A. West (eds) *Women at Work*, Milton Keynes: Open University Press.

Alban-Metcalfe, J. and Alimo-Metcalfe, B. (2007) Development of a private sector version of the (Engaging) Transformational Leadership Questionnaire. *Leadership & Organization Development Journal*, *28*(2), 104–121.

Alban-Metcalfe, J. and Alimo-Metcalfe, B. (2009) Engaging leadership part one: Competences are like Brighton Pier. *The International Journal of Leadership in Public Care*, *5*(1), 10–18.

Alimo-Metcalfe, B. (1992) Gender and appraisal: Findings from a national survey of managers in the British National Health Service, paper presented at the Global Research Conference on Women in Management, Ottawa.

Alimo-Metcalfe, B. (1994) Waiting for fish to grow feet! Removing organisational barriers to women's entry into leadership positions, in M. Tanton (ed.) *Women in Management*, London: Routledge.

Anderson, K. L. (2005) Theorizing gender in intimate partner violence research. *Sex Roles*, *52*(11), 853–865.

Anderson, R., Brown, J. and Campbell, E. A. (1993) Aspects of sex discrimination in police forces in England and Wales, London: Home Office.

Anonymous (1992) Personal View: Unprofessional behaviour, *British Medical Journal*, *305*, 962.

Apter, T. (1993) *Professional Progress: Why Women Still Don't Have Wives*, Basingstoke: Macmillan.

Archer, J. (1986) Gender roles and developmental pathways, *British Journal of Social Psychology*, *23*, 245–256.

Archer J. (1989) Childhood gender roles: Structure and development. *The Psychologist*, *9*, 367–370.

Archer, J. and Coyne, S. M. (2005) An integrated review of indirect, relational, and social aggression. *Personality and Social Psychology Review*, *9*(3), 212–230.

Archer, J. and Lloyd, B. (1982/2002) *Sex and Gender*, London: Penguin.

Archer, J. and Rhodes, V. (1993) The grief process and job loss: A cross-sectional study. *British Journal of Psychology*, *84*, 395–341.

Arulampalam, W., Booth, Alison L. and Bryan, M. L. (2007) Is there a glass ceiling over Europe? Exploring the gender pay gap across the wage distribution. *Industrial and Labor Relations Review*, *60*(2), 163–186.

Association of University Teachers (1990) *Goodwill under Stress: Morale in UK Universities*, London: AUT.

Auster, C. and Ohm, S. (2000) Masculinity and femininity in contemporary American society: A reevaluation using the Bem sex-role inventory. *Sex Roles*, *43*(7), 499–528.

Aziz, A. (1990) Women in UK universities: The road to casualisation? in S. Stiver Lie and V. E. O'Leary (eds) *Storming the Tower: Women in the Academic World*, London: Kogan Page.

Baillien, E. and De Witte, H. (2009) Why is organizational change related to workplace bullying? Role conflict and job insecurity as mediators. *Economic and Industrial Democracy*, *30*(3), 348–371.

Barge, J. K. and Fairhurst, G. T. (2008) Living leadership: A systemic constructionist approach. *Leadership*, *4*(3), 227–251.

Barnes, C. (2002) Book review: Gender, identity and place: Understanding feminist geographies. *Ethics, Place and Environment*, *5*(2), 157–175.

Baron-Cohen, S. and Wheelwright, S. (2004) The empathy quotient: An investigation of adults with Asperger syndrome or high functioning autism, and normal sex differences. *Journal of Autism and Developmental Disorders*, *34*(2), 163–175.

Bass, B. M., Avolio, B. J., Jung, D. I. and Berson, Y. (2003) Predicting unit performance by assessing transformational and transactional leadership. *Journal of Applied Psychology*, *88*(2), 207–218.

Beasley, B. and Collins Standley, T. (2002) Shirts vs. skins: Clothing as an indicator of gender role stereotyping in video games. *Mass Communication & Society*, *5*(3), 279–293.

Beckett, H. (1986) Cognitive developmental theory in the study of adolescent development, in S. Wilkinson (ed.) *Feminist Social Psychology: Developing Theory and Practice*, Milton Keynes: Open University Press.

Bee, H. (1981) *The Developing Child* (third edition), New York: Harper and Row.

Bell, C. and Newby, H. (1976) Husbands and wives: The dynamics of the deferential dialectic, in D. Barker and H. Allen (eds) *Dependence and Exploitation of Women in Work and Marriage*, London: Longman.

Bell, D. N. F. and Blanchflower, D. G. (2013) Underemployment in the UK revisited. *National Institute Economic Review*, *224*(1), F8–F22.

Beloff, H. (1992) Study reported in *The Times Higher Education Supplement*, 17 April 1992: 5.

Bem, S. L. (1974) The measurement of psychological androgyny, *Journal of Consulting and Clinical Psychology*, *42*, 155–162.

Bem, S. L. (1981) Gender schema theory: A cognitive account of sex typing, *Psychological Review*, *88*, 354–364.

Bem, S. L. (1993) *The Lenses of Gender*, London: Yale University Press.

Bendelow, G. and Williams, S. J. (1998). *Emotions in Social Life: Critical Themes and Contemporary Issues*, London: Routledge.

Benokraitis, N. V. and Feagin, J. R. (1995) *Modern Sexism: Blatant, Subtle and Covert Discrimination* (second edition), Englewood Cliffs, NJ: Prentice Hall.

Berger, P. and Kellner, H. (1964/1982) Marriage and the construction of reality, in M. Anderson (ed.) *Sociology of the Family*, Harmondsworth: Penguin.

Berger, P. (1966) Identity as a problem of knowledge, *Archives europeaennes de sociologie*, 7, 105–115.

Berger, P. and Luckman, T. (1985) *The Social Construction of Reality*, Harmondsworth: Pelican.

Bernard, J. (1981) *The Female World*, New York: The Free Press.

Bettinger, E. P. and Long, B. T. (2005) Do faculty serve as role models? The impact of instructor gender on female students. *The American Economic Review*, *95*(2), 152–157, *Papers and Proceedings of the One Hundred Seventeenth Annual Meeting of the American Economic Association*, Philadelphia, PA, 7–9 January.

Bettman, C. (2009) Patriarchy: The predominant discourse and fount of domestic violence. *Australian and New Zealand Journal of Family Therapy (ANZJFT)*, *30*(1), 15–28.

Bhavnani, K. and Phoenix, A. (1994) *Shifting Identities Shifting Racisms*, London: Sage.

Bifulco, A., Figueiredo, B., Guedeney, N., Gorman, L. L., Hayes, S., Muzik, M. and Henshaw, C. A. (2004) Maternal attachment style and depression associated with childbirth: Preliminary results from a European and US cross-cultural study. *The British Journal of Psychiatry*, *184*(46), s31–s37.

Bifulco, A., Mahon, J., Kwon, J. H., Moran, P. M. and Jacobs, C. (2003) The Vulnerable Attachment Style Questionnaire (VASQ): An interview-based measure of attachment styles that predict depressive disorder. *Psychological Medicine*, *33*(06), 1099–1110.

Bion, W. (1961) *Experiences in Groups*, London: Tavistock.

Birke, L. (1986) *Women, Feminism and Biology: The Feminist Challenge*, Hemel Hempstead: Harvester.

Bleier, R. (1984) *Science and Gender: A Critique of Biology and Its Theories on Women*, Oxford: Pergamon.

Black, P. and Sharma, U. (2001) Men are real, women are 'made up': Beauty therapy and the construction of femininity. *The Sociological Review*, *49*(1), 100–116.

Bocock, R. (1983) *Sigmund Freud*. London: Tavistock.

Bolden, R. and Gosling, J. (2006) Leadership competencies: Time to change the tune? *Leadership*, *2*(2), 147–163.

Bolton, S. C. (2000) Who cares? Offering emotion work as a 'gift' in the nursing labour process. *Journal of Advanced Nursing*, *32*(3), 580–586.

Bolton, S. C. (2001) Changing faces: Nurses as emotional jugglers. *Sociology of Health & Illness*, *23*(1), 85–100.

Bouchier, D. (1983) *The Feminist Challenge*. Basingstoke: Macmillan.

Bowlby, J. (1977) The making and breaking of affectional bonds. II. Some principles of psychotherapy. The Fiftieth Maudsley Lecture. *British Journal of Psychiatry*, *130*, 421–431.

Bowlby, J. (1982) Attachment and loss: Retrospect and prospect. *American Journal of Ortho-psychiatry, 52*(4), 664–678.

Bowlby, J. (1988) Developmental psychiatry comes of age. *American Journal of Psychiatry, 145*(1), 1–10.

Braidotti, R. (2008) In spite of the times: The postsecular turn in feminism. *Theory, Culture & Society, 25*(6), 1–24.

Brant, C. and Too, Y. L. (1994) *Rethinking Sexual Harassment*, London: Pluto.

Breakwell, G. B. (1985) *The Quiet Rebel: Women at Work in a Man's World*, London: Century Publishing.

Brennan, T. (1992) *The Interpretation of the Flesh*, London: Routledge.

Brennan, T. (ed.) (1993) *Between Feminism and Psychoanalysis*, London: Routledge.

British Medical Association (1993) *Patronage in the Medical Profession*, London: BMA.

British Psychological Society (1990) Sexual harassment and unethical intimacy between teachers and trainees: Discussion and policy, unpublished document, Division of Criminological and Legal Psychology Training Committee.

Brittan, A. (1989) *Masculinity and Power*, Oxford: Blackwell.

Britton, R. (1994) The blindness of the seeing eye: Inverse symmetry as a defense against reality. *Psychoanalytic Inquiry: A Topical Journal for Mental Health Professionals, 14*(3), 365–378.

Broverman, I. K., Broverman, D. M., Clarkson, F. E., Rosenkrantz, P. S. and Vogel, S. R. (1970) Sex role stereotypes and clinical judgments of mental health, *Journal of Consulting and Clinical Psychology, 34*, 1–7.

Brown, A. and Testa, M. (2008) Social influences on judgments of rape victims: The role of the negative and positive social reactions of others. *Sex Roles, 58*(7), 490–500.

Brown, B., Nolan, P., Crawford, P. and Lewis, A. (1996) Interaction, language and the 'narrative turn' in psychotherapy and psychiatry. *Social Science & Medicine, 43*(11), 1569–1578.

Brownmiller, S. (2013). *Femininity*. New York: Simon & Schuster.

Burman, E. (1989) Feminisms and feminists in psychology, paper presented at the Critical Psychology Symposium: British Psychological Society's London Conference.

Burman, E. (1990a) *Feminists in Psychological Practice*, London: Sage.

Burman, E. (1990b) Differing with deconstruction, in I. Parker and J. Shotter (eds) *Deconstructing Social Psychology*, London: Routledge.

Burman, E. and Parker, I. (1993) *Discourse Analytic Research: Repertoires and Readings of Texts in Action*, London: Routledge.

Burns, J. (1990) Women organising within psychology, in E. Burman (ed.) *Feminists in Psychological Practice*. London: Sage.

Burns, J. (1992) The psychology of lesbian health care, in P. Nicolson and J. M. Ussher (eds) *The Psychology of Women's Health and Health Care*, London, Macmillan.

Burrell, G. (1988) Modernism, post modernism and organizational analysis 2: The contribution of Michel Foucault. *Organization Studies, 9*(2), 221–235.

Burton, C. (1991) *The Promise and The Price*, Sydney: Allen & Unwin.

Buss, D. M. (1994) The strategies of human mating, *American Scientists, 82*, 238–249.

Buss, D. M. (2000) The evolution of happiness. *American Psychologist, 55*(1), 15–23.

Butler, A. and Landells, M. (1995) Taking offence: Research as resistance to sexual harassment in academia, in L. Morley and V. Walsh (eds) *Feminist Academics: Creative Agents for Change*, London: Taylor & Francis.

Butler, J. (1990) *Gender trouble: Feminism and the Subversion of Identity*, New York; London: Routledge.

Byers, A. and Fitzgerald, M. A. (2002) Networking for leadership, inquiry, and systemic thinking: A new approach to inquiry-based learning. *Journal of Science Education and Technology, 11*(1), 81–91.

Callaghan, G. and Thompson, P. (2002) We recruit attitude: The selection and shaping of routine call centre labour. *Journal of Management Studies, 39*, 233–254.

Cameron, D. (1992) *Feminism and Linguistic Theory* (second edition), Basingstoke: Macmillan.

Campbell, D., Coldicott, T. and Kinsella, K. (1994) *Systemic Work with Organizations: A New Model for Managers and Change Agents*, London: Karnac Books.

Campbell, J., Maxey, V. and Watson, W. (1995) Hawthorne effect: Implications for prehospital research. *Annals of Emergency Medicine, 28*(5), 590–594.

Campbell, K. (1992) *Critical Feminism: Argument in the Disciplines*, Milton Keynes: Open University Press.

Campbell, L. M., Sullivan, F. and Murray, T. S. (1995) Videotaping of general practice consultations: Effect on patient satisfaction. *British Medical Journal, 311*(6999), 236.

Campbell-Breen, T. and Poland, F. (2006) Using a biographical-narrative-interpretive method: Exploring motivation in mental health, in Linda Finley and Clair Ballinger (eds) *Qualitative Research for Allied Health Professionals: Challenging Choices*, Chichester: Wiley & Sons.

Capezza, N. and Arriaga, X. (2008) Why do people blame victims of abuse? The role of stereotypes of women on perceptions of blame. *Sex Roles, 59*(11), 839–850.

Caplan, P. (1994) *Lifting a Ton of Feathers: a Woman's Guide to Surviving in the Academic World.* Toronto: University of Toronto Press.

Carless, S. (1998) Gender differences in transformational leadership: An examination of superior, leader, and subordinate perspectives. *Sex Roles, 39*(11–12), 887–902.

Carroll, B., Levy, L. and Richmond, D. (2008) Leadership as practice: Challenging the competency paradigm. *Leadership, 4*(4), 363–379.

Carroll, M. (1994) in C. Morris (ed.) *Bearing Witness: Sexual Harassment and Beyond. Everywoman's Story,* New York: Little Brown & Company.

Carter, D. B. and Levy, G. D. (1988) Cognitive aspects of early sex-role development: The influence of gender schemas on preschoolers' memories and preferences for sex-typed toys and activities. *Child Development, 59*(3), 782–792.

Carter, P. and Jeffs, T. (1995) The Don Juans, *Times Higher Education Supplement,* 10 March, 16–17.

Cassell, C. and Walsh, S. (1991) Towards a woman-friendly psychology of work: Gender, power and organisational culture, paper presented to the British Psychological Society's Annual Occupational Psychology Conference, Liverpool University.

Cassell, C. and Walsh, S. (1993) Being seen but not heard: Barriers to women's equality in the workplace. *The Psychologist: Bulletin of the British Psychological Society, 6,* (3), 110–114.

Charney, D. A. and Russell, R. C. (1994) An overview of sexual harassment, *American Journal of Psychiatry, 151,* 10–17.

Cherney, I. D. and London, K. (2006) Gender-linked differences in the toys, television shows, computer games, and outdoor activities of 5- to 13-year-old children. *Sex Roles, 54*(9–10), 717–726.

Chetwynd, J. and Hartnett, O. (1978) *The Sex Role System*, London: Routledge and Kegan Paul.

Chodorow, N. (1978) *The Reproduction of Mothering*, Berkeley: University of California Press.

Chodorow, N. (1994) *Femininities, Masculinities and Sexualities: Freud and Beyond*, London: Free Association Books.

Chodorow, N. J. (2000) Reflections on the reproduction of mothering: Twenty years later. *Studies in Gender and Sexuality, 1*(4), 337–348.

Chodorow, N. and Contratto, S. (1982) The fantasy of the perfect mother, in B. Thorne and M. Yalom (eds) *Rethinking the Family: Some Feminist Questions*, New York: Longman.

Choi, P. Y. L. (1994) Women's raging hormones, in P. Y. L. Choi and P. Nicolson (eds) *Female Sexuality: Psychology, Biology and Social Context*, Hemel Hempstead: Harvester.

Choi, P. Y. L. and Nicolson, P. (eds) (1994) *Female Sexuality: Psychology, Biology and Social Context*, Hemel Hempstead: Harvester.

Choi, P. Y. L. and Salmon, P. (1995) Stress responsivity in exercisers and non-exercisers during different phases of the menstrual cycle. *Social Science & Medicine, 41*(6), 769–777.

Chrisler, J. C. and Ferguson, S. (2006) Violence against women as a public health issue. *Annals of the New York Academy of Sciences, 1087*, 235–249.

Church, J. and Summerfield, C. (1995) *Social Focus on Women*, London: HMSO.

Cinamon, R. G. and Rich, Y. (2002) Gender differences in the importance of work and family roles: Implications for work–family conflict. *Sex Roles, 47*(11–12), 531–541.

Cockburn, C. (1993) *In the Way of Women: Men's Resistance to Sex Equality in Organisations*, Basingstoke: Macmillan.

Collier, J. and Esteban, R. (2000) Systemic leadership: Ethical and effective. *Leadership & Organization Development Journal, 21*(4), 207–215.

Collinson, D. (2005) Dialectics of leadership. *Human Relations, 58*(11), 1419–1442.

Collinson, D. and Hearn, J. (1994) Naming men as men: Implications for work, organisation and management, *Gender, Work and Organisation, 1*(1), 2–22.

Condor, S. (1991) Sexism in psychological research: A brief note. *Feminism and Psychology, 1*(3), 430–434.

Conley, F. (1994) in C. Morris *Bearing Witness: Sexual Harassment and Beyond: Everywoman's Story*, New York: Little, Brown and Company.

Connell, R. W. (1993) *Gender and Power*, Cambridge: Polity Press.

Cooper, V. W. (1997) Homophily or the queen bee syndrome: Female evaluation of female leadership. *Small Group Research, 28*(4), 483–499.

Cooper, C. and Lewis, S. (1993) *The Workplace Revolution: Managing Today's Dual Career Families*, London: Kogan Page.

Coote, A. and Campbell, B. (1982) *Sweet Freedom*, London: Picador.

Coplan, R. J., Gavinski-Molina, M. H., Lagace-Seguin, D. G. and Wichmann, C. (2001) When girls versus boys play alone: Nonsocial play and adjustment in kindergarten. *Developmental Psychology, 37*(4), 464.

Cortina, L. M., Swan, S., Fitzgerald, L. F. and Waldo, C. (1998) Sexual harassment and assault. *Psychology of Women Quarterly, 22*(3), 419–441.

Cotter, D. A., Hermsen, J. M., Ovadia, S. and Vanneman, R. (2001) The glass ceiling effect. *Social Forces, 80*(2), 655–681.

Coward, R. (1993) *Our Treacherous Hearts*, London: Faber and Faber.

Coyle, A. (1996) Using the counselling interview to collect research data on sensitive topics, *Journal of Health Psychology*.

Coyne, S. M. and Archer, J. (2005) The relationship between indirect and physical aggression on television and in real life. *Social Development, 14*(2), 324–338.

Craib, I. (2001) *Psychoanalysis: A Critical Introduction*, Cambridge: Polity.

Crawford, D. (1989) The future of clinical psychology: Whither or wither? *Clinical Psychology Forum, 20*, 29–31.

Crawford, M. and Maracek, J. (1989) Psychology reconstructs the female: 1968–1988. *Psychology of Women Quarterly, 13*, 147–166.

Cross, S. and Bagilhole, B. (2002) Girls' jobs for the boys? Men, masculinity and non-traditional occupations. *Gender, Work and Organization, 9*, 204–226.

Cushway, D. (1992) Stress in clinical psychology trainees. *British Journal of Clinical Psychology, 31*(2), 169–179.

Cutrer, P. (1994) in C. Morris *Bearing Witness: Sexual Harassment and Beyond: Everywoman's Story*, New York: Little, Brown and Company

Dallos, R. and Draper, R. (2010) *An Introduction to Family Therapy: Systemic Theory and Practice* (third edition), Maidenhead: McGraw Hill.

Dangor, Z., Hoff, L. A. and Scott, R. (1998). Woman abuse in South Africa: An exploratory study. *Violence Against Women, 4*(2), 125–152.

Dasborough, M. T. (2006) Cognitive asymmetry in employee emotional reactions to leadership behaviors. *Leadership Quarterly, 17*(2), 163–178.

Davidson, M. J. and Cooper, C. L. (1992) *Shattering the Glass Ceiling: The Woman Manager*, London: Paul Chapman Publishing Ltd.

Davidson, M. J. and Cooper, C. L. (eds) (1993) *European Women in Business and Managment*, London: Paul Chapman Publishing Ltd.

Davidson, N. (1988) *The Failure of Feminism*, Buffalo, NY: Prometheus Books.

Davies, K. (2003) The body and doing gender: The relations between doctors and nurses in hospital work. *Sociology of Health & Illness, 25*(7), 720–742.

de Board, R. (1978) *The Psychoanalysis of Organisations*, London: Tavistock.

DeLamater, J. and Fidell, L. S. (1971) On the status of women, in L. S. Fidell and J. DeLameter (eds) *Women in the Professions: What's All the Fuss About?* London: Sage.

Delmar, R. (1986) What is feminism? in J. Mitchell and A. Oakley (eds) *What is Feminism?* Oxford: Blackwell.

Department of Health (1991) Report of the Joint Working Party Women doctors and their careers, London: Department of Health.

Department of Health (1992) Report of the Joint Working Party Women doctors and their careers, London: Department of Health.

Department of Health (1991/2) Medical and dental staffing prospects in the NHS in England and Wales 1990, *Health Trends, 23*(4), 132–141.

Dewsbury, J. D. (2000) Performativity and the event: Enacting a philosophy of difference. *Environment and Planning D: Society & Space, 18*(4), 473–496.

Dias, K. and Blecha, J. (2007) Feminism and social theory in geography: An introduction. *Professional Geographer, 59*(1), 1–9.

DiLillo, D. and Peterson, L. (2001) Behavior therapy with children, in J. S. Neil and B. B. Paul (eds) *International Encyclopedia of the Social & Behavioral Sciences*, Oxford: Pergamon.

Doherty, K. (1994) Subjectivity, reflexivity and the analysis of discourse, paper presented at the British Psychological Society London Conference, University of London Institute of Education.

Dougary, G. (1994) *The Executive Tart and Other Myths*, London: Virago.

Dryden, C. (2014) *Being married, doing gender: A critical analysis of gender relationships in marriage*, London: Routledge.

Dryden, C., Doherty, K. and Nicolson, P. (2009) Accounting for the hero: A psycho-discursive approach to children's experience of domestic violence and the construction of masculinities. *British Journal of Social Psychology, 49*(1), 189–205.

Dutton, D. G. (2008) My back pages: Reflections on thirty years of domestic violence research. *Trauma Violence Abuse, 9*(3), 131–143.

Dworkin, A. (1992) *Pornography*, London: The Women's Press.

Eagley, A. H. (1987) *Sex Differences in Social Behaviour: A Social Role Interpretation*, Hillsdale: Earlbaum.

Eagly, A. H. and Carli, L. L. (2003) The female leadership advantage: An evaluation of the evidence. *The Leadership Quarterly, 14*(6), 807–834.

Eagly, A. H. and Johannesen-Schmidt, M. (2003) Transformational, transactional, and laissez-faire leadership styles: A meta-analysis comparing women and men. *American Psychological Association, Psychological Bulletin, 129*(4), 569–591.

Edley, N. (2001) Analysing masculinity: Interpretative repertoires, ideological dilemmas and subject positions. *Discourse as Data: A Guide for Analysis, 189–228*.

Edmunds, L. and Ingber, R. (1977) Psychoanalytical writings on the Oedipus legend: A bibliography. *American Imago, 34,* 374–386.

Ehrenreich, B. (1983) *The Hearts of Men,* New York: Pluto.

Ehrenreich, B. and English, D. (1979) *For Her Own Good: 150 Years of the Experts' Advice to Women,* London: Pluto.

Eichenbaum, L. and Orbach, S. (1982) *Outside In . . . Inside Out,* Harmondsworth: Penguin.

Elston, M. (1993) Women doctors in a changing profession: The case of Britain, in E. Riska and K. Wegar (eds) *Gender, Work and Medicine,* London: Sage.

Ely, R. J. (1995) The power in demography: Women's social constructions of gender identity at work. *Academy of Management, 38*(3), 589–634.

Ely, R. J., Ibarra, H. and Kolb, D. M. (2011) Taking gender into account: Theory and design for women's leadership development programs. *Academy of Management Learning & Education, 10*(3), 474–493.

Eriksen, S. and Jensen, V. (2009) A push or a punch: Distinguishing the severity of sibling violence. *Journal of Interpersonal Violence, 24*(1), 183–208.

Erikson, E. (1958/1963) *Childhood and Society,* New York: Norton.

Erikson, E. (1968) *Identity, Youth and Crisis,* London: Faber and Faber.

Erikson, E. (1980) *Identity and the Life Cycle* (Vol. 1). New York: W. W. Norton & Company.

Ernst, S. (2003) From blame gossip to praise gossip? Gender, leadership and organizational change. *European Journal of Women's Studies, 10*(3), 277–299.

European Parliament Working Paper (1994) Measures to combat sexual harassment in the workplace, Luxembourg: Directorate General for Research.

Evans, D. and Adams, L. (2007) Through the glass ceiling – and back again: The experiences of two of the first non-medical directors of public health in England. *Public Health, 121*(6), 426–431.

Evans, J. A. (2002) Cautious caregivers: Gender stereotypes and the sexualization of men nurses' touch. *Journal of Advanced Nursing, 40*(4), 441–448.

Evetts, J. (ed.) (1994) *Women and Career: Themes and Issues in Advanced Industrial Societies,* London: Longman.

Fairhurst, G. T. (2005) Reframing the art of framing: Problems and prospects for leadership. *Leadership, 1*(2), 165–185.

Fairhurst, G. T. (2009) Considering context in discursive leadership research. *Human Relations, 62*(11), 1607–1633.

Fairhurst, G. T. and Grant, D. (2010) The social construction of leadership: A sailing guide. *Management Communication Quarterly, 24*(2), 171–210.

Faith, K. (1994) Resistance: Lessons from Foucault and feminism, in H. L. Radtke and H. J. Stam (eds) *Power/Gender,* London: Sage.

Faludi, S. (1992) *Backlash,* London: Vintage.

Fambrough, M. J. and Hart, R. K. (2008) Emotions in leadership development: A critique of emotional intelligence. *Advances in Developing Human Resources, 10*(5), 740–758.

Ferguson, K. E. (1984) *The Feminist Case Against Bureaucracy.* Philadelphia, PA: Temple University Press.

Fierman, J. (1990) Do women manage differently? *Fortune, 122*(15), 115–118.

Fine, C. (2011) *Delusions of Gender: The Real Science behind Sex Differences*, London: Icon Books.

Fineman, S. (ed.) (1993) *Emotion in Organisations*, London: Sage.

Firth-Cozens, J. (1991) Sources of stress in junior house officers, *British Medical Journal, 301*, 89–91.

Firth-Cozens, J. and West, M. A. (eds) (1990) *Women and Work*, Milton Keynes: Open University Press.

Flanders, M. L. (1994) *Breakthrough: The Career Woman's Guide to Shattering the Glass Ceiling*, London: Paul Chapman Publishing Ltd.

Fletcher, J. K. (2004). The paradox of postheroic leadership: An essay on gender, power, and transformational change. *The Leadership Quarterly, 15*(5), 647–661.

Fogarty, M. P., Allen, I. and Walters, P. (1981) *Women in Top Jobs*, London: Heinemann Educational Books.

Fonagy, P. and Target, M. (2000) Playing with reality: III. The persistence of dual psychic reality in borderline patients. *International Journal of Psychoanalysis, 81*, 853–873.

Ford, J. (2006) Discourses of leadership: Gender, identity and contradiction in a UK public sector organization. *Leadership, 2*(1), 77–99.

Ford, J. (2010) Studying leadership critically: A psychosocial lens on leadership identities. *Leadership, 6*(1), 47–65.

Forster, P. (1992) Sexual harassment at work. *British Medical Journal, 305*, 944–946.

Foster, A. (2001) The duty to care and the need to split. *Journal of Social Work Practice: Psychotherapeutic Approaches in Health, Welfare and the Community, 15*(1), 81–90.

Foucault, M. (1973) *The Archaeology of Knowledge*, London: Tavistock.

Foucault, M. (1978) *The History of Sexuality, Vol. 1*, Harmondsworth: Penguin.

Foucault, M. (1980) *Power/Knowledge: Selected Interviews and Other Writings 1972–1977*, Brighton: Harvester Press.

Foucault, M. (1982) The subject and power. *Critical Inquiry, 8*(4), 777–795.

Fox, N. J. (1993) *Post Modernism, Sociology and Health*, Milton Keynes: Open University Press.

Fox, S. and Lituchy, T. R. (2012) *Gender and the Dysfunctional Workplace*, Cheltenham: Edward Elgar.

French, J. R. P. Jnr. and Raven, B. H. (1959) The bases of social power, in D. Cartwright (ed.) *Studies in Social Power*, Ann Arbour, MI: University of Michigan.

Freud, S. (1921) Group psychology and the analysis of the ego, in *The Standard Edition of the Complete Psychological Works of Sigmund Freud* (Vol. XVIII), New York: W. W. Norton and Company.

Freud, S. (1922) Some neurotic mechanisms in jealousy, paranoia and homosexuality, *18*, 22–232, in T. Brennan (1992) *The Interpretation of the Flesh*, London: Routledge.

Freud, S. (1983) On Sexuality, in R. Bocock (ed.) *The Pelican Freud Library* (vol. 7), Harmondsworth: Penguin

Freud, S. (1933/2010) Lecture XXXIII: Femininity. *On Freud's Femininity*, 7.

Freud, S. (1917/1977) The taboo of virginity in The Pelican Freud, S. (1931) Female Sexuality in *Three Essays on the Theory of Sexuality*, trans. J. Strachey, New York: Norton.

Freud, S. (1933/1965) *New Introductory Lectures in Psychoanalysis*, trans. J. Strachey, New York: Norton.

Frosh, S. (1992) Masculine ideology and psychological therapy, in J. M. Ussher and P. Nicolson (eds) *Gender Issues in Clinical Psychology*, London: Routledge.

Frosh, S. (1994) *Sexual Difference: Masculinity and Ideology*, London: Routledge.

Frosh, S. (2003) Psychosocial studies and psychology: Is a critical approach emerging? *Human Relations, 56*(12), 1545–1567.

Fursland, E. (1993) Veterans of the consulting room share their traumas, *Independent*, 8 June.

Gallagher, H. L. and Frith, C. D. (2003) Functional imaging of 'theory of mind'. *Trends in Cognitive Sciences*, 7(2), 77–83.

Gallagher, H. L. and Frith, C. D. (2003) Functional imaging of 'theory of mind'. *Trends in Cognitive Sciences*, 7(2), 77–83.

Gannon, L. (1994) Sexuality and the menopause, in P. Y. L. Choi and P. Nicolson (eds) *Female Sexuality: Psychology, Biology and Social Context*, Hemel Hempstead: Harvester.

Gardiner, M. and Tiggerman, M. (1999) Gender differences in leadership style, job stress and mental health in male- and female-dominated industries. *Journal of Occupational and Organizational Psychology*, 72, 301–315.

Gartrell, N., Herman, J., Silvia, O., Feldstein, M. and Localio, R. (1986) Psychiatrist–patient sexual contact: Results of a national survey, I: Prevalence, *American Journal of Psychiatry*, 143(9), 1126–1231.

Gay, P. (1995) *The Freud Reader*, London: Vintage.

Genovese, M. A. and Steckenrider, J. S. (2013) *Women as Political Leaders: Studies in Gender and Governing*, London: Routledge.

Georgakopoulou, A. (2005). Styling men and masculinities: Interactional and identity aspects at work. *Language in Society*, 34(2), 163–184.

Gerber, G. (1991) Gender stereotypes and power: Perceptions of the roles in violent marriages. *Sex Roles*, 24(7–8), 439–458.

Giddens, A. (1979) *Central Problems in Social Theory*, Basingstoke: Macmillan.

Giddens, A. (1984/2003) *The Constitution of Society*, Cambridge: Polity Press.

Giddens, A. (1993) *The Transformation of Intimacy*, Cambridge: Polity Press.

Gill, J., Mills, J., Franzway, S. and Sharp, R. (2008) 'Oh you must be very clever!' high-achieving women, professional power and the ongoing negotiation of workplace identity. *Gender and Education*, 20(3), 223–236.

Gilligan, C. (1982) *In a Different Voice: Psychological Theory and Women's Development*. Cambridge, MA: Harvard University Press.

Gillis, J. R., Diamond, S. L., Jebely, P., Orekhovsky, V., Ostovich, E. M., MacIsaac, K. et al. (2006) Systemic obstacles to battered women's participation in the judicial system: When will the status quo change? *Violence Against Women*, 12(12), 1150–1168.

Girard, A. L. (2009) Backlash or equality? The influence of men's and women's rights discourses on domestic violence legislation in Ontario. *Violence Against Women*, 15(1), 5–23.

Goldin, C. (1990) *Understanding the Gender Gap: An Economic History of American Women*, Oxford: Oxford University Press.

Goldner, V., Penn, P., Sheinberg, M. and Walker, G. (1990) Love and violence: Gender paradoxes in volatile attachments. *Family Process*, 29(4), 343–364.

Goodwin, V. L., Wofford, J. C. and Whittington, J. L. (2001) A theoretical and empirical extension to the transformational leadership construct. *Journal of Organizational Behavior*, 22(7), 759–774.

Gordon, M. (2003) Roots of empathy: Responsive parenting, caring societies. *Keio Journal of Medicine*, 52(4), 236–243.

Gough, B. (2004) Psychoanalysis as a resource for understanding emotional ruptures in the text: The case of defensive masculinities. *British Journal of Social Psychology*, 43, 245–267.

Gough, B. (2006) Try to be healthy, but don't forgo your masculinity: Deconstructing men's health discourse in the media. *Social Science & Medicine*, 63(9), 2476–2488.

Gough, B. and Edwards, G. (1998) The beer talking: Four lads, a carry out and the reproduction of masculinities. *The Sociological Review*, 46(3), 409–455.

Grabe, M. E. and Kamhawi, R. (2006) Hard wired for negative news? Gender differences in processing broadcast news. *Communication Research, 33*(5), 346–369.

Gray, I., Field, R. and Brown, K. (2010) *Effective Leadership, Management and Supervision in Health and Social Care*, Exeter: Learning Matters Ltd.

Griffin, C. (1995) Feminism, social psychology and qualitative research. *The Psychologist, 8*(3), 119–121.

Griffin, C. (1989) 'I'm not a women's libber but'. . . feminism, consciousness and identity, in S. Skevington and D. Baker (eds) *The Social Identity of Women*, London: Sage.

Grosz, E. (1990) *Jacques Lacan: A Feminist Introduction*, London: Routledge.

Grint, K. (2005) *Leadership: Limits and Possibilities*, Basingstoke: Palgrave Macmillan.

Hansen, A. M., Hogh, A., Persson, R., Karlson, B. et al. (2006) Bullying at work, health outcomes, and physiological stress response. *Journal of Psychosomatic Research, 60*(1), 63–72.

Grove, J. (2013) *The Times Higher Education*, 13 June.

Gutek, B. (1989) Sexuality in the workplace: Key issues in social research and organisational practice, in J. Hearn, D. L. Sheppard, P. Tancred-Sheriff and G. Burrell (eds) *The Sexuality of Organisation*, London: Sage.

Hall, M. (1989) Private experiences in the public domain: Lesbians in organisations in J. Hearn, D. L. Sheppard, P. Tancred-Sheriff and G. Burrell (eds) *The Sexuality of Organisation*, London: Sage.

Halton, W. (1994) Some unconscious aspects of organisation life: Contributions from psychoanalysis, in A. Obholzer and V. Z. Roberts (eds) *The Unconscious at Work*, London: Routledge.

Hansard Society Commission (1990) *Women at the Top*, London: Hansard Society for Parliamentary Government.

Harding, S. (1986) *The Science Question in Feminism*, Milton Keynes: Open University Press.

Hargreaves, D. (1986) Psychological theories of sex-role stereotyping, in D. J. Hargreaves and A. M. Colley (eds) *The Psychology of Sex Roles*, London: Harper & Row.

Harré, R., Clarke, D. and DeCarlo, N. (1985) *Motives and Mechanisms: An Introduction to the Psychology of Action*, London: Methuen.

Harré, R. (1993) Foreword to J. Shotter, *Cultural Politics of Everyday Life*, Milton Keynes: Open University Press.

Harré, R. and Gillett, G. (1994) *The Discursive Mind*, London: Sage.

Harré, R. and Secord, P. F. (1972) *The Explanation of Social Behaviour*, Oxford: Blackwell.

Haslam, A., Reicher, S. and Platow, M. J. (2011) *The New Psychology of Leadership: Identity, Influence and Power*, London: The Psychology Press.

Health Trends (1991/2) WIST (Women in Surgical Training) Scheme, London: HMSO.

Hearn, J. (2004) From hegemonic masculinity to the hegemony of men. *Feminist Theory, 5*(1), 49–72.

Hearn, J. and Parkin, W. (1987) *'Sex' at 'Work': The Power and Paradox of Organisation Sexuality*, Brighton: Wheatsheaf Books.

Henriques, J., Hollway, W., Urwin, C., Venn, C. and Walkerdine, V. (1984/1998) *Changing the Subject: Psychology, Social Regulation and Subjectivity*, London: Routledge.

Henwood, K. and Pidgeon, N. (1995) Remaking the link: Qualitative research and feminist standpoint theory. *Feminism and Psychology, 5*(1) 7–30.

Higgs, M. (2002) Leadership – the long line: A view on how we can make sense of leadership in the 21st century. Henley Working Paper Series, Henley Management College, HWP (7).

Hill, C. and Silva, E. (2005) *Drawing the Line: Sexual Harassment on Campus.* ERIC.

Hill, P. S. and Ly, H. T. (2004) Women are silver, women are diamonds: Conflicting images of women in the Cambodian print media. *Reproductive Health Matters, 12*(24), 104–115.

Hiller, N. J., Day, D. V. and Vance, R. J. (2006) Collective enactment of leadership roles and team effectiveness: A field study. *Leadership Quarterly, 17*(4), 387–397.

Holland, L. and Spencer, L. (1992) Without prejudice? Sex equality at the bar and in the judiciary, Bournemouth: TMS Management Consultants.

Hollway, W. (1989) *Subjectivity and Method in Psychology*, London: Sage.

Hollway, W. and Jefferson, T. J. Eliciting narrative through the in-depth interview. *Qualitative Inquiry, 3*(1), 53–70.

Hollway, W. and Mukarai, L. (1990) The position of women managers in the Tanzanian Civil Service, University of Bradford: Report to the Civil Service Department Government of Tanzania.

Horney, K. (1967/93) *Feminine Psychology*, London: Norton.

Hunter, B. (2005) Emotion work and boundary maintenance in hospital-based midwifery. *Midwifery, 21*(3), 253–266.

Hvas, L. (2006) Menopausal women's positive experience of growing older. *Maturitas, 54*(3), 245–251.

Hyde, J. S. (2007) New directions in the study of gender similarities and differences. *Current Directions in Psychological Science, 16*(5), 259–263.

Iles, P. and Preece, D. (2006). Developing leaders or developing leadership? The academy of chief executives' programmes in the north east of England. *Leadership, 2*(3), 317–340.

Jaques, E. (1955) Social systems as a defence against persecutory and depressive anxiety, in M. Klein, P. Heimann, and R. Money-Kyrle (eds) *New Directions in Psychoanalysis*, London: Tavistock.

Jeffreys, S. (1990a) *Anticlimax*, London: The Women's Press.

Jones, C. (2006) Drawing boundaries: Exploring the relationship between sexual harassment, gender and bullying. *Women's Studies International Forum, 29*(2), 147–158.

Kagan, C. and Lewis, S. (1990a) Where's your sense of humour? Swimming against the tide in higher education, in E. Burman (ed.) *Feminists in Psychological Practice*, London: Sage.

Kagan, C. and Lewis, S. (1990b) *Transforming psychological practice. Australian Psychologist, 25*, 270–281.

Kaiser, B. L. and Kaiser, I. H. (1974) The challenge of the women's movement to American gynaecology. *American Journal of Obstetrics and Gynaecology, 120*(5), 653–655.

Kantor, R. M. (1977) *Men and Women of the Corporation*. New York: Basic Books.

Kardener, S. H. (1974) Sex and the physician–patient relationship. *American Journal of Psychiatry, 131*(10), 1135–1137.

Kath, B. (2004) Genderism and the bathroom problem: (Re)materialising sexed sites, (re)creating sexed bodies. *Gender, Place and Culture: A Journal of Feminist Geography, 11*, 331–346.

Kimura, M. (2008) Narrative as a site of subject construction: The 'Comfort women' debate. *Feminist Theory, 9*(1), 5–24.

Kirsten, R. and Tamar, M. (2009) Attitudes and attributions associated with female and male partner violence. *Journal of Applied Social Psychology, 39*(7), 1481–1512.

Kitch, S. L. (1994) 'We're all in this alone': Career women's attitudes towards feminism, in C. W. Konek and S. L. Kitch (eds) *Women and Careers: Issues and Challenges*, London: Sage.

Kitzinger, C. (1990) Resisting the discipline, in E. Burman (ed.) *Feminists in Psychological Practice*, London: Sage.

Kitzinger, C. (1992) Interview with Sandra Lipsitz Bem: Feminist psychologist, *The Psychologist, 5*(5), 222–224.

Kitzinger, C. (1994) Anti-lesbian harassment, in C. Brant and Y. L. Too (eds) *Rethinking Sexual Harassment*, London: Pluto.

Klein, M. (1946) Notes on some schizoid mechanisms. In H. Segal (ed.) *Envy and Gratitude and Other Works 1946–1963*, London: Virago.

Klein, M. (1953) *Love, Hate and Reparation*, London: Hogarth Press.

Klein, M. (1959/1975) Our adult world and its roots in infancy, in *The Writings of Melanie Klein: Envy and Gratitude and Other Works 1946–1963*, London: Hogarth Press.

Klein, M. (1975/1993) *Envy and Gratitude*, London: Hogarth Press.

Kohlberg, L. (1966) A cognitive developmental analysis of children's sex role concepts and attitudes, in E. E. Maccoby (ed.) *The Development of Sex Differences*, Stanford, CA: Stanford University Press.

Kolb, D. M. (1992) Women's work: peacemaking in organisations, in D. M. Kolb and J. M. Bartunek (eds) *Hidden Conflict in Organisations*, London: Sage.

Kolb, D. M. (2009) Too bad for the women or does it have to be? Gender and negotiation research over the past twenty-five years. *Negotiation Journal*, 25(4), 515–531.

Konek, C. W. and Kitch, S. L. (1994) *Women and Careers: Issues and Challenges*, London: Sage.

Krane, V., Choi, P. Y., Baird, S. M., Aimar, C. M. and Kauer, K. J. (2004) Living the paradox: Female athletes negotiate femininity and muscularity. *Sex Roles*, 50(5–6), 315–329.

Lacan, J. (1977) *Ecrits: A Selection*. London: M. Tavistock.

*Lancet* Editorial (1991) Monopoly of middle aged men, *The Lancet*, 27 April, 337: 1007–1008.

Laws, S. (1983) The sexual politics of pre-menstrual tension. *Women's Studies International Forum*, 6, 19–31.

Lefford, F. (1987) Women in medicine. Women doctors: A quarter century track record, *The Lancet*, 30 May, 1254–1256.

Lehman, C. (1990) The importance of being earnest: Gender conflicts in accounting, *Advances in Public Interest Accounting*, 3, 137–158.

Lempers, J. D. and Clark-Lempers, D. S. (1997) Economic hardship, family relationships, and adolescent distress: An evaluation of a stress–distress mediation model in mother–daughter and mother–son dyads. *Adolescence*, 32(126), 339–356.

León, M. and Mills, S. (2006) ECPR: Workshop 1 Parental, Maternity and/or Paternity Leave: comparative European perspectives. Paper prepared for the workshop 1 'EU Social Policy: Europeanisation or the Persistence of National Difference?' European Consortium for Political Research, Joint Sessions of Workshops, Nicosia, Cyprus 30th April.

Leonard, P. (1984) *Personality and Ideology*, Basingstoke: Macmillan.

Lester, J. (2008) Performing gender in the workplace: Gender socialization, power, and identity among women faculty members. *Community College Review*, 35(4), 277–305.

Levinson, D. (1986) A conception of adult development, *American Psychologist*, 41(1), 3–13.

Lewis, P. (2008) Emotion work and emotion space: Using a spatial perspective to explore the challenging of masculine emotion management practices. *British Journal of Management*, 19, S130–S140.

Lewis, S. E. (1994) The pathologisation of gender: The case of depression, paper presented at the 2nd International Conference on Qualitative Health Research, Penn State.

Lewis, S. E. (1995) The social construction of depression: Experience, discourse and subjectivity, unpublished PhD thesis, University of Sheffield.

Liden, R. C. and Antonakis, J. (2009) Considering context in psychological leadership research. *Human Relations*, 62(11), 1587–1605.

Lim, S. and Cortina, L. M. (2005) Interpersonal mistreatment in the workplace: The interface and impact of general incivility and sexual harassment. *Journal of Applied Psychology*, 90(3), 483.

Llewellyn, S. (1992) The sexual abuse of clients by therapists, paper presented at the British Psychological Society Annual Conference, Scarborough.

Lockwood, P. (2006) 'Someone like me can be successful': Do college students need same-gender role models? *Psychology of Women Quarterly*, *30*(1), 36–46.

Loewald, H. W. (2000) The waning of the Oedipus complex. *Journal of Psychotherapy Practice and Research*, *9*(4), 239–249.

Lopes, P. N., Grewal, D., Kadis, J., Gall, M. and Salovey, P. (2006) Evidence that emotional intelligence is related to job performance and affect and attitudes at work. *Psicothema, 18*, 132–138.

Loughrey, M. (2008) Just how male are male nurses . . . ? *Journal of Clinical Nursing*, *17*(10), 1327–1334.

Luscombe, B. (2013) The queen of lean. *Time*, *181* (10), 20–29.

Luyt, R. (2003) Rhetorical representations of masculinities in South Africa: Moving towards a material-discursive understanding of men. *Journal of Community & Applied Social Psychology*, *13*(1), 46–69.

Maccoby, E. E. and Jacklin, C. N. (1974) *The Psychology of Sex Differences*, Stanford, CA: Stanford University Press.

Mackinnon, C. A. (1979) *Sexual Harassment of Working Women*, London: Yale University Press.

Maguire, M. (1995) *Men, Women, Passion and Power: Gender Issues in Psychotherapy*, London: Routledge.

Mandell, B. and Pherwani, S. (2003) Relationship between emotional intelligence and transformational leadership style: A gender comparison. *Journal of Business and Psychology*, *17*(3), 387–404.

Markham, G. (1993) When women doctors behave as men, *British Medical Journal*, *307*, 11 September, 686.

Marris, P. (1986) *Loss and Change*, London: Tavistock.

Marshall, J. (1986) Exploring the experience of women managers, in S. Wilkinson (ed.) *Feminist Social Psychology*, Milton Keynes: Open University Press.

Marshall, H. and Nicolson, P. (1991) Why choose psychology? Mature and other students' accounts at graduation, in J. Radford (ed.) *The Choice of Psychology*, Leicester: British Psychological Society.

Marshall, J. (1984) *Women Managers: Travellers in a Male World*, New York: Wiley.

Marshall, J. (1994) Why women leave senior management jobs, in M. Tanton (ed.) *Women in Management*, London: Routledge.

Martin, C. L. and Ruble, D. N. (2010). Patterns of gender development. *Annual Review of Psychology*, *61*(1), 353–381.

Martin, C. L., Ruble, D. N. and Szkrybalo, J. (2002) Cognitive theories of early gender development. *Psychological Bulletin*, *128*(6), 903.

Martin, E. (1987) *The Woman in the Body*, Milton Keynes: Open University Press.

Maupin, R. J. (1993) How can women's lack of upward mobility in accounting organisations be explained? *Group and Organisational Management*, 18(2), 132–152.

McDowell, L. (1993) Space, place and gender relations: Part II. Identity, difference, feminist geometries and geographies. *Progress in Human Geography*, *17*(3), 305–318.

McDowell, L. (2001) Men, management and multiple masculinities in organisations. *Geoforum*, *32*(2), 181–198.

McFarlane, J. M., Groff, J. Y., O'Brien, J. A. and Watson, K. (2005) Prevalence of partner violence against 7,443 African American, white, and Hispanic women receiving care at urban public primary care clinics. *Public Health Nursing*, *22*(2), 98–107.

McKenzie Davey, K. (1993) Women balancing power and care in early career: Am I feminine or just one of the lads? Presented at the BPS Psychology of Women Section Annual Conference, University of Sussex.

McLoughlin, J. (1992) *Up and Running: Women in Business*, London: Virago.

McNay, L. (1992) *Foucault and Feminism*, Cambridge: Polity.

McRobbie, A. (2004) Post-feminism and popular culture. *Feminist Media Studies*, 4(3), 255–264.

Mead, G. H. (1934) *Mind, Self and Society*. Chicago: University of Chicago Press.

Mead, G. H. (2009) *Mind, Self, and Society: From the Standpoint of a Social Behaviorist* (Vol. 1), Chicago: University of Chicago Press.

Medical Manpower and Education Division, Department of Health (1991/2), Medical and dental staffing prospects in the NHS in England and Wales 1990. *Health Trends 23*(4), 132–141.

Medsoc Editorial, Northwing (1991) Sheffield University Student Union.

Mick, C. (2006) Taking a lead on stress: Rank and relationship awareness in the NHS. *Journal of Nursing Management, 14*(4), 310–317.

Mitchell, J. (1974) *Psychoanalysis and Feminism*. Harmondsworth: Pelican.

Molloy, J. T. (1977) *The Woman's Dress for Success Book*, New York: Warner Books.

MORI (1994) Sex in the professions, Report for Hays Personnel Services Ltd.

Morrell, K. and Hartley, J. (2006) A model of political leadership. *Human Relations, 59*(4), 483–504.

Morris, C. (1994) *Bearing Witness: Sexual Harassment and Beyond. Everywoman's Story*. New York: Little, Brown and Company.

Morris, P., Holloway, J., and Noble, J. (1990). Gender representation within the BPS. *The Psychologist, 9*, 408–411.

Morris, S. and Thomas, C. (2005) Placing the dying body: Emotional, situational and embodied factors in preferences for place for final care and death in cancer, in J. Davidson, L. Bondi and M. Smith (eds) *Emotional Geographies*, Aldershot: Ashgate.

Mowrer, O. H. (1950) *Learning Theory and Personality*, New York: Wiley.

Morris, S. and Thomas, C. (2005) Placing the dying body: Emotional, situational and embodied factors in preferences for place for final care and death in cancer. In J. Davidson, L. Bondi and M. Smith (eds) *Emotional Geographies*, Aldershot: Ashgate.

Nasrullah, M., Haqqi, S. and Cummings, K. J. (2009) The epidemiological patterns of honour killing of women in Pakistan. *European Journal of Public Health, 19*(2), 193–197.

NHS Management Executive (1992) Women in the NHS: An implementation guide to Opportunity 2000, London: NHS Management Executive.

Nicolson, P. (1988) The social psychology of post natal depression, unpublished PhD thesis, University of London.

Nicolson, P. (1991a) Vicki Bruce: Chair of the Scientific Affairs Board, *The Psychologist, 4*(6), 261–262.

Nicolson, P. (1991b) Heroines, *Changes: An International Journal of Psychology and Psychotherapy, 9*(3) 181–182.

Nicolson, P. (1992a) Towards a psychology of women's health and health care, in P. Nicolson and J. Ussher (eds) *The Psychology of Women's Health and Health Care*, Basingstoke: Macmillan.

Nicolson, P. (1992b) Menstrual cycle research and the construction of female psychology, in J. T. E. Richardson (ed.) *Cognition and the Menstrual Cycle: Research, Theory and Culture*. London: Springer Verlag.

Nicolson, P. (1992c) Feminism and academic psychology, in K. Campbell (ed.) *Critical Feminism: Argument in the Disciplines*, Milton Keynes: Open University Press.

Nicolson, P. (1993a) Public values and private beliefs: Why do women refer themselves for sex therapy? In J. M. Ussher and C. D. Baker (eds) *Psychological Perspectives on Sexual Problems*, London: Routledge.

Nicolson, P. (1993b) The social construction of motherhood, in D. Richardson and V. Robinson (eds) *Introducing Women's Studies*, Basingstoke: Macmillan.

Nicolson, P. (1993c) Doctoring the records, *Guardian*, 6 September, 11.

Nicolson, P. (1994) Is anatomy destiny? Sexuality and the female body, in P. Choi and P. Nicolson (eds) *Female Sexuality: Psychology, Biology and Social Context*, Hemel Hempstead: Harvester Wheatsheaf.

Nicolson, P. (1995a) The menstrual cycle, science and femininity: Assumptions underlying menstrual cycle research. *Social Science & Medicine*, *41*(6), 779–784.

Nicolson, P. (1995b) Interview with Nadine Radford, *Independent*, 18 January, 31.

Nicolson, P. (1995c) Interview with Geraldine McCool, *Independent*, 1 March, 30.

Nicolson, P. (1996) *Gender, Power and Organisation: A Psychological Perspective*. London: Routledge.

Nicolson, P. (1998) *Postnatal Depression: Psychology, Science and the Transition to Motherhood*, London: Routledge.

Nicolson, P. (2003) *Having It All? Choices for Today's Superwoman*. Chichester: Wiley.

Nicolson, P. (2010) *Psychology and Domestic Violence: A Critical Perspective*. London: Taylor & Francis.

Nicolson, P. (2012) Oedipus at work: A family affair? *Psychodynamic Practice*, *18*(4), 427–440.

Nicolson, P. (2014) *A Critical Approach to Human Growth and Development: A Textbook for Social Work Students and Practitioners*, Basingstoke: Palgrave/Macmillan.

Nicolson, P. and Welsh, C.L. (1992) Gender inequality in medical education, Preliminary Report to Trent Regional Health Authority.

Nicolson, P. and Welsh, C.L. (1993a) From larva to queen bee, paper presented at the British Psychological Society's Psychology of Women Section Conference, Sussex University.

Nicolson, P. and Welsh, C.L. (1993b) Sexual harassment, male dominated organizations and the role of counselling psychology: The case of medical school. *Counselling Psychology Quarterly*, *6*(4), 291–301.

Nicolson, P. and Welsh, C.L. (1994) Undermining equal opportunities in medical education: The case of 'blindness' to sexual harassment, paper presented at the 8th Conference of the European Health Psychology Conference, University of Alicante.

Nicolson, P., Rowland, E., Lokman, P.F.R., Gabriel, Y., Heffernan, K., Howorth, C. et al. (2011) *Leadership and Better Patient Care: Managing in the NHS*. London: HMSO.

Niederle, M. and Vesterlund, L. (2007) Do women shy away from competition? Do men compete too much? *The Quarterly Journal of Economics*, *122*(3), 1067–1101.

O'Leary, V.E. and Ryan, M.M. (1994) Women bosses: Counting the changes or changes that count, in M. Tanton (ed.) *Women in Management: A Developing Presence*, London: Routledge.

Orbach, S. (2010) *Bodies*, London: Profile Books.

Organisation for Economic Co-operation and Development (1979) *Equal Opportunities for Women*, Paris: OECD.

Paechter, C. (2006) Reconceptualizing the gendered body: Learning and constructing masculinities and femininities in school. *Gender and Education*, *18*(2), 121–135.

Paludi, M., Nydegger, R., Desouza, E., Nydegger, L. and Dicker, K.A. (2006) International perspectives on sexual harassment of college students. *Annals of the New York Academy of Sciences*, *1087*(1), 103–120.

Parker, I. (1993) *Discourse Dynamics: Critical Analysis for Social and Individual Psychology*, London: Routledge.

Parlee, M.B. (1990) Premenstrual syndrome and menstrual cycle research, paper presented at a research seminar, University of Sussex.

Paustian-Underdahl, S.C., Halbesleben, J.R.B., Carlson, D.S. and Kacmar, K.M. (2013) The work–family interface and promotability: Boundary integration as a double-edged sword. *Journal of Management*, *20*(10), 1–22.

Philp, M. (1985) Madness, truth and critique: Foucault and anti-psychiatry. *PsychCritique*, 1, 155–170.

Pillinger, J. (1993) *Feminising the Market*, Basingstoke: Macmillan.

Potter, J. and Wetherell, M. (1987) *Discourse and Social Psychology*, London: Sage.

Potts, M. (2005) Why can't a man be more like a woman? Sex, power, and politics. *Obstet Gynecol*, *106*(5 Pt 1), 1065–1070.

Prather, J. (1971) Why can't women be more like men?, in L. S. Fidell and J. DeLameter (eds) *Women in the Professions: What's All the Fuss About?* London: Sage

Pringle, R. (1989) Bureaucracy, rationality and sexuality: The case of secretaries, in J. Hearn, D. L. Sheppard, P. Tancred-Sheriff and G. Burrell (eds) *The Sexuality of Organisation*, London: Sage.

Purkiss, D. (1994) The lecherous professor revisited: Plato, pedagogy and the scene of harassment, in C. Brant and Y. L. Too (eds) *Rethinking Sexual Harassment*, London: Pluto.

Radtke, H. L. and Stam, H. J. (1994) *Power/Gender*, London: Sage.

Raitt, S. (1994) Sexual harassment and sexual abuse: When girls become women, in C. Brant and Y. L. Too (eds) *Rethinking Sexual Harassment*, London: Pluto.

Rapoport, R. and Rapoport, R. N. (1976) *Dual Career Families Re-examined*, London: Martin Robertson.

RCOG (1991) Training Brochure published by the Royal College of Obstetricians and Gynaecologists.

Reay, D. and Ball, S. J. (2000) Essentials of female management: Women's ways of working in the education market place? *Educational Management Administration & Leadership*, *28*(2), 145–159.

Rees, C. E. and Monrouxe, L. V. (2010) 'I should be lucky ha ha ha ha': The construction of power, identity and gender through laughter within medical workplace learning encounters. *Journal of Pragmatics*, *42*(12), 3384–3399.

Reinhartz, S. (1985) Feminist distrust: Problems of context and content in sociological work, in D. N. Berg and K. K. Smith (eds) *The Self in Social Inquiry: Researching Methods*, California: Sage.

Reskin, B. F. and Padavic I. (1994) *Women and Men at Work*, London: Pine Forge Press.

Richardson J. T. E. (1992) The menstrual cycle, cognition and paramenstrual symptomatology, in J. T. E. Richardson (ed.) *Cognition and the Menstrual Cycle: Culture, Theory and Practice*, London: Springer Verlag.

Richardson, D. and Robinson, V. (1993) *Introducing Women's Studies*, Basingstoke: Macmillan.

Richey C. A., Gambrill, E. D. and Blythe B. J. (1988) Mentor relationships among women in academe, *Affilia: Journal of Women and Social Work*, 3(1), 34–47.

Riger, S. (1992) Epistemological debates, feminist voices: Science, social values, and the study of women. *American Psychologist*, 47(6), 730–740.

Riggio, R. E. and Reichard, R. J. (2008) The emotional and social intelligences of effective leadership: An emotional and social skill approach. *Journal of Managerial Psychology*, *23*(2), 169–185.

Riska, E. (2001) Towards gender balance: But will women physicians have an impact on medicine? *Social Science & Medicine*, *52*(2), 179–187.

Rix, S. E. and Stone, A. J. (1984) Work, in S. M. Pritchard (ed.) *The Women's Annual*, Boston: G. K. Hall

Roazen, P. (1991) *Helene Deutsch: Psychoanalysis of the Sexual Functions of Women*, London: Karnac Books.

Robbins, I., Bender, M. P. and Finnis, S. J. (1997) Sexual harassment in nursing. *Journal of Advanced Nursing*, *25*(1), 163–169.

Rohrbaugh, J. B. (1981) *Women: Psychology's Puzzle*. Reading: Abacus.

Roiphe, K. (1993) *The Morning After*, London: Vintage.

Rosenberg, J., Perlstadt, H. and Phillips, W. R. (1993) Now that we are here: Discrimination, disparagement, and harassment at work and the experience of women lawyers. *Gender and Society*, 7(3), September, 415–433.

Rossi, A. (1977) A biosocial perspective on parenting. *Daedalus, 106*, 1–32.

Rostosky, S. S. and Travis, C. B. (1996) Menopause research and the dominance of the bio-medical model 1984–1994. *Psychology of Women Quarterly, 20*(2), 285–312.

Ruigrok, A. N., Salimi-Khorshidi, G., Lai, M. C., Baron-Cohen, S., Lombardo, M. V., Tait, R. J. et al. (2014) A meta-analysis of sex differences in human brain structure. *Neuroscience and Biobehavioral Reviews, 39*, 34–50.

Sambrook, S. (2007) Exploring HRD in two Welsh NHS trusts: Analysing the discursive resources used by senior managers. *Journal of Health, Organisation Management, 21*(4–5), 418–31.

Sampson, E. E. (1989) *The Deconstruction of the Self*, London: Sage.

Scase, R. and Goffee, R. (1989) *Reluctant Managers: Their Work and Lifestyles*, London: Unwin Hyman.

Sanders, C. (1995) The Don Juans, *The Times Higher Education Supplement*, 10 March, 16–17.

Sarcevic, A. and Burd, R. S. (2009) Information handover in time-critical work. *Proceedings of the ACM 2009 International Conference on Supporting Group Work*, Sanibel Island, Florida.

Savage, W. (1986) *A Savage Enquiry: Who Controls Childbirth?* London: Virago.

Sayers, J. (1986) *Sexual Contradictions*, London: Tavistock.

Sayers, J. (1982) *Biological Politics*, London: Tavistock.

Sayers, J. (1990) Psychoanalytic feminism: Deconstructing power in theory and therapy, in I. Parker and J. Shotter (eds) *Deconstructing Social Psychology*, London: Routledge.

Sayers, J. (1992) Feminism, psychoanalysis and psychotherapy, in J. M. Ussher and P. Nicolson (eds) *Gender Issues in Clinical Psychology*, London: Routledge.

Schafer, E. (2011) There's no good reason for this inequality, *The Times Higher Educational Supplement*, 20 June, 32–34.

Schilling, J. (2009) From ineffectiveness to destruction: A qualitative study on the meaning of negative leadership. *Leadership, 5*(1), 102–128.

Schnurr, S. (2008) Surviving in a man's world with a sense of humour: An analysis of women leaders' use of humour at work. *Leadership, 4*(3), 299–319.

Schore, A. N. (2001) The effects of early relational trauma on right brain development, affect regulation, and infant mental health. *Infant Mental Health Journal*, 22(1–2), 201–269.

Schwarz, N. (1990) Feelings as information: Informational and motivational functions of affective states. In R. Sorrentino and E. T. Higgins (eds) *Handbook of Motivation and Cognition*, New York: Guilford Press.

Sealy, R. and Vinnicombe, S. (2013) The female FTSE board report 2013: False dawn of progress for women on boards? International Centre for Women Leaders at the Cranfield School of Management.

Segal, H. (1973) *Introduction to the Work of Melanie Klein*, London: Hogarth Press and the Institute of Psychoanalysis.

Segal, J. (1992) *Melanie Klein*, London: Sage.

Segal, H. (1993) Countertransference, in A. Alexandris and G. Vaslamatzis (eds) *Countertransference: Theory, Technique, Teaching*, London: Karnac.

Segal, L (1994) *Straight Sex*, London: Virago.

Seidler, V. J. (2004). *Rediscovering Masculinity: Reason, Language and Sexuality*, Abingdon: Routledge.

Shapiro, J. R. and Applegate, J. S. (2000) Cognitive neuroscience, neurobiology and affect regulation: Implications for clinical social work. *Clinical Social Work Journal*, *28*(1), 9–3.

Sharp, R., Franzway, S., Mills, J. and Gill, J. (2012) Flawed policy, failed politics? Challenging the sexual politics of managing diversity in engineering organizations. *Gender Work and Organization*, *19*(6), 555–572.

Shemmings, D., Shemmings, Y. and Cook, A. (2012) Gaining the trust of 'highly resistant' families: Insights from attachment theory and research. *Child & Family Social Work*, *17*(2), 130–137.

Sheppard, D. (1989) Organisation, power and sexuality: The image and self-image of women managers, in J. Hearn, D. L. Sheppard, P. Tancred-Sheriff and G. Burrell (eds) *The Sexuality of Organisation*, London: Sage.

Sheppard, D. (1992) Women managers' perceptions of gender and organisational life, in A. J. Mills and P. Tancred (eds) *Gendering Organisational Analysis*, London: Sage.

Sherif, C. (1987) Bias in psychology, in S. Harding (ed.) *Feminism and Methodology*, Milton Keynes: Open University Press.

Shotter, J. (1993) *Cultural Politics of Everyday Life*, Milton Keynes: Open University Press.

Shotter, J. (1995) In conversation joint action, shared intentionality and ethics. *Theory & Psychology*, *5*(1), 49–73.

Simpson, S. M. (1991) Women entrepreneurs, in J. Firth-Cozens and M. A. West (eds) *Women at Work*, Milton Keynes: Open University Press.

Silver, G. (1990) The Lancet Editorial: Monopoly of middle-aged men, *335*, 1149–1150.

Simpson, S. M. (1991) Women entrepreneurs, in J. Firth-Cozens and M. A. West (eds) *Women at Work*, Milton Keynes: Open University Press.

Smith, D. E. (1978) A peculiar eclipsing: Women's from men's culture. *Women's Studies International Quarterly*, 1, 281–295.

Smith, J. A. (1993) Persons, text and talk: Subjectivity, reflexivity and qualitative research in psychology. Paper presented at the BPS Social Psychology Section Conference, University of Oxford.

Smith, N., Smith, V. and and Verne, M. (2011) The gender pay gap in top corporate jobs in Denmark: Glass ceilings, sticky floors or both? *International Journal of Manpower*, *32*(2), 156–157.

Smithson, J. and Stokoe, E. H. (2005) Discourses of work–life balance: Negotiating 'gender-blind' terms in organizations. *Gender, Work & Organization*, *12*(2), 147–168.

Snitow, A. Stansell, C. and Thompson, S. (1984) *Desire: The Politics of Sexuality*, London: Virago.

Sommer, B. (1992) Cognitive performance and the menstrual cycle, in J. T. E. Richardson (ed.) *Cognition and the Menstrual Cycle: Research, Theory and Culture*, London: Springer Verlag.

Squire, C. (1990) Feminism as 'anti psychology', in E. Burman (ed.) *Feminists in Psychological Practice*, London: Sage.

Stacey, J. (1993) Untangling feminist theory, in V. Robinson and D. Richardson (eds) *Introducing Women's Studies*, Basingstoke: Macmillan.

Stanley, L. and Wise, S. (1983) *Breaking Out: Feminist Consciousness and Feminist Research*, London: Routledge & Kegan Paul.

Stockdale, M. S., Logan, T. K. and Weston, R. (2008) Sexual harassment and posttraumatic stress disorder: Damages beyond prior abuse. *Law and Human Behavior*, *33*(5), 405.

Stordeur, S., D'Hoore, W. and Vandenberghe, C. (2001) Leadership, organizational stress, and emotional exhaustion among hospital nursing staff. *Journal of Advanced Nursing*, *35*(4), 533–542.

Stouten, J., Baillien, E., Van den Broeck, A., Camps, J., De Witte, H. and Euwema, M. (2010) Discouraging bullying: The role of ethical leadership and its effects on the work environment. *Journal of Business Ethics*, 95(1), 17–27.

SUSU (1992) Sheffield University Student's Union Sexual Harassment Survey, Sheffield University.

Swan, E. (1994) Managing emotion, in M. Tanton (ed.) *Women in Management*, London: Routledge.

Sy, T., Tram, S. and O'Hara, L. A. (2006) Relation of employee and manager emotional intelligence to job satisfaction and performance. *Journal of Vocational Behavior*, 68(3), 461–473.

Tajfel, H. (ed.) (1978) *Differentiation Between Social Groups: Studies in the Social Psychology of Intergroup Relations*, London: Academic.

Tannen, D. (1993/2007) *You Just Don't Understand: Women and Men in Conversation*, London: Virago.

Tanton, M. (1992) Developing authenticity in management development programmes. *Women in Management Review*, 7(4). http://dx.doi.org/10.1108/09649429210014351

Tanton, M. (1994) *Women in Management*, London: Routledge.

Thom, D. (1992) A lop-sided view: feminist history or the history of women? in K. Campbell (ed.) *Critical Feminism: Argument in the Disciplines*, Milton Keynes: Open University Press.

Thomas, A. M. (1985) The meaning of gender in women's self-conceptions, paper presented at the British Psychological Society's Social Psychology Section Annual Conference, Clare College, University of Cambridge.

Thomas, A. M. (1986) The personal and the political in women's self-conceptions, paper presented as part of the symposium on Social Factors in Gender Identity, held at the British Psychological Society's Annual Conference, University of Sheffield.

Thoms, J. C. (2008) Ethical integrity in leadership and organizational moral culture. *Leadership*, 4(4), 419–442.

Thorne, B. (1986) Boys and girls together . . . But most apart: Gender arrangements in elementary schools, in W. W. Hartup and Z. Rubin (eds) *Relationships and Development*, Hillsdale, NJ: Erlbaum.

Tourish, D. and Vatcha, N. (2005) Charismatic leadership and corporate cultism at Enron: The elimination of dissent, the promotion of conformity and organizational collapse. *Leadership*, 1(4), 455–480.

Tsouroufli, M., Özbilgin, M. and Smith, M. (2011) Gendered forms of othering in UK hospital medicine: Nostalgia as resistance against the modern doctor. *Equality, Diversity and Inclusion: An International Journal*, 30(6), 498–509.

Tunaley, J. R. (1994) Young women, self and the thin ideal, paper presented at the 2nd International Conference on Qualitative Health Research, Penn State.

Tunaley, J. R. (1995) Body size, food and women's identity: A lifespan approach, unpublished PhD thesis, University of Sheffield.

Uhl-Bien, M. (2006) Relational leadership theory: Exploring the social processes of leadership and organizing. *The Leadership Quarterly*, 17(6), 654–676.

Unger, R. K. (1979) Female and male: Psychological perspectives, London: Harper & Row.

Urwin, C. (1984) Power relations and emergence of language, in J. Henriques, W. Holloway, C. Urwin, C Venn, U. V. Walkerdine (eds) *Changing the Subject*, London: Methuen.

Ussher, J. M. (1989) *The Psychology of the Female Body*, London: Routledge.

Ussher, J. M. (1990a) Choosing psychology or not throwing the baby out with the bath water, in E. Burman (ed.) *Feminists and Psychological Practice*, London: Sage.

Ussher, J. M. (1990b) Sexism in psychology, *The Psychologist*, 13(9), 31–33.

Ussher, J. M. (1991) *Women's Madness: Misogyny or Misunderstanding*, Brighton: Harvester Wheatsheaf.

Ussher, J. M. (1992a) Science sexing psychology, in J. M. Ussher and P. Nicolson (eds) *Gender Issues in Clinical Psychology*, London: Routledge.

Ussher, J. M. (1992b) Reproductive rhetoric and the blaming of the body, in P. Nicolson and J. M. Ussher (eds) *The Psychology of Women's Health and Health Care*, Basingstoke: Macmillan.

Ussher, J. M. (1993) The construction of female sexual problems: Regulating sex, regulating women, in J. M. Ussher and C. D. Baker (eds) *Psychological Perspectives on Sexual Problems*, London: Routledge.

Ussher, J. (ed.) (2002) *Body Talk: The Material and Discursive Regulation of Sexuality, Madness and Reproduction*, London: Routledge.

Ussher, J. M. (1995) Masculinity as masquerade: Deconstructing phallic illusions in pornographic representation, paper presented at the British Psychological Society's Annual Conference, University of Warwick.

Ussher, J. M. (2003) The role of premenstrual dysphoric disorder in the subjectification of women. *Journal of Medical Humanities*, *24*(1–2), 131–146.

Ussher, J. M. (2006) *Managing the Monstrous Feminine: Regulating the Reproductive Body*, London: Taylor & Francis.

Valverde, M. (1985) *Sex, Power and Pleasure*, Toronto: The Women's Press.

Van Roosmalen, E. (2000) Forces of patriarchy: Adolescent experiences of sexuality and conceptions of relationships. *Youth Society*, *32*(2), 202–227.

Van Vianen, A. E. M. and Fischer, A. H. (2002) Illuminating the glass ceiling: The role of organizational culture preferences. *Journal of Occupational and Organizational Psychology*, *75*(3), 315–337.

von Bertalanffy, L. (1950) The theory of open systems in physics and biology, *Science*, *111*(2872), 23–29.

Wager, M. (1995) Constructions of femininity in academic women, paper presented at the British Psychological Society's Women and Psychology Annual Conference, University of Leeds.

Walker, A. (1995) Theory and methodology in pre-menstrual symptom research. *Social Science and Medicine*, 41(6), 793–800.

Walker, A. (1997/2008) *The Menstrual Cycle*. London: Routledge.

Walkerdine, V. (2003) Reclassifying upward mobility: Femininity and the neo-liberal subject. *Gender and Education*, *15*(3), 237–248.

Walt, V. (2013) Rescuer in chief. *Time*, *181* (13), 16–19.

Walter, C. A. (2000) The psychosocial meaning of menopause: Women's experiences. *Journal of Women & Aging*, *12*(3–4), 117–131.

Warner, P. and Walker, A. (1992) Editorial: Menstrual cycle research – Time to take stock, *Journal of Reproductive and Infant Psychology*, 10, 63–66.

Weedon, C. (1987) *Feminist Practice and Poststructuralist Theory*, Oxford: Blackwell.

Weitzman, L. (1979) Sex role socialisation, Palo Alto, CA: Mayfield.

Western, S. (2013) *Leadership: A Critical Text*. London: Sage.

Wetherell, M. (1993) Discussant paper for symposium: Subjectivity, Reflexivity and Qualititative Psychology, BPS Annual Social Psychology Section Conference, Jesus College, University of Oxford.

Wetherell, M. and Edley, N. (1999) Negotiating hegemonic masculinity: Imaginary positions and psycho-discursive practices. *Feminism Psychology*, *9*(3), 335–356.

White, B. Cox, C. and Cooper, C. (1992) *Women's Career Development: A Study of High Flyers*, Oxford: Blackwell Business.

Whitford, M. (1993) *The Irigaray Reader*, Oxford: Blackwell.

Wilkinson, S. J. (1986) *Feminist Social Psychology: Theory and Method*, Milton Keynes: Open University Press.

Wilkinson, S. J. (1990) Women organising in psychology, in E. Burman (ed.) *Feminists in Psychological Practice*. London: Sage.

Williams, J. A. and Giles, H. (1978) The changing status of women in society: An intergroup perspective, in H. Tajfel (ed.) *Differentiation between Social Groups: Studies in the Social Psychology of Intergroup Relations*, London: Academic Press.

Wilson, E. O. (1978) *On Human Nature*, Cambridge, MA: Harvard University Press.

Wise, S. and Stanley, L. (1987) *Georgie Porgie: Sexual Harassment in Everyday Life*. London: Pandora Press.

WIST (Women in Surgical Training) Scheme, *Health Trends* 1992.

Witz, A. (1992) *Professions and Patriarchy*, London: Routledge.

Witz, A. and Savage, M. (1992) The gender of organisations, in M. Savage and A. Witz (eds) *Gender and Bureaucracy*, Oxford: Blackwell.

Wolf, N. (1990) *The Beauty Myth*, London: Vintage.

Wolf, N. (1994) *Fire with Fire*, London: Vintage.

Wood, J. T. (2001) The normalization of violence in heterosexual romantic relationships: Women's narratives of love and violence. *Journal of Social and Personal Relationships*, *18*(2), 239–261.

Woollett, A., Choi, P.Y.L. and Nicolson, P. (1995) Teaching Psychology: The Perspective of Women Academic Psychologists. Workshop presented at the Women in Psychology Conference, University of Leeds.

Yardley, L. (1996) Reconciling discursive and materialist perspectives on health and illness: A reconstruction of the biopsychosocial approach. *Theory & Psychology*, *6*(3), 485–508.

Yarnal, C. M., Dowler, L. and Hutchinson, S. (2004) Don't let the bastards see you sweat: Masculinity, public and private space, and the volunteer firehouse. *Environment and Planning A*, *36*(4), 685–699.

Zaretsky, E. (2000). Charisma or rationalization? Domesticity and psychoanalysis in the United States in the 1950s. *Critical Inquiry*, *26*(2), 328–354.

# INDEX

abuse 15, 25, 92, 109, 122–124, 125
academia 8, 11–12, 65–67, 82, 83–85;
    complaints against male staff 117–
    118; 'promotion game' 5; sexual
    objectification of women 111–113;
    sexual relationships 114, 116–117
accounting 8
affirmative action 79
age-related prejudice 41
aggression 27, 30, 33, 57, 63, 66, 132
Alimo-Metcalfe, Beverly 13, 128
Allsopp, Kirstie 78–79
anatomy 26, 27, 35, 38–39, 48, 76; *see also*
    biology
androgyny 51–52
anti-feminism 22
anxiety 79–80, 105, 134; defence
    mechanisms 82, 84, 104, 105–106; Klein
    on 81
Archer, John 57, 58, 59, 60–61, 63, 64, 68
arrogance 4
aspirations 9
attachments 23, 24
attitudes towards bosses 96

backlash to rise of women's power 98, 100
Bank of England 5, 8
Barber, Lynn 120
Barnsley, Victoria 130
barriers 10, 135, 143; discursive 91;

structural 91–93; unconscious 102–104;
    *see also* boundaries
*The Beano* 59
beauty 40, 41–42, 111
beliefs 30, 31, 50, 51, 91, 140, 144
Bell, C. 132
Bem, Sandra 51–52, 54
Benokraitis, N. V. 94, 120
Berger, P. 53
Bettelheim, Bruno 107n10
Bhutto, Benazir 9, 89
bio-material context 35
biography 17–18, 19, 24, 77, 131–132, 135
biology 17–18, 35, 38–39, 63; material
    context 19; sex and sex roles 25, 26;
    social meaning 27; *see also* body
Bion, Wilfred 14
bitterness 49, 50
Blair, Tony 4
Blyton, Enid 59
body 26, 27, 38–39, 40–43; gendered 35;
    meaning of the 40; sexual abuse 123;
    sexual objectification of women 111, 112
boundaries: between self and other 134–
    136, 138; psychological 131; with other
    women 143
'boundary-marker' role 142
Bowlby, John 14, 24
Breakwell, Dame Glynis 25–26, 29, 53
breast 80

Brennan, Teresa 44–45
British Army 130
British Broadcasting Corporation (BBC) 41, 127, 128
British Medical Association 101
British Psychological Society 149
Brittan, A. 2
Broverman, I. K. 31
Brown, Gordon 129
bullying 5, 15, 109
Buss, David 40–41

care professions 7
career 17–18, 29, 77
Carroll, Majorie 112–113, 114, 117–118
Carter, P. 112, 116–117, 118
castration 44, 45, 46, 48, 105
chief executive officers (CEOs) 2, 5, 8
child-care: lack of child-care facilities 10, 91, 92; reproduction of mothering 61–63; sex roles 28
child development 29–30
childhood experiences 18; see also infancy
Chodorow, Nancy 47, 61–63, 64, 138
Choi, Precilla 40
Church of England 104
Clark, Marcia 111
class 24
clinical psychology 98, 104–105, 124
Clinton, Bill 110
Clinton, Hillary 5, 9, 88, 145
clothes 42–43, 111, 119
co-operation between women 147, 148, 149
Cockburn, Cynthia 76
cognitive-neuropsychology 57
Collinson, D. 74, 75
company boards 2, 4, 102–103
competition 14–15, 39; with men 72; with women 147
complaints 97–98, 117–118, 121
conflict 140–141
'conformist' role 143
Conley, Frances 125
connection 137–138, 141, 147
conscious self-awareness 135
consensual sex 113–117
Contratto, S. 64
conversation analysis 137–138
Cooper, Cary 13, 63, 68, 74, 100
coping strategies 10, 146–147
countertransference 82, 84
*Countryfile* 41
court cases 102, 121

Crawford, D. 104–105
Crompton, Richmal 60
'culture trap' 68–69, 73
Cutrer, Pamela 116

Dallos, R. 18
Daly, Helena 99, 102
Davidson, Marilyn 13, 63, 68, 74, 100
deconstruction 22, 23, 33
defence mechanisms 82, 84, 85, 103, 105–106
deference 28–29, 131–134
DeLamater, J. 9
demographic changes 6–8, 130
denial 81, 105–106
'departmental mascot' role 69
depressive position 80, 81, 82
desire 48, 110
'destiny' 27, 28
difference 2, 47, 131; academic women 67; gender-role development 57; image management 43; Lacan 48
discourse analysis 22, 33, 53; see also language; the 'discursive'
discrimination 5, 29, 71–72, 109, 146; covert 99; *Hansard* report 10; legislation against 88, 145; medical profession 13, 78; multiple levels of 98; overt sexist attitudes 94–96; processes of 91; subjectivity 32; toxic context of 125; 'unofficial' 90; see also sexual harassment
the 'discursive' 20–23, 35; see also discourse analysis; language
discursive barriers 91
discursive masculinity 77–78
'display professions' 111
division of labour 61, 62
doctors 7–8, 69, 98, 102; see also medical profession
domestic labour 92
domestic violence 25, 29, 92
Dougary, Ginny 13, 120
Draper, R. 18

education 21, 30
ego 44, 48, 135, 136, 139
Ehrenreich, B. 119
Eichenbaum, L. 131–132, 133, 134, 138
emotion 15, 74, 103, 137, 138–140
emotional antennae 134
emotional intelligence 4, 71, 129, 138
emotional segregation 63
empathy 23, 57
English, D. 119

envy 14–15, 79–80, 103; defence
    mechanisms 82, 84, 104; Klein on 81–82;
    sexual relationships 117
equal opportunities 6, 25, 54, 78, 90, 104,
    145, 148
equal pay 6, 67, 88
equality 86, 132; barriers to 10; battle for 5;
    illusions of 3
Erikson, Erik 24
essentialism 63, 131
Esteve-Coll, Elizabeth 73–74
ethnicity 24
evaluation of women 99
exclusion 100
expectations 28, 32, 57, 138, 144; academic
    women 65, 66; leadership 129–130;
    motherhood 65; teachers 30
'extra-visible manager' role 142

Facebook 5
failure 49
Fairbairn, R. 135
Faludi, S. 42
family 18, 29; gender-role development 61;
    reasons for leaving a job 130; sex-role
    spill-over 63–65; *see also* motherhood
*Family Guy* 59
*Famous Five* 59
fantasies 104–105
fashion industry 42
Fawcett Society 88
Feagin, J. R. 94, 120
fear, male 104–105, 106, 149
femininity: beliefs and behaviours 51–52;
    bio-material context 35; career success
    144; as contradictory experience 33;
    conventional 29; definitions of 37;
    essential 68; expressed through anatomy
    27; failed 40; Freud 43, 45–46; gender-
    role development 58, 59, 60, 62; Lacan
    48; lack of clarity about 68; leadership
    131, 134; loss of subjective sense of 54;
    motherhood 27, 64; sex-role stereotyping
    31; shifting power dynamic 36; social
    construction of 34; socialization into
    9, 129; as subjective position 47; under
    surveillance 28; traits 36; unconscious
    processes 36
feminism 36–37, 103, 147, 148; discursive
    change 21–22; essential femininity 68;
    heterosexuality 118; liberal 63; meaning
    of the body 40; organizational culture 86;
    psychoanalysis 43, 45, 46–47
fertility 39

Fidell, L. S. 9
Finch, Janet 73
Fine, Cordelia 21
Firth-Cozens, Jenny 13
Flanders, M. L. 68, 73
Flowers, Paul 128–129
*Fortunata and Jacinta* 20
Foucault, M. 53, 54
Freud, Sigmund 14, 31, 37, 43–48, 61, 79,
    80, 81, 138
Frosh, S. 47, 49, 51, 58
FTSE companies 4, 5

Galdós, Benito Pérez 20
Gallup Survey 96
Gandhi, Indira 89
gay men 109
gender: anatomical and biological aspects of
    38–39; 'becoming gendered' 38; biology
    and 17; definitions of masculinity and
    femininity 37; Freud 44; gender-power
    relations 6, 22, 28, 36, 53–55, 56, 133,
    144, 146; gender-role development
    57–63; gendered experience 47–48,
    51, 63; hard-wiring of 21, 25; informal
    peacekeeping 141; lifespan development
    29–30; material context 19–20;
    MDI approach 24; meaning of 52; as
    social construction 21, 26–27; *see also*
    femininity; gender relations; masculinity;
    sex
gender-deference 28–29, 131–134
gender identity 9, 29, 34, 38, 62; *see also*
    identity
gender politics 6
gender relations 2, 4–5, 27–28; dynamics of
    6; power-related practices 140; sex-typed
    behaviours 50–53
Genovese, M. A. 89
Gillard, Julia 89, 91
Gilligan, Carol 68
glass ceiling 5, 15, 88–89, 102, 145
gossip 94, 101
Grosz, E. 48
Grove, Jack 3, 5
guilt 79, 134
Guntrip, Harry 135

Halton, W. 103, 105–106
Hansard Society 3, 8, 10, 88, 90
Harman, Harriet 41
Harper-Collins 130
Harré, R. 33, 53
*Harry Potter* 60

Hearn, J. 74, 75
heterosexuality 43, 108–109, 117, 118, 126, 134
Higgs, Marietta 102, 128
Hill, Anita 121, 125
Hollway, Wendy 13, 22, 54
homosexuality 46
Horlick, Nicola 5
Horney, K. 47, 50, 138
House of Commons 3, 90; *see also* members of parliament
House of Lords 90, 122
Howe, Baroness 3
*Hunger Games* 60

id 44
idealization 80
identity 9, 22–23, 29, 33, 104; 'becoming gendered' 38; equated with personality 'style' 62; feminine 10, 34; masculine 10, 75, 134; shifts in 51; *see also* subjectivity
ideology 63
image management 10, 42–43
independence 141–142
inequalities 29, 43
infancy 23, 44, 80, 135
informal mentoring 93–94
informal peacekeeping 140–141
International Monetary Fund (IMF) 5
interpersonal environment 19
intersubjectivity 52
intimacy 141–142
the 'intrapsychic' 23, 36, 91
intuition 138
isolation 5, 13, 141–143, 148; case example 83, 84; as emotional experience 138; exclusion from male networks 100; successful women 91, 102

jealousy 81–82
Jeffs, T. 112, 116–117, 118
jokes 66, 75, 76, 94–95, 121, 122, 123
Judd, Ashley 111
judges 8
*Just William* 60

Kagan, Carolyn 92, 112
Kellner, H. 53
King, Christine 74
Klein, Melanie 14, 80–82, 135
knowledge: patriarchal 138; power and 53, 54; scientific 27–28
Kolb, Deborah 140–141

Lacan, Jacques 48–49, 55n7
Lagarde, Christine 5, 37–38
Lamont, Norman 120
language 22, 32, 48, 55n7
leadership 25, 66, 127–144; boundaries between self and other 134–136; conflict resolution 140–141; emotionally intelligent 4, 71, 129, 138; gender-deference 131–134; invisible masculinity 75; isolation and loneliness 141–143; masculine and feminine leadership styles 134; National Health Service 3, 69–70; qualities 70; studies on 128; *see also* managers
leaving a job 130
legislation 25, 88, 121, 145
Leonard, Peter 28, 54
lesbian women 113
Lewinsky, Monica 110
Lewis, Sue 92, 112
lifespan 24, 29–30
Llewellyn, Sue 124
'logic' 104, 105
loneliness 138, 142, 143
low pay 7

MacKinnon, C. A. 108, 110, 111, 115, 120, 121
Maguire, M. 37
Major, John 120
management styles 68, 69, 71, 136
managers: gender-role development 68; invisible masculinity 75; lack of women 90; role descriptions 142–143
marginalization 34
Markham, G. 102
marriage 63
Marshall, Judi 13
'martyr' role 143
masculinity 9, 10, 39–40, 74–79, 134; aping of 37; beliefs and behaviours 51–52; bio-material context 35; defined through 'what it is not' 28; definitions of 37; discursive 77–78; expressed through anatomy 27; failed 40; Freud 31, 43, 44, 46; gender-role development 58–61, 62; leadership styles 134; masculine standards 50; old-boy networks 100; phallus 48–49; power dressing 42; practical 75–77; problematic 33; shifting power dynamic 36; as subjective position 47; success at work 30; threat to 82; traits 36; unconscious 36, 78–79

material context 19–20
material-discursive-intrapsychic (MDI)
    approach 14, 15, 17, 18–24, 33–34
maternity leave 92
McCool, Geraldine 71
McKenzie Davey, Kate 69, 72
McLoughlin, Jane 13, 72
MDI *see* material-discursive-intrapsychic
    approach
Mead, G. H. 53
media 4, 21, 41, 90
medical profession 2, 7–8, 13, 69, 78, 90;
    patriarchal structure and culture 97–98,
    99; patronage 101; practical masculinity
    76; sexual harassment 123, 125; sexual
    relationships 115; *see also* National Health
    Service
Meir, Golda 89
Mellor, David 120
members of parliament (MPs) 3, 4, 8, 10, 90
menstruation 28, 30, 35, 39, 119
mentors 91, 93–94, 148
Merkel, Angela 9
minority groups 101
misconduct cases 102
misogyny 39, 64, 78, 89, 98, 102, 104, 105
Mitchell, J. 46–47, 48
Moffat, Nicky 130
Molloy, John 42
Morris, Celia 13, 112–113, 114, 115–116,
    117–118, 125, 147
Morris, Estelle 4
'mother confessor' role 68
motherhood 27, 31, 45, 59, 92; academic
    women 66; Freud 46; reproduction of
    mothering 61–63; sex-role spill-over
    64–65; *see also* family
motivation 91

National Health Service (NHS) 3, 5, 13,
    128, 146; leadership 69–70; Opportunity
    2000 programme 90, 97; patriarchal
    culture 98; *see also* medical profession
negotiation 24, 140
neuroscience 57
neurosis 45, 46, 51
Newby, H. 132
newspapers 8
NHS *see* National Health Service
Nicolson, Paula 3, 71, 118–119, 121
non-sexist behaviour 6
nursing 7, 82, 111
nurturance 52, 62, 100, 137

object relations theory 80–81, 135
objects of desire, women as 48–49, 50,
    110
Oedipus complex 44–45, 79, 80
old-boy networks 100–101, 109
'one of the boys' role 143
Orbach, S. 131–132, 133, 134, 138
O'Reilly, Miriam 41
organizational culture: feminist analysis
    of 86; norms 144; patriarchal 74, 91,
    98–100, 102, 108–109, 143
organizational dynamics 2
organizational structures 89–90

paranoid-schizoid position 80, 81, 82
part-objects 80–81
part-time employment 7
passivity 27, 31, 34, 36, 37, 46, 63, 117
paternity leave 92
patriarchy 9, 15, 28, 34, 86, 147, 149; career
    success 5; constraints of 106; 'culture trap'
    73; female sexuality 119; Freud 46–47;
    gender roles 27; medical profession
    97–98; mothering 62; patriarchal culture
    74, 91, 98–100, 102, 108–109, 143;
    patriarchal power relations 2–3, 37, 50;
    political elite 20; power and knowledge
    54; resistance to 32; science 39; symbolic
    order 48
patronage 101
pay 68, 104–105; *see also* equal pay
peacekeeping, informal 140–141
'penis envy' 31, 44, 45, 46, 79
Penny, Laurie 109
people skills 37
performance, organizational 128–129
persecutory anxiety 81, 84
personality 32
phallus 48–49, 79
physical environment 19
political correctness 113–114
political elite 20, 110; *see also* members of
    parliament
popular culture 59
positivism 22
post-feminism 21, 22, 88–89
post-modernism 22, 33
post-structuralism 40
potency 49, 82, 117
Potter, J. 53
power 2, 36, 53–55, 56, 86, 110, 146, 147;
    access to 137, 140, 141; gender-power
    balance 6, 8; gender relations as power

relations 27–28; husbands and wives 132; imbalanced sexual relationships 114–115; linguistic repertoires 22; male bastions of 89–90; masculinity equated with 50, 51; mentor relationships 93; patriarchal power relations 2–3, 37, 50; phallic 49, 50; sexual harassment 120; social environment 47; women's deference 132, 133; women's negotiation skills 140
power dressing 42
practical masculinity 75–77
Prather, J. 100
Pringle, R. 119
professors 8; *see also* academia
projection 82, 84
projective identification 82, 84
promotion 5, 11–12, 83, 139, 143, 148
psychiatry 11
psychoanalysis 23, 31, 53, 56, 63, 138; Freud 43–47; Klein 80–82; Lacan 48–49; meaning of the body 40; motherhood 64; object relations theory 135
psychological boundaries 131
psychological development 29–30, 31, 32, 40, 50–51
psychology 6, 27, 32; clinical 98, 104–105, 124; critique of mainstream 33; feminist 22; motherhood 64; Psychology of Women Section 149; sex roles 36
Psychology of Women Section (POWS) 149
psychosocial development 24
psychotherapy 47, 82, 124
publishing industry 90
Purkiss, D. 117

Radtke, H. L. 2
rape 25, 121, 123
rationality 138
recession 7
reflexivity 72, 130, 131–132, 135
relationships 23, 132, 133, 138; caution regarding 142; emotional 139–140; family 18; misunderstandings about 144; sexualized 133–134; *see also* sexual relationships
Rennard, Lord 122
reproductive role 27, 28, 35, 39
researchers 8
Rice, Condoleeza 9
Roiphe, K. 113, 122
role models 9, 73, 91, 93, 122
Roman Catholic Church 104

Royal College of Obstetricians and Gynaecologists 90, 99
Rudd, Kevin 89

Sampson, E. E. 32
Sandberg, Sheryl 5, 9, 37, 145
Sanders, C. 118
Savage, M. 2
Savage, Wendy 97–98, 99, 101, 102
Sayers, Janet 38, 47, 62–63
Schafer, Liz 67
science 39
Sealy, R. 4
secretaries 111, 119
Segal, Julia 80, 81
Segal, Lynne 117, 118
self 32, 33, 47, 129–130, 131, 134–136; *see also* identity; subjectivity
self-awareness 135
self-concept 52
self-confidence 4
self-esteem 9, 10, 91, 106, 132
self-worth 139
sex: biology and 17, 26; Freud 44
sex roles 25–26, 28–29, 36; 'culture trap' 68; sex-role spill-over 63–65; stereotyping 29, 30–31
sex-typed behaviours 50–53
sexism 41, 76, 89, 106, 121; anti-sexism policies 97; constant exposure to 122; medical profession 13, 125; overt sexist attitudes 94–96; political elite 20; politicians 110; *see also* discrimination; misogyny
sexual abuse 109, 122–124, 125; *see also* abuse
Sexual Discrimination Act (1975) 88
sexual harassment 15, 42, 71–72, 94, 96–97, 109, 120–122; anti-harassment procedures 113; definitions of 120–121; legislation against 121, 145; male views on 78; politicians 110; sexual abuse distinction 123; surveys on 85; toxic context of 125–126
sexual innuendo 75, 76
sexual relationships 113–117, 139
sexuality 15, 26, 35, 108–126; consensual sex 113–117; construction of 109–113; female 118–120; Freud 44, 45, 46; male 113–114, 122; mentor relationships 93; passivity 31; sexualized relationships 133–134
Shafik, Nemat 5, 6, 88

Sheppard, D. 119–120, 142
Shotter, J. 53
signifiers 48, 55n7
Simpson, S. M. 91
Smith, Dorothy 75, 99
social constructionism 53, 56, 129
social context 63
social work 82, 124
socialization 9, 26, 27, 63, 129; career
    131–132; childhood experiences 18,
    30; differential 131, 138; gender-role
    development 57–58, 61; men 134, 143–
    144; motherhood 64; old-boy networks
    100; patriarchal culture 98; patriarchal
    power relations 50; professional 74,
    75; sex-role stereotyping 31; women's
    deference 133; work organizations 50–51
splitting 81, 82, 84
Stam, H. J. 2
Starkey, Carole 102
Steckenrider, J. S. 89
stereotyping 14, 25, 29, 30–31, 36, 50, 57
'sticky door' concept 5, 6, 88, 145
stress 6, 63, 130–131, 143
structural barriers 91–93
'subjective/interactive' perspective 54
subjectivity 32–33, 43, 48, 104, 129–130;
    complexity of women's 134; feminist
    psychology 22; fluidity of women's 138;
    masculine 77, 78, 79; shifts in 51; social
    nature of 135; women's deference 132,
    133; see also identity
success 8–10, 73; barriers to 10; beliefs
    about 144; male 10, 51; masculine traits
    30; personal growth 143
superego 44, 45, 80
support 147, 148–149
surveillance 28
surveys 85, 96, 97

Swan, E. 138–139
systems theory 24–25

Tannen, Deborah 137–138, 141–142
Tanton, M. 132–133
teaching 7
Thatcher, Margaret 148
Thomas, Alison 52
Thomas, Clarence 121, 125
Thorne, B. 60, 73
tokenism 69
'tomboys' 58, 59
'traitor' role 143
traits 27, 30, 36, 52

unconscious masculinity 78–79
unconscious processes 36, 40, 43, 85, 91,
    103–104
unemployment 75
Unger, Rhoda 50
United States (US) 8, 88, 96, 100, 110, 112,
    121
'unrecognized explorer' role 143
Ussher, Jane 38, 39, 49, 79, 109–110

values 75, 133
Valverde, M. 118

Wager, Maaret 34, 65–66
Welsh, Christopher 13, 121
Wetherell, M. 53
whistle blowing 124
White, Barbara 13, 92, 93
Williams, Shirley 122
Winnicott, Donald 14, 135
Witz, A. 2
Wolf, Naomi 40–41, 42, 111, 147, 148,
    149
Women in Surgical Training (WIST) 90